What Mama Couldn't Tell Us About Love

What Mama Couldn't Tell Us About Love

HEALING THE EMOTIONAL LEGACY OF SLAVERY, CELEBRATING OUR LIGHT

◆

**Brenda Lane Richardson
and Dr. Brenda Wade**

HarperCollins*Publishers*

HarperCollins books may be purchased for educational, business, or sales promo-
tional use. For information please write: Special Markets Department, HarperCollins
Publishers, Inc., 10 East 53rd Street, New York, NY 10022.

FIRST EDITION

Designed by Nancy B. Field

Library of Congress Cataloging-in-Publication Data

Richardson, Brenda Lane, 1948–
    What mama couldn't tell us about love : healing the emotional legacy of slavery,
celebrating our light / Brenda Lane Richardson and Brenda Wade. — 1st ed.
      p. cm.
    ISBN 0-06-019296-8
    1. Afro-American women—Psychology. 2. Afro-American women—Attitudes.
3. Afro-American women—Mental health. Man-woman relationships—United
States. 5. Intimacy (Psychology)—United States. 6. Oppression (Psychology)—
United States. 7. Slavery—United States—History. 8. Healing—United States.
I. Wade, Brenda. II. Title.
E185.86.R53 1999
158.2'082—dc21   99-12127

99 00 01 02 03 ❖ / RRD 10 9 8 7 6 5 4 3 2 1

To my spiritual model of abundance, Jesus Christ,
who fed five thousand from five loaves and two fish.
And to my human model of abundance, T. J. Robinson,
who used love and her grandmother's cookie recipe to create
the world-renowned Gingerbread House restaurant
in Oakland, California.

—BLR

To those who have taught me the most about love:
my daughters, Kena and Kai; my mother, Lizzella Scott Wade;
and my entire family.

—BW

"Everything I learned about love, I learned from my mother. For it is mothers who bend, twist, flex, and break most dramatically before our uninitiated eyes . . . It is only now, inside the fluid boundaries of a good, loving marriage, that I can face and recompose the lessons my mother taught me about love. Her legacy to me is stark and contradictory. I watched the drama of my parents' turbulent, tortured union and learned that it isn't love unless it hurts."

—Marita Golden, *Wild Women Don't Wear No Blues*

"Our life is shaped by our mind; we become what we think."

—from the teachings of the Buddha, the *Dhammapada*, translated by Eknath Easwaran

Contents

PART THREE
The Keys to Self–Love

Acknowledgments

This book was created with the support and encouragement of my beloved husband and best friend, W. Mark Richardson, and our children, Mark Jr., Carolyn, and H. P., and my grandson, Tiger, and his mother Shanti.

I am equally indebted to William and Audrey Richardson for financing the research for this book; Gail Winston, the kind of editor writers dream of having; Candice Fuhrman, agent par excellence; Roy Carlisle, whose early advice made this work a reality; Dorothy and April Provost, friends and pillars of strength; Carl and Joan Stockbridge, whose generosity to the world has brought them an abundance of everything good; and Dr. Brenda Wade, my friend and a gifted therapist.

Finally, I would like to thank the members of our San Francisco abundance group, who shared their stories so that others might heal; Blanche Richardson, the manager of Marcus Books in Oakland, who has supported and encouraged us and numerous black authors; and Niravi Payne, a brilliant therapist whose research on shadow grief influenced the creation of this work.

—BRENDA LANE RICHARDSON

My thanks to Stephen and Ondrea Levine for their compassionate work with grief and loss and their generous assistance with this work. Thanks and deepest appreciation to Joyce Gillis for emotional and administrative support. My gratitude to my Essence Communications Family for their encouragement and support, Edward Lewis, CEO, Susan Taylor, editor-in-chief, and Ziba Kasheef, my insightful senior editor. Thank you to our editor Gail Winston for "getting it" and to my friend and our literary agent Candace Fuhrman for carrying the ball and Roy Carlisle for hours of editorial guidance. To Reverend Dr. Dorsey Blake, Professor at the University of Creation Spirituality and Pastor of Fellowship for All Peoples Church who contributed scholarly data and inspiration, thank you. I am grateful to my colleague Dr. Jesse "In Your Face" Miller for many curbside consultations. Thanks also to Yvonne Moss, Ph.D, for her assistance, and to Catherine Bremer, manager of the Presidio branch of the San Francisco Public Library. Finally, grateful acknowledgment to Chow Chow Imamoto, R.N., for friendship and spiritual mentorship, to my Dear Sister friend Brenda Richardson for traveling this journey with me, and love always to Sathya Sai Baba.

—DR. WADE

Authors' Note:
To You from Us

We started this book more than a decade ago. It was a late-night phone conversation between two sista/friends. You know the kind of discussion we're talking about; women have been whispering intimacies about troubles in their relationships since humankind first set up housekeeping in caves. But our conversation, during which we stopped to pray, became something far greater than the sum of who we are.

Brenda Lane Richardson studied to be a Baptist minister, but she left her religious work believing that God had indeed called her though not necessarily to preach to congregations. She has since written several books. Dr. Brenda Wade, widely recognized as an *Essence* columnist and as a frequent guest on several daytime talk shows and on national network news, is a family psychologist who has been in private practice for twenty years. For fifteen years Dr. Wade had a personal mentorship with Dr. Virginia Satir, the founder of family therapy, who taught her that so much of what occurs in relationships, from the way we attract or discourage possible mates to the way we interact in a union, is connected to patterns of feeling and behavior that have been passed on by family members from one generation to the next. So when Brenda Richardson admitted that she and her husband weren't getting along, Dr. Wade suggested she look to her past to discover the true source of her difficulties.

We've been buddies for about seventeen years, and this book is an outgrowth of that friendship and our professional expertise. It reflects our commitment to our own healing and growth, which forms the foundation of our work. Both of us have been in therapy, attended healing retreats and classes, and meditated and prayed a lot. As Dr. Wade said to twelve hundred of her colleagues in her keynote address to the 1993 California Convention of Marriage, Family, and Child Therapists, people who work as healers need to engage in their own personal growth work.

The pain that is inherent in the human experience is amplified in the United States. We are a "nation of immigrants," a nation of people who have experienced disruption and loss. This is true whether the traumatic historical experience is the loss of tribal lands and culture by Native Americans, the isolation and discrimination experienced by newly arrived immigrants, the enslavement of African people, the anti-Chinese "Yellow Peril" laws, Japanese American internment camps, or the Holocaust. None of this pain can simply be "put behind us."

Our belief that everyone needs to heal specific historical losses is exemplified in a comment by Secretary of State Madeleine K. Albright. Although raised as a Roman Catholic, Albright learned in 1997 that she was of Jewish heritage and that her Czech grandparents and other relatives were Holocaust victims. Though she had never met these relatives, when she spoke publicly about her ties to the past, she said, "When I was young I didn't often think about grandparents. I just knew I didn't have any."[1] As she continued speaking, her voice broke and she had to struggle to maintain her composure.[2] Albright's sense of loss over family members she never knew was a reminder that unspent grief spans time. We carry it with us like invisible baggage.

We, the authors, are proud descendants of slave ancestors we never knew. We realize we've been blessed. We have good lives and are grateful for them, but we dare to ask for more. This book is our effort toward that end.

Prologue: A Letter to Mama

Dear Mama:

I'm writing because I didn't want people to assume from the title of this book that I was dissing you. I've written you many letters since that day, more than a decade ago, when you placed a pillow and a blanket on the floor, stretched out on your back, and died. People were amazed at the way you left this world—"If she wasn't sick, how'd she know when she'd die?" they asked—but I wasn't a bit surprised.

You are, after all, the same Mama who at twenty-two bought your first house, a building so antiquated it had no electricity. When you showed my father your acquisition, he thought you were crazy because he didn't know "how to wire no house." Not to worry, you told him, and brandished a flashlight and a book on how to install electricity. Mama, you taught me that we can give ourselves anything we can imagine.

By the time we'd moved to a thirteen-room house in a fashionable neighborhood in Brooklyn, Daddy had taken off, and you were rearing me and my sister on your own. You held down a full-time secretarial job, and you were always dreaming up new pursuits. First, you self-published a book of children's stories and convinced a chain of five and dime stores to purchase all 10,000 copies. Another time, the phone kept ringing with folks asking for the Able Moving and Storage Company. That night, I told you about all the wrong numbers people had dialed, and you said, "Oh, I forgot to tell you, I've gone into the moving and storage business." Years later, when my sister and I went to college, decades before there was anything called "dance aerobics," you paid our tuition by producing a record that taught people how to dance and lose weight. You wrote the lyrics, rented a recording studio and a band, and, when the vocalist didn't show, you sang the songs yourself.

Mama, through this and other experiences, you taught me how a black woman could survive and prevail in this world, but only if we are stronger than everyone else. You taught me that no matter how bad the experience, it was to be viewed as a lesson, that every loss should be seen as a gain. You took me right where I should be so I could learn what I had to in this world.

But the one thing I desperately needed that you couldn't teach me caused you so much pain that, even with your strength, at sixty-four years old you lay down to die. You were so starved for love it must have felt as if the loneliness in your heart would devour you. Your marriages lasted only long enough to teach you that the one thing worse than being lonely is the ache of living with someone without intimacy.

After my father left, when I was eight months old, you waited a while before marrying again. I was five years old when I met your new husband, my "Daddy Billy." We moved into a just-built suburban house and our family felt complete. But after three years, when that union failed, there were no good-byes for us. You didn't tell Billy you were leaving because you didn't "want any trouble out of him." He left for work and then your brother pulled up with a big truck that we all filled with our belongings. Little was left behind besides your note telling Daddy Billy he had ten days to vacate your house. You told me to pretend I'd never met him. Over the years I thought my longing for him had been bled out of me, and yet all these years later when I see a newly built house something tightens in my chest. Your steely determination could regulate every aspect of my life except the chambers of my heart.

Mama, you taught me real good how to leave a man. But because you never learned yourself, you couldn't teach me how to make love work. Not only could you not teach me to love a man, you couldn't teach me to love myself because you couldn't love yourself. I don't mean any disrespect, Mama, and I worried that you'd think I was somehow looking down on your life. Then I had a dream about wearing your clothes and my concerns were chased away.

In my dream I was walking in a rainstorm, along a road near your childhood home in Holland, Virginia, dressed in your real alligator shoes and one of those fancy sequined dresses you and your girlfriends used to buy when you went searching for Mr. Right. Strangely, I wasn't troubled about getting filthy and I continued to move easily, even when the dust turned into huge mud puddles that reached to my chin. By the time I arrived at my destination high on a rock looking out over the muddy fields, the dress was ruined, but the emerging sun shone down on your shoes, which were so sparkling clean they seemed illuminated.

When I considered that dream, I knew the rain signified a washing clean, a transformation, and that the sun was God, the giver of light. Later, I understood why your shoes had remained untouched by the mud. Shoes, of course, are made for walking, for moving on. Your message was clear. I don't have to be stuck in your pattern: looking good outside but feeling empty on the inside. Nor do I have to make a choice, as you had, between having love or being strong. I can have both.

You were right, Mama (and you probably know that). You were smiling fifteen years ago on my wedding day, and I absolutely know you were with me two years ago when, in the middle of a workday, my fax machine went off with a note from my husband. He'd written, "I love you and I can't wait to see you tonight." Reading the note, I could have sworn I heard you shouting "hallelujah!"

I'm saying now what I told you that day. I love you, Mama. Thank you for being the school I was born into, for teaching me to honor God, for supporting me even when I saw things differently from you. You didn't like it when I talked about slavery. You'd say, "Even God can't change the past." I certainly didn't know that the past would one day be the key to my healing.

We've never known your great-great grandmother, but during one of my healing exercises, I knew I'd come closer to understanding the despair and hopelessness I'd felt concerning my love life when I wrote her a letter. Because I didn't know her name, I called her Emma and pictured her waking in the slave quarter, starting her day by gritting her teeth, bracing for trouble, and knowing she could expect only two responses from men: The one who was white would rape or beat her; the one who was black would have to look the other way. I asked her about her life and told her about mine, including the lingering grief I have felt over losses she could never mourn. I sobbed as I said her name aloud and thanked her for taking the lash for me, for bearing the pain and then pulling herself up and carrying on. Because Emma refused to give up, I live. Her strength is the jewel of my slave legacy.

When emancipation came, Emma must have continued on even in

the face of her depression, exhaustion, and disappointment over her spurious freedom. Surely by then her rage had become a habit. Unknowingly, she passed on to her children her belief in scarcity, her fears about men and love. Her fears about love affected her daughter's life; yours, Mama; and mine. Now I have children of my own, and in a loud revolutionary voice, I declare to the universe: The pain stops here. Thanks be to God for lasting love.

Your daughter always, BLR

Introduction

*"I wouldn't trade my experiences for anything,
as painful as some of them have been. I'm even grateful for the abuse,
because it brought me to where I am and made me who I am today."*

—OPRAH WINFREY

We open with this quote from Oprah Winfrey, because we too believe that even our most pain-filled experiences are priceless gifts that offer us opportunities to grow and to learn to live abundantly. If we can correctly interpret and resolve our hurtful experiences, we can discover and expand into our highest and best selves. Most of us identify our wrenching experiences as being personal and singular, beginning and ending with our own lives, but we would like to suggest that our most painful experiences are rooted in our history. This is a reality that Oprah Winfrey identified when she first read Toni Morrison's Pulitzer-prize-winning novel, *Beloved*. As she has explained, she recognized this work as a turning point in our nation's coming to terms with our tragic past. Whereas, before, the focus was on the historical details of the slave experience, *Beloved* forced us to confront what slavery *felt* like. Ms. Winfrey decided to produce and star in the critically acclaimed film adaptation of *Beloved* because she recognized that the real legacy of the slave experience is emotional.

The shame that white as well as black people still feel about slavery (because the racism it unleashed continues to haunt us) meant that Ms. Winfrey, one of the most powerful and popular people in the entertainment business, couldn't convince most of her fans to see *Beloved*. Long before the movie was made, Toni Morrison said she expected people to resist reading *Beloved* because the emotional impact of slavery is "something black people don't want to remember, white people don't want to remember. I mean, it's national amnesia."[1]

While the novel and film adaptation of *Beloved* were powerful and beautifully rendered, we believe you'll find that *What Mama Couldn't Tell Us About Love* takes a very different approach. We show you how the past can help you in the here and now. We're certain that you'll feel empowered as you identify your inherited strengths. You may also feel reluctant about exploring the more hurtful aspects of our history. But turning your back on those feelings would be particularly unfortunate if it means you remain deeply conflicted about the faulty beliefs that evolved during slavery. As you will learn in this book, when we humans feel emotional pain because of events, we often create unconscious beliefs that help us cope. But coping isn't all it's cracked up to be. While it's true that it's better than giving up, there's a high price to pay for adaptability. Sometimes people use coping tactics when they're no longer necessary. Beliefs that were once coping strategies can become burdensome,[2] and these burdens can affect personal relationships.

People of all races operate on the basis of a belief system made up of familial, cultural, and personal messages, as well as those that can be traced back to specific historical events. As a way of justifying slavery, for instance, many whites developed beliefs about people of African descent, as well as their own place in society, and, consciously as well as unconsciously, passed those messages on to their children, who in turn communicated them to their children, and then onto newly arriving immigrants. Black people are negatively affected by those beliefs—especially the fallacious doctrine of white supremacy—every day. We African Americans have also naturally internalized beliefs about ourselves from that period.

What Mama Couldn't Tell Us about Love examines our emotional legacy, a legacy of feelings and beliefs that developed from our collective experiences, beginning with the kidnapping of our African ancestors when they were dragged in chains to the "New" World, and continuing as their descendants suffered through the violence and humiliations of the Jim Crow laws passed across the South around 1914, and latter-day racism. All of this impacted us financially and socially. These historical events, fraught as they were with complex and diverse highs and lows, tragedies and triumphs, have cast a long shadow over our lives. We know that to give and receive love fully demands that we first appreciate our own inner beauty and learn to love ourselves. Yet getting in touch with our true selves, and with the shame, anger, and fear that certain aspects of our history have caused us to feel, can be overwhelmingly difficult. These emotions are connected to grief, and it is grief that keeps people from fully loving and being loved.[3] If we are to cherish ourselves and create abundance in our lives, we must allow ourselves to grieve our brutal history and ultimately to make peace with it by embracing its lessons.

Given our history, what is most admirable is that we have retained our great capacity for love, as depicted in songs that top the charts, in poetry, and in novels and films that win us international recognition. Yet in our personal lives, our need for intimacy often goes unfulfilled.

A barrage of statistics indicate that most black women will never have lasting romantic love in their lives. But we believe that for every one of us who is ready for love, there are enough good men who are willing to heal and grow. We believe that God, who *is* love, wants us to have love in abundance. After all, the Creator wouldn't give love to some of us and leave the rest of us wanting. The big piece that has been missing for us is an integration of spirituality in areas of our lives that have been deprived. Divine power is real, as so many recent studies on the power of prayer demonstrate. In addition to the spiritual work that we need to do, many of us must examine what we have learned about romantic relationships, sorting through the love lessons passed on to us through the generations.

Although it seemed quite apparent to us that we could gain power by exploring our ancestral legacy, we were initially startled when a few people we knew, and some we didn't, were opposed to us writing this book. A few of their milder comments included:

"Honey, don't go there."

"Why dig up those old bones?"

"How could my love life be connected to slavery and today's racism?"

We were initially startled by these responses, but on reflection they made sense. After all, many of us go to work each day dressed in our Masters of the Universe suits. We aren't wearing rags that may be stripped from our breasts by a slaveholder who parades us and our children on an auction block. Yet our unknown great-great grandparents' shame lives on in our collective memory.[4] Our history didn't just happen to a group of anonymous people. These people were our ancestors, and in many respects, they are part of us.

The subject of transmitting intergenerational patterns has been discussed in relation to other groups. In *The Dance of Anger*, Harriet Lerner examines female patterns in relationships, and in *I Don't Want to Talk about It*, Terrence Real demonstrates how depression can be passed on from father to son. The idea that a culture born of the slavery experience has been passed from generation to generation was first suggested by psychiatrists William Grier and Price Cobb in their groundbreaking book, *Black Rage*, published in 1968. More recently, bell hooks and sex therapist Dr. Gail Elizabeth Wyatt makes the connection. In *Sisters of the Yam: Black Women and Self-Recovery*, hooks connects "our difficulties with the art and act of loving" to our emotional deprivation and the unending grief resulting from slavery.[5] In *Stolen Women*, Dr. Wyatt writes: "Given the passage of time, you might assume, African American women should be very different from their ancestors in their vulnerability as members of society. But a group simply cannot walk away from such a systematic assault unscathed, particularly if the assault continues in new ways."[6]

What Mama Couldn't Tell Us About Love takes this approach a step further. It acknowledges the hidden belief system that grew out of slavery and shows how those beliefs are reinforced, and how they interfere with self-esteem and love. Engaging in this healing program is like getting involved in a diamond excavation; and it's no coincidence that we use this gem to make our point. The world's richest diamond fields are in South Africa. Our inner strengths originated with our African ancestors, and like carbon that transforms into diamonds after being subjected to monumental pressure, our ancestral gems lie deep within us. In healing, we remove barriers to love—which are damaging beliefs formed in response to slavery and racism—so we can reveal and polish our jewels to their greatest brilliance.

So we begin by learning from past hurts, reading between the lines of our history. Millions of our people lived and died and had children born into bondage, and after emancipation others suffered through another hundred years of bitter racism. Although the most egregious discrimination declined a few decades ago, racism continues to wear away at us in more subtle forms. This history of loss is part of our emotional and psychic heritage. Slavery set the tone for us to be treated as inferiors, explains Dr. Nancy Boyd-Franklin. She writes: "The process of discrimination is evident at all class levels. It does not disappear or lessen with advances in economic status, education, the neighborhood in which one lives, career, or job level."[7]

Over the decades a few whites have altered their appearance in an attempt to look like African Americans so they could study and understand our experience. In one much-discussed case, in 1994, Joshua Soloman, a twenty-year-old white student from the University of Maryland, shaved his head and took doses of a medication that darkened his skin temporarily because he planned to spend several months living as a black man. Soloman said he conducted the experiment because, like many white people, when he heard African Americans complain about racism, he "played a sympathetic role, but deep down, I had my suspicions." Wanting to learn the truth, he traveled to Washington, D.C., Atlanta, and Gainesville, Georgia, with plans for eventually heading North. But after a few days, he ended the experiment saying, "I just couldn't take being constantly pounded with hate. It never seemed to stop." Writing of his experience in the *Washington Post*, Solomon told of store keepers following him around and being rude, of women locking their car doors and rushing into their homes as he innocently passed by, and of whites refusing to give him directions when he tried to find a friend's apartment.[8]

Soloman's experiences were corroborated in 1998 by President Clinton's race advisory board, which reported widespread evidence of "white privilege." After fifteen months of study and hundreds of dialogues around the country, the board concluded that white privilege is built into the daily indignities that minorities endure and whites generally do not. They were referring to a world in which we are often unfairly targeted by the police and made to pay more for big-ticket items such as cars, and a country in which the median annual family income for whites is approximately $47,000 versus $26,000 for African Americans.[9]

Dr. Boyd-Franklin would not be surprised by this panel's findings. She has written: "It is difficult to convey fully to someone who has not experienced [it] the insidious, pervasive, and constant impact that racism and discrimination have on the lives of Black people in America today. Both affect a Black person from birth until death and have an impact on every aspect of family life, from child-rearing practices, courtship, and marriage, to male-female roles, self-esteem, and cultural and racial identification. They also influence the way in which Black people relate to each other and to the outside world."[10]

Psychologists such as Virginia Satir and Harriet Lerner have recognized that the cumulative effect of unconscious pain can destroy relationships even before they begin. Despite our unwavering belief in these theories, we understand why some of our people may be wary if they misunderstand this book's message. After all, if we admit there's room for improvement, that message might be thrown back in our faces, as so much information, valid and fallacious, has been used against us. That was certainly the case in 1965 when future senator Daniel Patrick Moynihan's report on black Americans was published. The now infamous Moynihan report narrowly focused on our history and portrayed us as pathology-ridden and self-destructive. Our work, which is dramatically different, focuses on our enormous well of inherited strengths and talents and our genius for survival. We acknowledge that, like all human beings, we have issues that require work, and that a lot of those issues relate to our particular history.

Acknowledging that we have any issues at all is taking a risk. Some people might say, "We've all had hard times; why don't they get over it?" or "I always knew black women were hard to get along with." The truth of course is that no one racial group has cornered the market on successful relationships. More than half of all marriages and more than 60 percent of second marriages, regardless of race, end in divorce. We are all looking for ways to make love work. And this year (the last of the millennium) is a time for completing unfinished business—we must be prepared to take some risks.

Like many therapeutic approaches, ours may provoke the resistance that typically comes up when anyone faces pain-filled subconscious issues. This is a normal part of the psychotherapy process. There's no such thing as confronting inner wounds without also needing to get past the automatic resistance to feeling pain. This is how the subconscious mind attempts to protect us from further suffering. We anticipate this response from black as well as white readers.

Despite any initial discomfort, we urge you to keep reading. Valuable energy and emotional resources are not available to us when kept underground. It's like dragging around a hundred-pound sack. Life is short, but it can feel excruciatingly long for those who must live without satisfying love. In the healing process, we empty the heavy sack, and as our load gets lighter, our energy is freed up so we can make love work in our lives.

The idea of choosing to live abundantly may even seem frightening. As bell hooks points out, many of us develop coping strategies based on imagining the worst and planning how to survive. She explains that accepting the notion that the world "is not an alien place, and that there are enough resources to meet everyone's needs . . . demands that we adapt a new mind-set, the belief that despite racism, we can find everything we need to live well in the universe."[11]

We recognize that many men of our race and both men and women of various races will benefit from reading this book, but we have chosen to speak directly to women like us, whose ancestors were kidnapped and transported to lives of slavery in the United States, the Caribbean, or Latin America. We are also aware that there's no single kind of black woman. Some of us hail from a long line of successful marriages or have broken through emotional barriers and created happy and satisfying relationships, while others have not. We are all unique individuals who can be found in remote towns in Japan, in corporate offices in major American cities and small towns, in projects not far from luxurious suburbs, on fashion runways in Europe, and on sultry Caribbean islands.

But the millions of descendants of the people stolen from sub-Saharan Africa and transported to countries throughout the Western Hemisphere (and that means most of us) have the experience of racism and oppression in common. One African-Caribbean sister, Ondine, a thirty-five-year-old surgeon who was raised in Haiti, realized how her ancestral history has affected her love life. Divorced from Dan, her husband of two years, Ondine discovered the connection between her marital difficulties and her parents' move to the United States, which included leaving Ondine, who was six, with her grandmother.

Ondine said, "My mother and father left me because they were chasing the American dream of greater material good. They didn't realize that by leaving me, they were repeating the pattern forced on our enslaved ancestors who were separated from their children. I've felt terrible shame about being abandoned. Learning to love myself has been like trying to draw water from a dry well. My parents didn't love themselves either. My lack of self-love has definitely kept me from forming a healthy relationship. I just wish I had known more about myself and my history before I even looked at a man."

You don't have to be a child of Mother Africa to identify with the concerns we raise. Women of other races have pointed out that they struggle with many of the same problems; obviously black women haven't cornered the market on grief. Adult children of immigrants, no matter from which country their ancestors hailed, will find these themes strike a particularly familiar chord. A similar sense of loss may be an enduring part of their consciousness, affecting the way they eat or spend or love or parent. Many white friends and colleagues who have read this work have begun to look closely at the issues in their lives that may be connected to their own ancestral grief. One woman in particular began crying as she recalled that her father experienced bitter discrimination after immigrating to the United States from Italy, and eventually changed his name so that it would not reflect his heritage. "He lost his name and any sense of who he was," she said. Adult children of parents who suffered during the Depression may also find scarcity themes familiar as well. But a major premise of our work is that our issues arise from circumstances that are unique.

Certainly other immigrant groups came to this country under severe duress and experienced tremendous prejudice on arrival. But they chose to come here. Moreover, the children of the Italian, Polish, Jewish, and Irish could assimilate into the American culture, and they became "white" in the eyes of society, whereas our color was used as an excuse for keeping us separate and isolated. Asian groups, despite the prejudice and discrimination they have faced, have found sustenance by being able to retain some of their family structure: customs, languages, and traditions. Irish and Italian people maintained continuity and cohesiveness through the Roman Catholic Church, just as Jewish people did through their culture and religion.[12]

Our ancestors were forcibly brought to a country where their oppressors forbade them to speak their language, practice their customs, or even keep their names. Their family lives, which had been the foundation of their governments and communities, were completely disrupted. Although legally sanctioned discrimination has ended, we have never been fully accepted. Doctors William Grier and Price Cobbs write that "the hatred of blacks has been so deeply bound up with being an American that it has been one of the first things new Americans learn."[13]

Their message sounds especially prescient when we hear the advice a U.S. customs clerk recently gave a young woman who was newly arrived from Ethiopia about how to succeed in this country. "He told me to stay away from black people, to keep my accent, and never let anyone assume I was a black American," she reports. As African Americans, we have grown up as outsiders in our own land.

Another reason the discrimination we face differs from that experienced by immigrant groups, explain researchers Joe R. Feagin and Melvin P. Sikes, is that there is a cumulative emotional toll that is "freighted with centuries of racial oppression of which [African Americans] are consciously or unconsciously aware." Feagin and Sikes point out that past injustices aren't forgotten because the indignities continue, creating a constant rewounding. They write: "Experiences with serious discrimination are stored not only in individual memories but also in family stories and group recollections."[14]

Most therapists don't take into account the social and historical contexts of African Americans nor the deeply buried intergenerational patterns. Dr. Wade's work has taken a different route. While many of her clients are African American, she also works with people of other ethnic backgrounds and encourages them all to examine their family histories.

In the quiet of her San Francisco office, her clients tell stories of forebears who escaped pogroms in Russia; famines in Ireland; wars in China, Korea, and Vietnam; and, here on American soil, the disruption of Native American family life caused by forced tribal relocations and boarding school separations. Young as well as older, often well dressed and professional, they weep and sometimes rage as they experience the grief their ancestors never had time to heal from because they had to push on to survive. Having resolved their anger, shame, and sorrow, which were compounded by their inherited patterns, many of her clients have moved on to healthier, happier lives.

How can we explain their transformation? All humans are of two minds. There is our rational mind, which doesn't take into account the feelings connected with our history. The other aspect of our mind holds onto pain-filled memories and feelings of those who came before us. And because those traumas were unresolved, they were passed on to us. An old adage says we're doomed to repeat whatever the generation before failed to complete.

Ninety percent of our beliefs and behaviors arise from the subcon-

scious. Right now, for example, your conscious mind is reading and processing these words, but your subconscious hears the traffic outside and
remembers your first-grade teacher's name, your birth, and the loud
argument that your mother had with your father when you were eight
months old. Traumatic memories need working through so we can
release the emotional energy connected with them and the faulty belief
system resulting from the unresolved pain.

Without emotional healing we would be like the escaped slave,
Sethe, a character in *Beloved* who tries unsuccessfully to "beat back the
past." She has an affair with Paul D., also a former slave, whom
Morrison describes as "blessed in his manner. Women saw him and
wanted to weep."[15] But Sethe and Paul D. struggle in their relationship
because a ghost from the past stands between them. Like Sethe, we can
be haunted by our grief.

The only way we can attain freedom is by bringing our past into the
light of understanding. What's required is a different sort of liberation
movement, one that allows us to work through the shame and guilt that
keeps us from embracing ourselves. Slaves were granted physical freedom. Emotional emancipation is a process we must choose for ourselves.

To that end, this work is user friendly. There are eleven chapters and
three parts. Part one includes chapters 1 and 2. Chapter 1 is a personal
narrative by Brenda Richardson. She discusses how her damaging
beliefs kept her from creating lasting love, and then, after marrying a
wonderful man, how she worked with Dr. Wade to use the positive messages of her ancestral legacy to create an abundance of love in her life.
In chapter 2 we describe how our ancestors' unexpressed feelings about
the trauma of slavery led them to form damaging beliefs, which in turn
produced coping mechanisms and led to behaviors that were repeated
through the generations.

In part two, chapters 3 through 9 fully delve into each of the damaging messages that we call "anti-intimacy" beliefs. At the start of these
chapters, we have included opportunities for recharging the spirit by

---

*The biographical details of their stories were found in the *Great African Americans
Knowledge Card* series; and the book A *Shining Thread of Hope*, by Darlene Clark
Hine and Kathleen Thompson; the autobiography of Rosa Parks, *My Story*, by Rosa
Parks with Jim Haskins, Dial Books, New York, 1992; as well as in *African American
Biographies*, edited by Barbara Levadi and Lynn W. Kloss.

recalling how other black women overcame obstacles and eventually triumphed. We present condensed bios focusing on women whom we call Sister Spirits, who are with us in spirit as we move toward emotional freedom. Their lives embody the positive principles emphasized in each chapter.*

Some of our information about slaves' lives and a few direct quotes come from early interviews of former slaves. Late in the 1920s, various black academic and state-funded teams initiated oral history projects with former bondpeople; and from 1937 to 1939, the Federal Writers Project conducted interviews that culminated in 2,300 typewritten narratives.[16] Many detailed such extensive horror that some white editors and readers doubted the veracity of the accounts.[17] Let it suffice to say that while some important details of the period may have been edited out of the final slave narratives, they remain a rich source of information about our ancestors' lives. In reading through many of the narratives as well as history books detailing that period, we came away with a heightened sense of pride and are confident their stories will affect you in a similar manner.

You'll find that we've interspersed our message with reference to spirituals, the religious songs created by our ancestors that offered them emotional release. Many spirituals were also encoded with communications that assisted escape plans. When you see familiar verses, we hope you will sing them aloud so they can comfort and inspire you on your journey to emotional freedom.

The chapters in part two are composed of four parts: (1) an exploration of how a particular anti-intimacy belief has affected the lives of one or more women who are either members of the therapy/support group we initiated for the purpose of practicing the processes we share here or who represent a composite of clients Dr. Wade has worked with through the years in workshops, clinics, groups, and private practice; (2) a discussion of historical events that led to a particular anti-intimacy belief; (3) an opportunity for you to consider how those long-ago events affected your childhood; and (4) exercises to help you transform your life.

We urge you to read the book straight through, beginning with chapter 1 and moving through each one progressively, without skipping, even if you initially feel a given chapter doesn't concern you. Even if your first response is "this isn't what I believe," we urge you to fight through what may be denial and continue reading. Each chapter will help you better understand the next.

Chapters 10 and 11 in part three focus on the remaining keys to self-love. These include learning to forgive genuinely those who have hurt us and strengthening "life-enhancing beliefs." These beliefs afford us certain strengths, such as creativity and intuition, which many of our people have harnessed to help them survive and prevail despite extremely difficult conditions. Life-enhancing beliefs can be used to their greatest advantage once we have worked through our anti-intimacy beliefs.

Also in part three are suggestions for starting support gatherings called "abundance groups." In the event that you choose to work collectively with the healing tools and ideas presented in this book—and we hope you will—we have included the stories of women in our San Francisco abundance group. The five sisters in this circle began meeting weekly in the fall of 1998, working through many of the principles we discuss in this work. We feel blessed to know them, and as we have watched them grow and transform, we are reminded of God's action in our lives. Marisa, one of the women in our group, said that knowing that other members had similar issues freed her for the first time to share details of her childhood without shame. You can work with this material individually or gather your own support group to assist you in your growth. Abundance group members can eventually introduce one another to potential mates. A member of one of Dr. Wade's womens groups met and married the cousin of another member.

When the opportunity presents itself, we have included humorous remarks, jokes, and even an amusing but informative self-test to lighten the mood. We are sisters who love to laugh. You might enjoy knowing that at the start of this project, Brenda Richardson was on the phone telling Dr. Wade that she had lost her mother's wedding ring. She expected a sympathetic response, but that's not what she got. Dr. Wade said, "Well, it isn't as if your mother was a role model for how to have a great marriage." After howling with laughter, Brenda Richardson said, "The universe gave us our title." We named our book *What Mama Couldn't Tell Us About Love*. As sisters who revere our mamas, we had healed enough to know it's okay not to follow in their emotional footsteps. Thanks to their sacrifices, we can choose to have better lives.

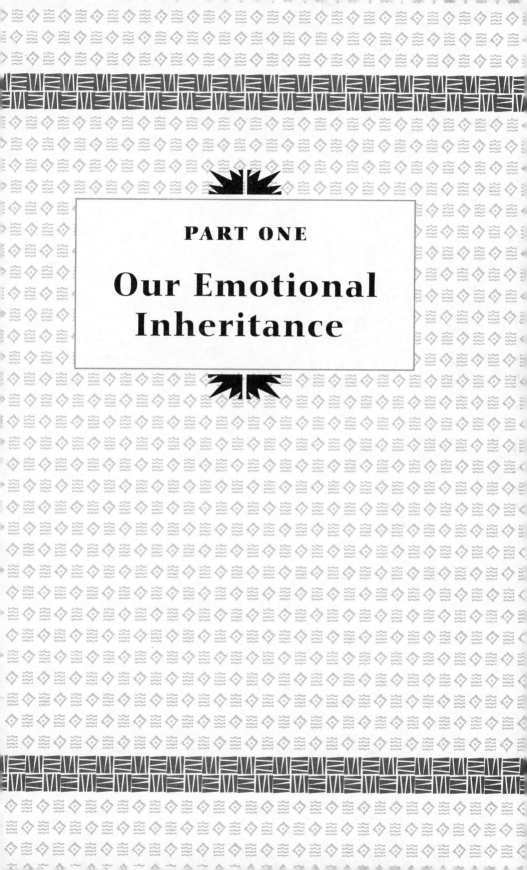

PART ONE

Our Emotional Inheritance

1

The Past as a Presence

It was a weekday morning with our children hurriedly preparing for school. My husband, Mark, and I were already preoccupied with details of the hectic day ahead. Just as we were about to rush out the front door, our eight-year-old son, Mark Jr., yelled, "Prayer!" and we thrust backpacks and bags out of the way. Arms circling one another, we bowed our heads. This was not the first time we'd interrupted the morning dash to pray, but it was the first time I could remember Mark Jr. being anxious to participate in a prayer. Just as we were finishing, little Mark stared meaningfully at me and then at his dad, and said, "Thanks so much, God, for a mom and dad who love each other." My husband squeezed my hand.

That scene occurred more than three years ago and was just a pause in a busy day, but I will always remember it as the official turning point in my life; after a lifetime of longing for lasting love, I knew we had created it. Mark and I have now been married for fifteen years, but in our early years together, we lost too much time in angry, tense moments.

I'm breaking my tradition of privacy to share details of my marriage, because I want to demonstrate through my personal experiences that a life of abundant love is possible for all of us. Whether you're married or single, lesbian or straight, I hope my story will encourage you to work toward satisfying love. I'm a perfect example of a difficult reality: If you get the love you've been praying for and you aren't ready for it, you can still lose out.

If you are not currently in a relationship, keep in mind that the right person can arrive at any time. When I met Mark, I was a divorced single mother. I'd had the strength to leave my first marriage only after working with a therapist. It was my only physically abusive relationship, but looking back, it seems as if I specialized in dating dysfunctional men of various races.

When I was thirteen, my first boyfriend, Carlos, was the "war-lord" of the Chaplains, a Brooklyn gang. Our times together were fleeting. I remember waiting for a bus to take me to junior high school, when Carlos ran by, saw me, and paused long enough to kiss me gently on the lips and tell me he loved me. When he sped off, I realized he was being chased by several knife-wielding members of a rival gang. Although the men I dated later in life were deemed more socially acceptable, the truth is, after Carlos my lack of self-love only led me downhill. At least Carlos told me he loved me.

I don't have to tell you about the kind of men I was attracted to. (Honey, you've probably dated some of them yourself.) Once my first son was born, though, I became more selective about the kind of men I dated, and aware of my lousy track record, I continued working on my issues in therapy and turned to God for help. I prayed for a highly principled man, one who put his spirituality into practice, and I also asked for my heart to be softened. I wanted to be able to trust a man again.

Many of my friends were scornful and advised me to be happy with what I could get, because "the pickings for sisters were slim to nothing." But I kept on praying, especially weekday mornings. My son's nursery was located in a church that opened at dawn, and I would drop him off before work and rush to the sanctuary to spend a few minutes in prayer. I believe that the Holy Spirit not only hears our prayers, but helps us when we help ourselves. My life changed because my prayers gave me the strength and opportunity to continue learning more about why I had chosen abusive men in the first place.

In 1979, as the editor of a women's magazine, I spent a week in Manhattan. On my last morning there, I had a horrible argument with a male colleague and said some terrible things to him. About an hour later, I realized my feelings toward men in general had fueled my anger. As I'd been doing for many months, I closed my eyes and asked God to show me how to let go of my rage. Opening my eyes, I saw it was only minutes before my scheduled interview, but I felt compelled to find the colleague I'd argued with and apologize to him.

When I found this man, he listened patiently as I apologized, but he also wanted a favor. He had to meet an old school friend but was worried about getting lost in Manhattan. Since I knew my way around the city, he suggested that I accompany him to Grand Central Station. I definitely didn't want to go, and it meant postponing my scheduled interview, but something told me to and I did.

At the stroke of noon, I was standing near the elevated clock in Grand Central Station waiting with my colleague, when I noticed, in the midst of the crowd, a tall, powerfully built, and dramatically handsome man dressed in a clergyman's shirt. I thought, that's the kind of man I need, someone who lives his faith. I was shocked as this stranger suddenly shifted direction, walked purposefully toward us, and extended his hand in greeting. He was the man for whom my colleague had been waiting. And because God always gives us more than we ask for, this was also the man I had been waiting for all my life.

A year later, when Mark, an Episcopal clergyman and academic, quit his job and moved to California where I lived, I introduced him to my friends, a few of whom had been questioning my sanity during what they called my "heavy praying" stage. As I made introductions, I noticed that one of my friends hung back. When she finally approached, she whispered, "Honey, give me the address of that church where you prayed."

What we didn't consider was that neither Mark nor I had a clue about how to make our relationship work. We certainly tried to learn. When we realized we had a tendency to argue over small things, even before we married, we consulted a therapist. We learned a great deal about ourselves and tools for discussing problems, but the benefits of our work did not last.

Throughout the years, I also joined the recovery movement, explored my childhood losses, and read scores of self-help books. (Mark also worked to change and grow, but I would not presume to tell his story for him.) My fascination with the psychology of relationships led me to coauthor three self-help books. One of them, written with Dr. Wade and published in 1993, was called *Love Lessons*. Written for people of every race, *Love Lessons* helps readers to understand how their love relationships mirror those of their parents, because behaviors are passed on intergenerationally, from grandparent to parent to child. Everyone, regardless of race, acts out an emotional script that was written generations before by her ancestors.

I subsequently completed another book with fertility therapist Niravi Payne. *The Language of Fertility* shows readers how unexpressed intergenerational grief is so powerful it can even interfere with reproductive functioning. I felt the universe was shouting at me to explore my deeper past for answers to my own dilemma: Mark and I didn't want to break up, but we didn't know how to stay together peacefully. I renewed my prayers, asking for a ray of light so I could see the right answers.

My transformation began when Dr. Wade urged me to go back to my earliest family history, and I listed all the players I could remember hearing of. Then I noted the difficult patterns they had passed on to me, as well as the strengths, such as faith in God, creativity, intuition, and determination. We discovered that the very attributes that could help me create a healthy marriage also existed in my ancestral legacy, but I needed to embrace them. Prayer, meditation, reading, and journal writing led me to understand that I was grappling with feelings of grief, such as depression, anger, shame, and fear. I'd spent my life unconsciously repressing those feelings, which can wreak havoc.

We are drawn to lovers whose personalities are dominated by characteristics similar to those we're trying to hide. This, as well as our family patterns, explains why we wind up with mates who have personality traits similar to those of our parents.

How do we attract someone healthier or improve an already existing relationship? We identify and name these hidden feelings, then connect them to the childhood and generational experiences from which they arose and work through them. For instance, in both of my marriages, I acted out the same scenario. If someone yelled, I would run around the house closing windows, telling others in the house not to get angry and to lower their voices. My fear of shouting was directly related to growing up in one of the first African American families on my block. The day we moved in, my sister and I excitedly raced to the backyard, and spotting an elderly white woman in the adjoining yard, greeted her with a cheery "Hi neighbor!" This woman hobbled toward the fence and growled, "Niggers!" I felt shame about being shunned, and that feeling was intensified by having a sister who flew into loud tantrums.

At some point in my childhood, I decided that acting angry was shameful, but I wasn't aware of that feeling. In my family, the message was that no matter how difficult life became, we were to focus on the good and ignore problems (and the emotions that went with them). So we were involved in an elaborate cover-up. Indoors, my sister acted out her rage, which we contained by shutting the windows and pretending it didn't matter. Instead, we focused on the physical aspects of our house, which was big and located in a lovely neighborhood. Appearances meant everything to us; the exterior details formed a wall behind which we hid our real feelings.

Knowing what had happened in my childhood was a start but not enough to begin healing. Dr. Wade kept encouraging me to learn as much as possible about the beginnings of my family's family history. She said my intergenerational cycles would hold the key to understanding my childhood experiences and my present-day life, so I looked back at my family history and researched information about slavery. One question that occupied my thoughts was why African people were enslaved. The answer I uncovered shed light on everything else I learned about my buried inheritance. I hope this information will do the same for you. What follows is a condensed version of what I learned.

A combination of circumstances occurred during the late seventeenth and early eighteenth centuries that led to our people being designated as slaves. There was a worldwide demand for crops such as tobacco and rice and indigo (a plant from which blue dye is obtained).[1] The south had hundreds of thousands of acres of prime, undeveloped land. New planting techniques had been introduced that required gang labor.[2] And developments in ship building provided the means to construct vessels that could transport hundreds of human beings.[3] Together, these factors created opportunities for colonial landowners to make more money than they'd ever dreamed of. And as they began to count their profits in their heads, they realized the highest possible revenues could be earned by not having to pay workers at all.

The first victims of this greed were impoverished people from England, Scotland, and Ireland—former prisoners, convicted criminals, kidnapped street urchins, prostitutes, and the homeless—as well as some Africans who were forced to work as indentured servants. The problem for the colonialists was that there weren't enough poor whites available to work the fields profitably, and a growing number of critics felt it was morally wrong to enslave Europeans.

Still in search of free labor, landowners enslaved Native Americans. But thousands died from diseases brought over by newly arrived Europeans, and furthermore, they were so familiar with the terrain that many managed to escape and then hide out with sympathetic tribes.[4] Our forebears became prisoners of brutal circumstances, therefore, when wealthy landowners turned their sights toward Mother Africa, where many of our people were already agrarian workers, accustomed to laboring long, hard hours in the bruising sun. At first Europeans kidnapped Africans themselves, but later they were able to find unscrupulous Africans to do it for them. But there's more to this story.

Africans customarily enslaved their prisoners of war, but unlike American slaveholders, they didn't separate families, and they allowed slaves eventually to earn their freedom.[5] The American brand of slavery was not only far more dehumanizing but also so extraordinarily profitable that many European merchants would stop at nothing to acquire humans to trade. For example, some merchants encouraged African village chiefs to declare war on one another to yield prisoners of war who could be offered for sale. In addition to supplying village leaders with guns and bribes, the merchants encouraged tribal crime because Africans punished their criminals with slavery. Eventually, many Africans wanted to end the practice of selling their people, but they found themselves in an impossible bind. They needed guns to protect themselves from slave raiders, and the only way to get guns was by trading other Africans for them.[6]

Perhaps you grew up hearing stories of African ancestors who had royal blood. There may be some truth to those stories. A surprising number of our people who were enslaved were tribal nobles who had been captured by rival tribes. Their enemies considered them too dangerous to keep as servants and were quick to sell them to whites so they could get rid of them for good.[7]

Another way in which we seemed to meet the brutal requirements for slavery was that once in the "New" World we could not easily escape and blend in with local inhabitants. There were a number of free and indentured Africans (some had voluntarily migrated to the colonies; others were captives who had been brought as "servants for life," but even these people were much freer and more independent than latter-day slaves would be[8]). Some Africans had married impoverished Europeans, and others eventually became people of standing. For the most part, however, we were largely unknown to the colonists. This would prove to be a bonanza for slaveholders, who were able to convince the populace that we were creatures without human feelings and could not be hurt the same way they were.

Over the next several decades, in much the same way that companies today spend millions on advertisements to convince consumers of their point of view, slaveowners engaged in the most sweeping propaganda campaign in the history of this country. Using the power of the printed word, including newspapers and pseudoscience books, as well as cartoons, minstrel shows, and passionate oratory, the message from the highest governmental offices to churches, schools, and homes across America was that people of African descent deserved to be enslaved. On the other hand, Irish, Scottish, and English people, as well as a number of others of European descent, were deemed "white." The deadly and insidious doctrine of white supremacy was born.

Ignoring our deep spirituality, proslavers convinced others that we were godless heathens. Though we were prized by landowners because we were such hard workers,[9] they portrayed us as inherently lazy. They passed laws prohibiting us from being educated, arguing that we were intellectually inferior. Although they made us the backbone of every plantation house, where we prepared meals, bathed and dressed whites, and even breast-fed their babies, they convinced others that we were filthy and dishonest. They ignored the cries and pleas of thousands of black mothers and fathers whose children were sold away from them and claimed we were happy and content with our lot. They pronounced us ugly, comparing us to apes and satanic figures, and yet, as our varying hues indicate, their men and women found us physically and sexually desirable.

W. E. B. Du Bois described this miseducation campaign as "one of the most stupendous efforts the world ever saw to discredit human beings, an effort involving universities, history, science, social life and religion."[10]

If there was ever proof that these slavers knew they were perpetuating falsehoods, it is in the recent results of DNA tests that indicate that President Thomas Jefferson fathered at least one of the children of his slave Sally Hemmings. For many historians, this latest evidence was the final piece of the equation that led them to conclude that Jefferson and Hemmings carried on a long-term affair. Some believe that Jefferson loved Hemmings. If so, he didn't let his affection stand in the way of protecting his profits. Through his writings, Jefferson worked to convince others that we lacked humanity.

Slaveholders represented only 30 percent of the Southern population, but they dominated the Supreme Court and the presidential cabinet. Their lies were all about protecting investments, and they saw to it that slavery became deeply embedded in the country's social, political, and economic fabric. By the 1830s, the two million slaves in the United States were worth an estimated billion dollars, at a time when annual federal revenues were less than $25 million. And it wasn't just the South that benefited. Captives were transported by Northern ships, Northern insurance companies financed the voyages, and slavery was the basis for ship building, banking, and many of the early factories.[11]

There were morally upstanding European Americans and Native Americans who saw through the falsehoods concerning black people. I recognized the names of white abolitionists such as John Brown, who led an armed revolt against slavery, and I learned more about the former indentured servant, William Lloyd Garrison, a journalist who with the support of free black people, made the Abolitionist movement a force to be reckoned with.[12] But I'd never heard of the great Seminole leader, Osceola of Florida, who risked not only his own life but also the lives of his people, for the sake of our ancestors' freedom. When the United States offered to end warfare, pay for the tribe's livestock, and give them new land in the West, Osceola refused: He would not have been permitted to take along black Seminoles. These were people of African descent who were escaped slaves; several had married into the tribe, others were offspring of these unions. Many were eventually caught and sold into slavery, and after numerous wars and Osceola's death, the defeated tribe did go West, taking along black brothers and sisters. But 300 Seminoles, including black tribespeople hid out in the Everglades, and never did sign the treaty.[13]

Despite the heroic efforts of many, the belief that we were inferior was nearly universally accepted in America.[14] The institution of slavery is objectionable in any form, but what made slavery in America different from bondage in other countries was our classification as chattel, which meant that rather than being human, we were "moveable property." Historians Darlene Clark Hine and Kathleen Thompson write that slave codes in Africa, as well as throughout the world, "usually recognized the essential humanity of the person enslaved and treated slavery as a temporary, economically dictated condition. The American South changed all that. Being a slave became part of the definition of a black person. And being a slave meant having absolutely no rights."[15]

The brutality that shaped our ancestors' lives determined how we would be regarded, in both the North and the South. The stories of our people have been unearthed, but their feelings have remained buried.

I began to see that the anger and depression my ancestors must have felt at this degrading, inhuman treatment had set a pattern in motion. I wished I could pick up the phone and call one of my unknown great-great grandmothers to confirm that her feelings of grief had ricocheted through my family to me. Since that was impossible, I decided to rely on my intuition. Breathing deeply, I closed my eyes and imagined I was one of my long-ago ancestors on the day she was kidnapped by slave traders. I saw my arms and legs bound in chains as I stood near the rail of a slave ship that was about to sail away. I began to weep, feeling desperately alone because my parents were gone and there was no one to protect me.

This image was certainly familiar. During my childhood, my father took off just after I was born. Soon thereafter, my fair-skinned mother was fired from her government job when her white boss discovered she was "colored." In the forties and fifties, even in so-called liberal cities, such as New York, African Americans could not easily get jobs in offices, stores, and even some factories, unless they were light enough to pass themselves off as white. As a result, many "passed" at work and "lived black" at home, in their segregated neighborhoods.[16] With no money coming in, my mother made a heart-wrenching decision. She sent me and my sister to live with my grandmother and aunts from the time I was a year old until I was five. As I considered my life against the backdrop of history, I realized I was crying because I knew how painful it was for my ancestors to have been kidnapped. I, who had lost my parents in my infancy, knew how it felt to have lost the first loves of my life.

I called Dr. B. (Dr. Wade), and she helped me understand why this grief from the past felt so present. "Bren," she said, "what our ancestors went through was an experience of wholesale abandonment. They usually lost their parents, husbands, wives, children, and everyone they'd known in their villages." I said, "I know there's a connection to the trouble in my marriage. If my great-great grandmother's mother was taken away from people she loved and then was constantly having people she loved sold away from her, she must have learned to protect herself by not letting anyone she loved get close because . . . "—on the same wavelength, we said together—"it hurt too much when they left." This is a key element in our work: Our ancestors developed beliefs that were passed down to us through words and actions.

Later that night, I reminded myself to focus on the issues I'd brought to my marriage and not to point an accusing finger at Mark. I told him that our arguments had been my way of pushing him away. I explained that I had unconsciously assumed he would leave me one day and that I had kept him from getting too close so it wouldn't hurt so much once he took off. I also told him, "I need you and I always will." He held me in his arms as I cried. I had never felt that close to him before.

Although I shed a lot of tears during that time of my life, I was convinced that I didn't feel depressed. I had read that depression affects more than half of African American women, but not me, I thought. Although I'd struggled with depression earlier in life, since then I'd developed a cheerful outlook on life; people were always complimenting me on my sunny nature. It was Mark Jr. who put my dilemma into perspective. He asked, "Mom, how come, when you think no one is watching, you look so sad and angry?" His question forced me to get in touch with more of my hidden despair and my lack of self-love.

Today, Mark and I communicate on a new level because I have recognized my grief and fear, and I have continued working through these emotions. In a couple, it takes only one person's changing to break negative patterns, because the other person then has emotional room to grow and change. I now think of Mark as a man who can be trusted, and I don't project my negative feelings onto him. I see him for who he really is. This has practical implications. Just recently, for instance, we were having a thorny conversation. I suggested that I needed more help around the house. Even though he was doing a lot, I couldn't handle the rest alone. We had talked about this before, to no avail. With children and a career to juggle, I needed all the help I could get. But this time, when we had the conversation, I didn't shame him or try in any other way to control him, so our conversation produced a different outcome.

I listened as Mark said he felt overworked with his own schedule. Speaking from the heart, I said, "I don't know what the answer is, but when I'm cleaning up after the children and spend so much of my time with housework, then time with my own work, I feel unsupported, as if there isn't anyone who cares enough about me to help out." He seemed to hear me.

Later that day, I returned home with Dr. B. from a meeting. We were discussing her recent trip to Senegal, on assignment for *Essence*. She had toured Goree Island, where many of our ancestors were held after they were kidnapped and before they embarked on the brutal voyage across the Atlantic. As we entered the house, the first thing I noticed was the smell of Pinesol, which told me that Mark had been scrubbing floors. The house, in fact, was spotless.

After greeting us with warm hugs, Mark went to the kitchen and soon returned with cups and a pot of steaming herbal tea, which he sat before us.

My greatest prayer for you, dear reader, is that as you begin to transform your damaging beliefs, and enhance your inherited strengths, you can create a relationship that will allow you to feel this heard, this nurtured, this loved.

2

Limiting Beliefs and Freeing Beliefs

"I am six years old, and I feel anger and sadness and shame." It was the voice of Mary Ann,[1] now forty-one, as she participated in a regression exercise during an abundance group meeting. Mentally traveling back to her past, she recalled a time when she felt overwhelmed by these painful feelings. Unable to express them, she had unconsciously hidden them away and adopted a secret belief system to help her survive. When we face traumatic or overwhelmingly hurtful events, our subconscious mind protects us by taking over and coming up with a way of thinking about the situation that mitigates the pain. The thoughts form the basis of our beliefs about ourselves, love relationships, and other aspects of our lives.

Mary Ann continued describing her memory: "Earlier that week, I went to church with a neighbor and accepted Christ as my savior. I thought Mommy would be glad, but she was angry that I hadn't joined our family church. She said she wouldn't go with me to my baptismal ceremony, that I'd have to go alone."

The incident might not have weighed so heavily if Mary Ann hadn't already felt alone and unloved, but this event crystallized much of what was wrong in her young life. She was only four when her parents

---

[1]For the sake of privacy, we have changed the names and biographical details of all of the women discussed in this book. In addition, for the sake of brevity, we have merged some individual stories.

divorced and her father moved to another state, leaving Mary Ann with her mother and two sisters. But her mother, a fair-skinned woman known in their small town as a "great beauty," was color struck and showed favoritism toward Mary Ann's almond-toned sisters. Mary Ann's skin is a beautiful chestnut brown.

"I remember getting up that morning and dressing myself in a little white dress. I left the house alone and walked to the church alone along a dirt road. I remember it so well." Her voice broke as she added, "The belief I formed that morning was that life is a lonely journey, that I would always be alone and have to make it on my own."

As an adult, she unknowingly lived out this conviction, never becoming involved in a committed relationship and shouldering overwhelming responsibilities at work. Identifying and transforming her beliefs took her closer to creating a balanced life. It seems bizarre that our lives can be determined by something we aren't even aware of and don't consciously remember, but every human being operates from hidden thought patterns. They are the wiring that affects the way we interpret things, how we feel about life and love, and our assumptions and behaviors.[1]

As Mary Ann's story demonstrates, we create our beliefs on the basis of our experiences. We internalized the messages of the people who raised us as we listened to what they said and watched what they did. Beliefs become entrenched as they travel through families from generation to generation, beginning with early ancestors. That's how our parents acquired their beliefs. This chain reaction stops when the buried beliefs become conscious. Then we can correct them and improve our lives.

We already have some tools, because we have benefited from a lot of what we learned. Take for instance the belief that if we stay strong, we can survive life's worst calamities. Someone who raised you may have taught you that, but this person also may have inadvertently passed on to you ideas that limited opportunities for abundance in love. If your mother rolled her eyes when your dad spoke, you received a negative message about men. If your mother lived alone, she may have communicated to you that partners are unnecessary or that they hurt or abandon you. If she ended up with lovers who abused her, she conveyed several messages, including that she didn't deserve better, that love hurts, or that all men are dangerous. If your father or brothers warned you that men are snakes, you didn't have to work hard to interpret that message.

Siblings also contribute to our belief systems, as do other close relatives and teachers. Brenda Richardson's older sister, Tamra, became convinced that Brenda could be a writer, and when Tamra was thirteen, she began paying Brenda a penny a page, from her baby-sitting earnings, to read classic literature (including *The Complete Works of Sigmund Freud* and *War and Peace*) so that Brenda could eventually become a writer. Brenda, who has a learning disability was struggling in school, but since her mother had written a book, the idea of becoming a writer seemed within reason. Later, a junior high school teacher confirmed Brenda's talent. That's why, a few years later, when a racist high school counselor insisted that Brenda was incapable of abstract thinking and recommended she go into domestic work, Brenda refused to accept his opinion. She believed she could write, so she persisted.

Although she didn't know Brenda Richardson at the time, across the country in San Francisco, Brenda Wade experienced something similar. She told her physician, who was white, that she wanted to be a psychologist, and the woman said, "You're trying to bite off more than you can chew." She encouraged Brenda to find a more traditional role for a young black woman. Obviously, this didn't slow Brenda down. Two generations before, a belief was formed in her family that essentially states: "With God's help, we will find opportunity where others see impossibility." As with so many of our people, her positive beliefs helped her to achieve her goals.

In both incidents, the white professionals operated out of racist imprinting. Belief in white superiority and black inferiority originated with slavery, and those beliefs have been passed down in families and on to each wave of newly arriving immigrants. Although those beliefs can usually be changed through positive personal interactions with black people and education regarding the nature of racism, the messages are deeply entrenched. Most whites say they don't have negative beliefs toward African Americans, but when some of the same people are given a test that taps into their unconscious beliefs, the results often tell a different story. Two Yale University researchers recently found that prejudice can be so pervasive and deeply rooted that many people are not consciously aware of their biases.[2]

Black people were not completely immune to these messages of black inferiority and white superiority, for we also were bombarded by the media, as the whole culture was, with ideas about how we should look, and we have internalized some of them. The implicit message, of course, is that anyone who doesn't have what the media is selling (including straight blonde hair and white skin) is flawed.

Damaging societal messages, coupled with beliefs Mary Ann had formed in response to her mother's neglect, convinced her she would always be alone. She rationalized, "I've traveled all over the world and never met a man who is reliable. There are no good ones." Rationalization is one of the ways we defend our unconscious beliefs. Denial constitutes another protective response. Before engaging in her healing work, Mary Ann convinced herself that she liked being single. She told friends, "I don't need a man."

Our beliefs and defense mechanisms operate in a vicious circle. Mary Ann couldn't resolve her fear because her belief told her the fear was legitimate. She then acted out her fear by pushing people away, which made her prophecy self-fulfilling. But recently her mother came to visit her in Sacramento, and Mary Ann decided she wasn't going to be one more in the long line of women in her family who had never had a satisfying relationship. She joined our abundance group soon thereafter and learned to sort through her experiences for clues to her beliefs and behaviors.

Joyce Nelson Patenaude, a psychologist who focuses on how beliefs affect our lives, writes: "We attract experiences that match our beliefs or we interpret experiences based on our beliefs. This is called *selective* focus. If we believe that we have to struggle to get what we want, we will attract countless ways to struggle. If we believe we don't deserve a happy relationship, we will choose and create a relationship in which we will be unhappy. If we believe all men are users, we will attract men who are users."[3]

The sisters in our abundance group listed what they discovered to be their beliefs about life and love: "My feelings don't count." "Men are dangerous." "Loved ones always leave." "I don't deserve anything." "I can't count on anyone but myself." Women in our group, as well as many of the hundreds of other sisters Dr. Wade has worked with, have a hidden theme in common: "I am somehow intrinsically flawed and unlovable." This is the most damaging of all our beliefs because it makes us unconsciously fearful that we deserve to be deserted by those we love. It causes anger, rage, and depression and leads to controlling behaviors; it leaves us either holding on too tightly or pushing away those we love.

Regarding the core thought of feeling unlovable, it's important to say that our limiting beliefs don't make us flawed. We don't need to be "fixed" so we can "get" lovers. As Dr. Wayne Dyer reminds us, since God is everywhere, including inside us all, we are "as divine as everyone and everything else on this planet now or that has ever been here or ever will be."[4] The goal is to know ourselves so we can reach that state of being Virginia Satir has described as "congruence," a state in which what we think and feel and the way we behave are in sync. To the extent that our body, emotions, and thoughts are in alignment, we feel peace and joy and a closeness to the Spirit. Then we radiate love and attract it with ease.

It's important to view our life experiences and our belief systems as the gifts they are. Consider what a wonderful entity the mind is, processing our experiences and creating messages to protect us. Our beliefs are like the musical composition "The Moldau," which the Czechoslovakian composer Smetana created to reveal the power and beauty of rushing water. The composition starts with just a flute, reminding us of the trickling of a stream, sounding wistful, filled with longing. Eventually, other instruments—the violin, oboe, bases, and brass—join in, just as one hidden spring joins into a larger stream, one warm and gushing, the other cold and tranquil, their waves flowing over rocky beds, uniting with a brook and rushing on. Finally, as the music gathers strength, power, and complexity, it ends in rich magnificent chords, as the water meets a river and then moves on.[5]

Our beliefs and experiences follow this pattern, with the messages of our ancestors flowing down through generations to join other family knowledge and experiences. The hidden springs and streams continued to converge, as our parents acted out of their needs and feelings, combining their messages with our innate genetic code and personality traits. Our individual highs and lows of childhood also contribute to this river as it grows in size and depth, and we need only remove the boulders that block the flow, so it can join with the majesty of the oceans.

Throughout literature, oceans have symbolized transformation, a washing clean, and death and rebirth. How perfectly appropriate these images are when one considers that the tears that fall from our eyes and the amniotic fluid in a mother's womb have the same components as the fluids in the oceans of Mother Earth. For it was across the great Atlantic, in the cradle of civilization, where the course of our ancestors' lives met unalterable change.

OUR HISTORY/OUR LIVES

Imagine that you are sitting alone in a peaceful African village. The other members of your tribe are out hunting and gathering food for a special ceremony. Your daughter is getting married tomorrow. The wedding ritual is among the most sacred, invoking the blessings of your ancestors and the Spirit of Life. This custom literally goes back to the dawn of humankind. As you sew decorations into your daughter's bridal wrap, you feel the peace of the village around you. Here, where you live, in an empire called the Songhai (or Mali, Katsina, or Kanem-Bornu),[6] your people are called the Bambara (or perhaps they are the Mende, the Ewe, the Akan, the Kimbundi, the Zulu, the Hausa, or the Teso).[7] Your family is looking forward to the celebration. You are known far and wide for your special yam dish. And you know your mate will be proud of you, not only because of the wedding wrap but because of the feast you have prepared.

Suddenly, a stranger bursts in, grabs you, and holds a knife under your throat, warning you not to cry out for help. But your first thought is for the safety of your thirteen-year-old son, who is somewhere close by, home today because of a minor ailment. You risk your life, calling out to warn him, shouting in Twi, Fula, Hausa, Shona, or one of a thousand other languages,[8] but to no avail. For as the stranger drags you to a clearing, you see your boy, his long legs covered in cuts and scratches from fighting his captors, joined with several others from neighboring tribes, arms chained together, and you join in this cruel lineup. What are you feeling? Shock, bewilderment, terror, and fury, but there's no time, no way to express any of this.

After miles of travel, you reach a coastal area, where your kidnapper strips off your clothing so you can be inspected and then traded to strange beings with pale pink skin. You know who they are; the stories have traveled far and wide. Some tribes call them the "stealers of souls." In exchange for you and other captives, your kidnappers are given beads, cloth, rum, iron bars, and some things you later learn are guns.[9] Once the bargain is sealed, you are branded with a searing hot iron and thrown into a stifling dungeon along with other women, where you remain for months until enough people are captured to fill a vessel.

Though you are terrified and ill from confinement, you keep hoping that someone who loves you will battle his way past the armed fortifications that surround the coastal area and rescue you and your boy. You long for your beloved mate, and your daughter, mother, father, siblings, and elders. Tears roll down your cheeks as you recall their dear faces. Any hopes of rescue are dashed as you are loaded onto a vessel and shoved into the dark hold of a ship, where you are chained into a space the size of a coffin.

For three months, your own body fluids mingle with the blood, vomit, and excrement of others. You hear the cries of babies being born, and in some cases mothers smothering them to protect them from this life that is no life. You witness the last gasps of people rotting from diseases or slowly starving from the rancid food your captors distribute to keep you alive. On occasions when you are led above for a few minutes of exercise, you see in the wake of the ship many brown bodies floating—sickly captives who were hurled overboard—the sharks encircling the vessel, filling their bellies with human flesh.

Your fellow captives respond in a number of ways. Some seethe and plan rebellion. Others become zombielike. Unlike some, you wouldn't consider making a dash for it and hurling yourself into the ocean. You don't know where you're going, and you're heartbroken over all that you have lost, but you're telling yourself to hold on for the sake of your son. You have seen him occasionally, and you recognize the rage and defiance in his eyes. You long to comfort and soothe him, knowing he has a fiery personality and that he's not going to take this quietly.

Against all odds, you arrive in a new land. Even more miraculous, as you are pushed to make room for other captives, you see that your son, though much thinner, is also alive. But despite the crack of the whip on his back, he's still struggling, while you, in your despair, have become more docile.

Buckets of cold water are thrown on you to wash off some of the stench that has settled on your body. You are led with other Africans toward a stage where the pale strangers check your teeth and prod and poke your body cavities. It isn't until you see that some of your people are being led off with separate pink people that you realize there is a possibility your son might be taken away without you. Your eyes grow wide as someone points at you and begins to lead you off. You try to communicate in your native language, gesture toward your son, but someone slashes you with a whip to silence you. Nothing will silence this anger. You rear up, stretching your arms toward your son. Though he stares ahead impassively, you can see by his eyes that he too is terrified. As you are crowded into the back of a cart, the rain begins to fall, and you know the spirits cry with you.

You never see your son again. The pain of losing him and all your other family and tribespeople is horrible, wrenching, almost beyond the limits of your endurance. Somehow you go on. But you never forget him or your other loved ones, even years later, after you have been raped by the man who makes you call him "master" and you give birth to another child, a daughter. You love this half-white child fiercely and protect her and care for her as best you can. You want to be close to her, knowing all too well that child is your heart, your soul, your lifeline. You cling to her ferociously, even though you know there's a good possibility that you'll lose her too. And that is what happens. She is sold away to pay off a debt for your "owner," despite your screams for mercy, your cries that you have worked hard and will work harder still. This loss reopens the old wound, which has never really healed.

Bitterness and despair show in your face and in your behavior. Now that your third child is gone, another young slave and her daughter share your hut. When you overhear the woman telling her daughter to work hard, you bitterly interrupt, saying it doesn't matter how hard any of you work, that you'll never have anything to show for it. This is something you have come to believe, based on your heartrending experiences. But you have learned to cover up those feelings of despair and ignore them.

In the meantime, both your son and daughter have grown into adulthood on other plantations, believing they can't count on anyone for closeness and warmth, that love is temporary. After all, they lost the first love of their lives, and heaped on this are the everyday cruelties and humiliations of being a slave. Under these conditions, they can't love themselves, and so it is impossible for them to teach their children to love themselves.

Slavery was a way of life that continued for more than two hundred years. Proud, free, independent human beings were reduced to positions of chattel and were made to swallow the pain of their losses. For many of us, the anger, shame, and depression are still at the core of our experiences. The beliefs formed to contain that core of unspent grief were reinforced through another hundred years of legally sanctioned racism for countless individuals and families. Though many of us still bear scars from generations of severe trauma, the wonder and miracle is that we survived and lived on to form families and communities and create music and art and make scientific breakthroughs.

Finally, still imagining yourself as one of your ancestors, see yourself as an elderly bondwoman standing at a stove shaping "master's" biscuits, singing out your defiance: "Cain't nobody turn me round, turn me round, turn me round." It was that fierce determination and other strengths that our people brought with them, including their spirituality, from which they drew an incomparable endurance and the will to survive. These strengths gave rise to an alternate set of beliefs that existed alongside the negative ones.

We have distilled, from Dr. Wade's work in her private practice, workshops, and retreats with black women, fourteen beliefs that emerged from our collective experience. We call the seven messages that interfere with our love "anti-intimacy beliefs." The seven messages that lend us particular strengths are called "life-enhancing" beliefs.

Our Emotional Inheritance

Here are the seven anti-intimacy beliefs:

1: *There will never be enough of anything I need, especially love:* This statement defined reality for our enslaved ancestors, as well as sharecroppers and those who worked in oppressive conditions. Our ancestors' lives were severely limited. Many who later migrated to the North found themselves in the larger urban ghettos. Today, 50 percent of our people still live at or below the poverty level. Although some of us have managed to rise above poverty, we don't necessarily have prosperity in our self-love or our relationships. Fear that we will never have enough influences our perception of ourselves as never having enough time or money and not even enough food.

2: *I'm not good enough to be loved:* From a slaveholder's point of view, the ideal slave had to have a deep sense of inferiority. If a slave exhibited any sense of self-worth, she was a candidate for "seasoning," a process of psychological and emotional abuse designed to strip our people of dignity. In addition, because being African was designated as the justification for our degradation, issues of skin color, hair, and features fed into our lack of self-love. The feeling of not being good enough was reinforced during childhood in our homes and in the larger society; the ongoing campaign by the media and entertainment industry continues to promote the idea of white skin being preferable to brown. Many of us remain conflicted about our hair, our skin, and our bodies—our very being. It is not surprising that it would be diffi-cult for us to accept a lover and believe this person could love what we reject.

3: *I'll lose anyone who gets close to me:* With our ancestors torn away from all that was familiar—their villages and their loved ones—and then experiencing the additional pain of loved ones being sold away, they learned that getting too close could mean more pain. After emancipation, millions of African Americans migrated North, and they were later followed by a tide of Caribbean immigrants, all of them searching for a way out of grinding poverty and racism. But this meant more losses for children who were left behind with relatives. Because our psyches lead us to recreate unresolved issues from our childhood, if we were abandoned, emotionally or physically, there's a good chance we have been attracted to men who also have aban-doned us.

4: *It's not safe for me to face my anger:* Our ancestors, who were tortured emotionally and physically, knew that slaveowners and, later, employers would heap more abuse on them if they dared to vent their anger. That situation holds true today. Whether we're in domestic work or corporate America, there are severe consequences for those of us who seem angry. Repressed anger is harmful because it goes underground and makes us prone to physical and emotional distress and passive-aggressive behavior, such as chronic tardiness. As a result, we can develop high blood pressure, become obese, or have other health problems. Whether we seethe silently, mask anger with a smile, or have an explosive temperament, festering anger is dangerous to ourselves and can hurt anyone who gets too close to us.

5: *No matter what I do, it won't make a difference:* With no future to look forward to, facing daily abuse and degradation, and not being able to express anger or grief over their profound losses, many of our ancestors felt hopeless and depressed. Slavery, Jim Crow, and institutionalized racism existed not for a few decades but for more than three hundred fifty years. Generations were born, lived through misery, and died never having experienced deep relief. While our lives are certainly different today from those of our ancestors, we encounter more subtle forms of racism, which, coupled with losses and feelings of isolation, fuel depression. Pain and joy are blocked out by depression, and depression can make us chronically negative toward our lives and our mates.

6: *I have to control everyone and everything around me to protect myself from being hurt again:* Show us someone controlling and you'll see someone who has been hurt and who is frightened of being hurt again. With all the emotional pain our ancestors endured, it should not be surprising that many of us have learned to be controlling. We may exert control by trying to change our partners, telling them what time to come home, correcting their speech or manners, or shaming them if they "misbehave." The biggest problem is that this behavior forces loved ones to run away or push away just to have space to breathe, which is the complete opposite of what we're hoping for.

7: *My body is not my own:* Enslaved women were used for breeding purposes and were the victims of rape. In addition, a mythology that portrayed us as sexually insatiable temptresses was created by slaveowners, who had to explain to their wives why so many of our ancestors were giving birth to biracial infants. That myth lives on, assisted by movies such as *Deconstructing Harry,* in which Woody Allen introduced his first major black character, a stereotypical hooker. We might assume that the belief "my body is not my own" died with our progenitors, but it still affects us today.[10] Some of us may use our sexuality as a way to attract or control lovers, doubting that they can find anything else about us to like. Or we might hide our pain and confusion about our sexuality by becoming overweight or by turning off to sex completely.

Whereas these negative beliefs may be painful to hear and may provoke rationalizations or outright denial, most of us are quite aware of the positive beliefs we have inherited. Here are the life-enhancing beliefs we have identified:

1: *God loves me:* Our people arrived in the "New" World with a deep spirituality, and they adopted Christianity, recognizing that there is one life force, or spirit. Our people created a form of worship that's an amalgam of African and Christian traditions. Faith in the divine, which sustained our ancestors, continues to be a source of joy and peace. For those of us who have never seen a healthy love relationship, our faith can be a motivating force. It can help us to change aspects of ourselves that need healing and free us to manifest divine love toward ourselves and others.

2: *I can make something from nothing:* Centuries of scarcity forced our people to make "something from nothing," which allowed us to cultivate our creativity. That's why so many of us are recognized as leaders in popular culture. Creativity not only boosts our attractiveness but enhances every aspect of our lives. What we can imagine, we can create for ourselves. Creativity is encouraged by self-nurturing, in turn creativity helps us to become more intimate with ourselves, and more trusting of the Great Creator, who is within each of us.

3: *I can make a way where there seems to be no way:* Determination and persistence were evident in our ancestors who risked their lives to escape, in slave teachers who organized secret schools, in those who participated in the Civil Rights Movement, and in many of us who, when doors were pushed open a crack, rushed through and succeeded professionally. In working toward emotional freedom, we also need determination. As with anything worthwhile, healthy lives and lasting love requires persistence.

4: *My heart will guide me if I listen:* Our intuition—which literally made the difference for our ancestors between life and death—as they sought out whites who would be sympathetic to their cause, for instance, or as they chose escape routes—can be an inner guidance system that can help us make the right choices about life and love. Through our "inner eye," we learn to look farther than we can see otherwise as we become more aware of the pulses that guide the universe. This truth, which is already within us, can provide us with a renewed awareness and understanding of those we love, and that includes ourselves.

5: *I bring humor and joy to my life:* We are the descendants of people who used humor in the Motherland to defeat enemies and to entertain friends. We can use our sense of humor to lift our spirits and those of others. Consider the times you've been with people with whom you can laugh easily and how you look forward to seeing them again. Laughter lifts us above despair, and helps to seal relationships because it brings the energy of joy into a union.

6: *I can inspire others to achieve:* Most people include the ability to inspire at the top of their list of qualities hoped for in a mate. Our motivational skills are legendary. Scores of powerful leaders have risen from our ranks who have inspired us not only in words but by example. This includes those who rallied for emancipation and civil rights as well as today's preachers, teachers, and legislators. When we inspire lovers, friends, and family they feel connected to us in a deeper, more meaningful way.

7: *My friends are my sisters:* Our notion of kinship ties was born in the African tribal system. It was nourished during slavery, when suddenly-sold mothers had to rely on other bondpeople to raise their children. That sense of kinship continued in our childhood homes, where we often lived with grandmothers, aunts, or cousins (or people we treated as such). Accustomed to forging "sisterly close" relationships, we can use our notion of extended family to create support groups, help one another to grow, and introduce one another to prospective mates.

What were you feeling as you read through the fourteen beliefs and, earlier in this chapter, when you were asked to imagine yourself in your ancestor's place? The historical section was painful for us to write. Did you perhaps experience revulsion? Outrage? Anger? Sorrow? Numbness? Remind yourself that your emotional responses occur for a reason: They call your attention to a truth that you need to stop and pay attention to. Author J. Keith Miller has written: "Our feelings, when allowed to function normally, constitute a signal system from the unconscious 'awareness' of our body to the consciousness of our minds, telling us what our reality is. When we pay attention to these signals, we can make congruent, reality-oriented decisions about our lives."[11] As you work through this book and reconnect with your ancestors, you will experience a range of emotional responses, essential first steps on your healing journey.

OPENING TO YOUR INNER LIGHT

The meditation–exercise that appears below will help you focus on your chakras—the energy centers in your body—so you can become aware of the flow of energy in your body, mind, emotions and spirit— and learn through images of color, sensations or impressions, what impeding beliefs you may have developed and still live by. The first law of metaphysics is, "energy follows thoughts." Just as laws govern physics, such as, "for every action there is an equal and opposite reaction," there are also laws governing anything that is not physical, such as emotions. Our thoughts and feelings, like everything else in the universe, are a form of energy.

For thousands of years, followers of Eastern religions and indigenous shamans have viewed the human being as a system of complex overlapping energy centers. The Eastern view of medicine and spirituality depends on what are called "chakras" and "meridians" which conduct the energy flow through our bodies. (Chakras are specific energy centers in the body, and meridians direct energy up and down through the body, like a traffic system.) The idea that our bodies react to specific emotional and physical energies form the foundation of Eastern medical practices. More recently, Western researchers, physicians and psychologists have validated this point of view. Those at the forefront of these teachings include Iyanla Vanzant, Deepak Chopra, Joan Borysenko, Andrew Weil, and Caroline Myss. They and many others have found evidence that thoughts have concrete effects in our lives.

You may want to read this meditation into a tape recorder, have someone close read it to you, or check our resource list for a recorded version.

The African Queen of Light

Find a place where you can be alone and sit comfortably. Breathe deeply and close your eyes. See before you a beautiful African queen, dressed in resplendent robes, her body giving off a light that is radiantly bright and comforting. Admire the color of her skin, her features; feel her peace and joy and tranquillity as she smiles and welcomes you, the light shimmering from her radiant brown skin and magnificent rainbow-colored, flowing robe. As you draw closer and closer still, you begin to meld into this queen. Her hands become yours, as do her face and body and robe. Realize that you are this queen of light. Sitting on your throne, you feel energy, in the form of light, flow through your body. Visualize this light as energy:[12]

See a clear red light starting at the base of your spine, filling every cell in your body and then rising up your spine, renewing your energy and vitality as you develop greater health and well-being.

Now picture a fire-orange light, moving in, around, and through you, especially a few inches below your navel, and warming every area of your body, imparting emotional well-being. Next, see a brilliant sunny yellow light, centering around your navel, as you feel your thoughts become positive. Say to yourself, "I have a bright and happy future."

We move now to the area of the heart, the balance point between the lower three chakras, which govern physical, emotional, and mental energies, and the upper chakras, which govern creative, individual, and spiritual strengths.

Visualize an emerald-green light flowing in and around and through your heart, enhancing your sense of balance and self-control, which in turn increases your intuitive powers.

Now see the blue of a summer sky, moving through you and centered in your throat. This is the power of your creativity. See yourself talking, writing, painting, dancing, singing, suffused in this blue light. The avenues through which you can channel your creativity are without limit.

See the light turning the indigo blue of a midnight sky, sending rays of light to the center of your brow, or your third eye, giving you the power to see who you really are as an individual and as part of all creation.

Finally, see a magnificent violet fire, equal parts red and blue, blazing down through the crown of your head, engulfing your entire body. This light manifests spiritual alchemy, changing darkness to light, negative energy to positive, and bringing you the power of forgiveness, spiritual freedom, and success in the world.

Now that you have cleared your energy centers, opening to the free flow of the divine power, it is time to bring the energy of your higher power more directly into the work of identifying your beliefs. Say aloud to your Higher Power: "Where in my body am I holding the energy that needs to be healed?" Put your hand on the first part of your body that comes to mind. Then ask your Higher Power: "What color is the energy under my hand?" Again, take the first answer that comes. Then ask, "What emotion or emotions are in this color?" After receiving the answer, ask: "What events occurred that triggered these emotions?" As memories begin to run through your mind, ask your Higher Power a final question: "As a result of these experiences, what did I come to believe about myself, my life, and about relationships?"

Continue to breathe deeply as the answer comes to you, and when you are ready, open your eyes and write down your answer to the last question. Spend time writing about the feelings and experiences to help clarify them. Then ask your Higher Power: "What color light or energy would wash away and heal the residue of this painful experience?" Whatever color comes to you, see it washing through your body in the form of light energy, pouring into each of your cells as if they were parched desert flowers soaking in rain. Finally, ask your Higher Power to show or tell you what else you need to do to complete this part of your healing. When you have finished, work on changing your belief into a positive affirmation. For instance, Mary Ann changed "Life is a lonely journey and I'll always be alone" to "God holds my hand on my journey. I am worthy. I deserve love, and I give and receive love freely." Write your affirmation on several slips of paper and tape the papers to your mirror, over your bed, and on your desk where your work. At first this statement will sound false. You might hear yourself saying, for instance, "Yeah, sure I deserve love. What a joke." Persist, despite this discouraging voice. Repeat or write this affirmation many times a day, for twenty-one days, envisioning yourself as the African Queen of Light. Affirmations work best when said with feeling; chanting them musically especially helps them penetrate the subconscious mind. See our resource list, page 223, for information on ordering this and other affirmations and meditations.

You will want to get a journal for your healing work. Record this affirmation, as well as others you will develop, and be sure to schedule saying them into your day.

As you continue working with this book, you will gather information about how to transform whatever flawed beliefs you have formed. And don't worry if your Higher Power doesn't offer you an answer the first time you try this meditation. Practice again, the next day, and the next, if necessary.

You'll discover your body does hold the answer to where painful emotions reside. As you work through the seven chapters in part two, which is designed to help you unearth and resolve painful memories, be sure to return to this Queen of Light exercise.

PART TWO

What Mama Couldn't Tell Us...

3

Believe in Abundance

The Sister Spirit guiding us to abundance is Madame C. J. Walker (1867–1919). Born four years after emancipation, she was raised in Mississippi, married at fourteen, and widowed at twenty. None of this stopped Madame Walker from creating the abundance she desired. She became a successful hair and cosmetics entrepreneur and, by the early twentieth century, a millionaire, the richest self-made woman in America.

The story of Madame Walker, like the condensed stories of African American women that introduce all the chapters in Part II, is part of our emotional legacy. The women described, whether living or dead, are with us in spirit, and we can use their stories as emotional power to take action in our lives. As we work to create abundance, Madame Walker's story reminds us that anything we desire is within our grasp.

**Anti-intimacy belief explored in this chapter:
There will never be enough of anything I need,
especially love.**

With a head full of red curls, Faizah, twenty-five, of Cleveland, who works as a clerk for the local public utilities commission, bears a strong resemblance to pop princess Janet Jackson. But on a Saturday evening, as she sat alone in a blues club waiting for a blind date to show up, she didn't feel like a superstar. "I was alone, surrounded by couples holding hands and whispering," Faizah told other participants at one of Dr. Wade's retreats.

Faizah recalled as she waited, "I felt I'd wasted money I didn't have to get my hair looking all good and to pay for a sitter to watch my son. My mom was working, so I'd had to hire someone at five dollars an hour. I was already into $2.50 of that, just sitting there waiting, getting angry, cause he didn't have the decency to call and say he couldn't make it. Girl, I pictured him looking into the club, seeing me, and cutting out quick before I saw him," she brayed, entertaining herself with her own joke. She added, "On the other side of my head, I was thinking that he was secretly married and his wife made him stay home."

Minutes later, when Marcus arrived, Faizah struggled to keep her eyes from opening like headlights as she admired his long frame, elegantly tailored suit, and lips she called "kissable." She recalled how, despite her cool demeanor, she was thrilled by what she saw. "Girl, I thought if I drink me some water, steam will be coming out of my ears. This brother was definitely blazing." Marcus had been profusely apologetic about having been caught in traffic.

Before the night was over, she learned he was a police detective who was on his way up in the department, and she was impressed that he asked provocative questions about her night school classes and her dreams of becoming a social worker. As she stood to go to the ladies' room, she sensed that he was admiring her body, and she was doubly grateful that she had continued going to the gym. At evening's end, he said he was going to thank their mutual friend for hooking them up. She made certain not to appear overly anxious. Funny, though, he never called her again.

Faizah admitted, "That one really hurt. I thought he would at least call. Things seemed to have gone so well." All traces of gaiety gone from her voice, she added, "The situation was like, well, since there are just a few brothers who've got it going on, all the good ones are 'playas' with ladies lining up, so why should they just choose one? My friends call men dogs. But I always said they're cats. At least dogs are loyal."

While waiting in the club, Faizah was engaged in an inner monologue filled with negative messages about men. Her thoughts were running without her being fully conscious of them. Although she may have been unaware of them, there's a good chance that Marcus "read her mind"—through her body language, choice of words, inflection, tone of speech, and perhaps especially facial expressions. There's a Guinean proverb that says, "For news of the heart, ask the face." Faizah's eyes and mouth were like a bulletin board broadcasting her deepest feelings. Later, she privately told Dr. Wade, "I'd had that conversation with myself so often, I could sum it up in a few words: "Men can't be trusted. I expect them to disappoint me."

Faizah's beliefs could have affected her interactions with Marcus in various ways. Listening to him astutely question the waiter about the wine, Faizah may have thought she was flirting when she asked him, "How do *you* know so much about wine?" But her words may have emerged from her mouth sounding contemptuous. Her body and mind working in tandem, she might have conveyed that she was furious about waiting, that she was terrified that he wouldn't like her, and that she expected the worst from him. He soon lived "down" to all her expectations.

We know little about Marcus, not even whether he was the right man for Faizah. She eventually learned from the friend who had set up the blind date that Marcus made only vague responses about what he thought of Faizah. There was something about her that put him off. Shortly after that meeting, he began dating someone who, the acquaintance said, looked a lot like Faizah. He later married that woman.

"That's when I decided to stop sitting around with my friends dishing men," Faizah said. "I heard Dr. Wade say on TV that the only way to make a change in your life is to stop pointing the finger at everyone else and to point toward your own heart to find the answer."

Faizah could be any one of us, a beautiful sister of the Motherland. Many of us are like her in that we have given ourselves permission to get the most stylish hairdos and to have our nails shaped and polished, and we may even take the time to eat better and exercise. Our efforts have paid off: Increasing numbers of us are at our physical best. But our secret conviction that there will never be enough of anything we need, certainly not love, dates back to our ancestors' experience of having to work their fingers to the bone but never having anything to show for it, an experience that persisted for generations in most families. This issue is deeply felt by many African Americans, especially those of us who, like Faizah, are single mothers.

Today, the message of insufficiency resonates through our daily lives with everything from salary inequities with white coworkers to the stark contrasts between the bleak urban landscapes often described as "black neighborhoods" and the lush comforts of "white" ones.

Despite all that we may see and experience that reinforces our scarcity beliefs, we can learn to neutralize the critical voices, either our own internal ones or those of friends or relatives, who might insist there couldn't possibly be enough good men out there. Keep reassuring yourself that there are. And if someone says, for instance, that you're not young enough, and maybe has the nerve to say, "You've already gone through menopause," just tell her what Minister Ava Mohammad likes to say: that you're willing to check out the men part, but that you do not intend to pause. Whatever your age or background, keep on keeping on in your quest for self-love and romantic love.

That's what Yvonne did after decades of being single. This high school principal was sixty-two when she met Ralph, fifty-eight, a divorced university professor, at a conference for black educators. After a whirlwind courtship and lavish wedding, their relationship quickly turned sour. Yvonne began working on her own issues, trusting that if she changed, Ralph would more closely examine his destructive pattern of growing cold and incommunicative when things didn't go his way. As she worked with Dr. Wade, Yvonne realized that despite her love for her husband, she had never really expected their relationship to be satisfying.

Raised by parents who had been respectful but unloving toward one another, that was about as much as Yvonne secretly expected from Ralph, and they both unconsciously anticipated that they would always feel unloved. Determined to have more than the loveless marriage she'd witnessed at home, after sharing what she'd discovered about her part in the conflicts, Yvonne invited Ralph to join her in her in a therapy session. With Dr. Wade's encouragement, she asked him this: "You stopped speaking to me yesterday and wouldn't tell me what you were feeling. I love you and I'm scared. Please tell me what I did to hurt you."

Ralph quickly answered: "I was telling you about my idea to have that addition built onto the back of the house, and you got the same look on your face that one of my little rich white students gets when he interrupts the class to debate a point with me—like he'd humor me but when the bell rings he'd go down the hall and get the right answer from a white professor."

Stunned by his response, Yvonne admitted she had tried to pretend she was listening to Ralph but had actually thought his idea frivolous. She apologized, saying, "It was as if you read my mind."

She eventually learned that contempt is one of the most corrosive elements in a relationship. According to Dr. John Gottman, a research scientist who studies marriages, "Contempt is an insult, any kind of statement that the partner is incompetent, morally inferior, and somehow reprehensible in some way. Unfortunately, contempt can also be communicated by very brief facial expressions that are cross-cultural."[1]

Ralph and Yvonne had more candid conversations, continued marital therapy, and learned to work through their scarcity beliefs and to expect an abundance of love. Their story is a reminder that a wedding ring is no guarantee that we have come to terms with our scarcity issues, but the story is also encouragement that it's never too late to get love right.

Three decades younger than Yvonne, Faizah was equally as determined to transform her life. She began by tracing her lineage back to her maternal grandparents, "dirt farmers" who earned a hardscrabble living. Her father's mother, a widow, took in laundry while raising twelve children. "My people weren't complainers," Faizah said. Looking into a faded photo of her maternal grandparents in Alabama standing before a "beat-up shack," Faizah observed, "No, they didn't look happy. People back then didn't care about that, just about serving the Lord and surviving. All they wanted was for their kids to do better in life."

Faizah's mother did forge a better life. She fought her parents to let her get out of the fields so she could finish high school, then divorced Faizah's father, an alcoholic who walked with a permanent limp. Early in his marriage to Faizah's mother, he had been returning from work when he was brutally beaten and left for dead by a group of white college students who were never charged with the crime. Unable to return to physical labor and unskilled, he was crushed by poverty and began to drink more and more. Despairing, Faizah's mother moved to Cleveland, where she worked as a laundress and eventually opened a check-cashing business.

"Her sisters came up and worked with her, and they bought their first house together, then seven more rental units. They taught themselves how to fix everything. I grew up surrounded by their love. Oh, Honey, now they were old-fashioned about discipline. You had to go out and break off those thin little switches from trees so they could beat you, but one aunt or another almost always came to my rescue. I was their baby. . . . But all that time, I never wondered why they only dated and never married. There was the feeling that if you brought in a man, he'd mess up till you didn't have nothing left."

Faizah's mother, Pat, believed that men could not be trusted, and she had a lot of reasons for feeling that way. At ten, she lost her father to cancer, and shortly afterward, her only brother, who had been expected to help support the family, had run away from home, leaving the others to fend for themselves. Pat's short-lived marriage to Faizah's father only confirmed the message, which she later passed on to her daughter.

Faizah decided not to marry her son's father after she became pregnant. She now attends college at night and hopes to become a social worker. "I thought all I needed was what my aunts and my mother have. They take good vacations, have closets of clothes, whoo! They've got cabinets with drawers built in for each pair of shoes. That's abundance. But now I want someone to share it with. I love my mom and my aunts, but I finally figured it out: They're as unhappy as my grandparents in that picture."

Her innate wisdom, coupled with her growing understanding of her needs, helped Faizah realize her family had created financial abundance but were blinded to their emotional vulnerabilities. Once we get this concept, we can recognize how scarcity manifests itself in numerous ways, not just in our relationships. For example, we might eat as if tomorrow will bring famine, even if our refrigerator is crammed with food. In the career arena, no matter how hard we work, some of us sabotage our careers, showing up late or overbooking clients so they get fed up and leave. We might be so irritable that managers view us as "unpromotable." In the area of finances, many of us spend more money than we earn, have to rely on credit, then scramble to keep up with payments. All of these behaviors fulfill the self-imposed prophecy: I won't ever have enough, and its secret companion, I don't deserve more.

That belief was reflected in the choices made by Lisa, a forty-one-year-old blues singer, concerning her love life. After ending her relationship with a physically abusive man, she decided she would simply stop dating because all men were "snakes." She'd left her former husband because he flew into jealous tantrums. Her father, a psychiatrist, moved away from the family when he fell in love with a white colleague. Although her father provided financial support and kept in touch with Lisa and her siblings, seeing them on weekends and holidays, Lisa watched her mother fall into an ever-worsening depression. "If I brought up the subject of men, Mommy's face would freeze over," said Lisa.

When Lisa swore she would spend her remaining years alone, she thought her worries were over, but in the end she was filled with regret. Over the years she had many suitors, one of whom was so persistent he convinced Lisa's friend to plead his case. "I told her that if she thought he was so great she should date him herself." That's exactly what her friend did, and they've been happily married for years. Lisa said, "I'm glad for my sista/friend, but that could have been me . . . if I'd been able to take off my blinders."

Fortunately for her, and for all of us, we can break patterns once we become conscious of them. Faizah, for instance, who became engaged in much of the healing work we've included throughout this book, is now in a committed relationship with a man who was in her statistics class. She says she feels more at peace, and more than ever she enjoys spending time with her son. She found that the first step toward transforming her scarcity beliefs was understanding how they evolved.

OUR HISTORY: LIVES OF SCARCITY

This country is made up of people of all racial backgrounds, many of whose forebears experienced dire poverty, including those whose parents weathered the Great Depression. But it was our progenitors who were taught by experience that abundance was possible for others but not for black people. Life for slaves was so devoid of emotional and material sustenance that even infants were sometimes forced to get by on the milk left over in their mothers' breasts after the "master's" children had filled their bellies. Their harshest lessons in scarcity, however, had to do with simple intangibles such as not having enough safety, respect, nurturing, or comfort. These deficiencies often led to disastrous consequences.

Author Linda Brent wrote of her Aunt Nancy, who, like so many house slaves, wasn't allowed a bed of her own. She slept on the floor of her mistress's bedroom, to be available at a moment's notice, so that if the mistress "should want a drink of water in the night, what could she do without her slave to bring it? So my aunt was compelled to lie at the door, until one midnight she was forced to leave, to give premature birth to a child. In a fortnight she was required to resume her place on the entry floor because Mrs. Flint's baby needed her attentions. She kept her station there through the summer and winter, [year after year] until she had given premature birth to six children, all of whom died."[2]

Although few of us have family stories that date back to slavery, details of not having enough were repeated to us, adding more planks to our scarcity beliefs. After emancipation, this deprivation was hammered home for millions of sharecroppers who participated in a system that was designed to tie them to a white farmer's land, making it nearly impossible for them to get ahead. The sharecropping system existed for about fifty years.

In many states, black people were legally barred from owning land.[3] Through miracles of industry, however, a few African Americans were able to save enough to purchase land, when they could find liberal white landowners willing to sell to blacks, often at greatly inflated prices.

It's important to note that even with these roadblocks, some African Americans managed to build modest homes, create small businesses, and run farms, even though they were paid less for their products. As ever, our people were eager to earn their keep, and in 1910, at a time when there was more work available for unskilled laborers, rates of employment were higher among African Americans than among whites. Whereas 82 percent of white men over the age of eighteen were employed, that figure was 90 percent among black males. Among females, 55 percent of black women worked outside their homes, whereas 20 percent of white women did.[4]

When African Americans used their hard-earned salaries to get ahead, they often became the targets of white supremacy groups, who either burned them out or lynched the husband and raped the wife. Leon Litwack writes: "The total effect of white terrorism and intimidation was to discourage blacks from accumulating enough to arouse white resentment, while forcing the more enterprising to abandon their homes and occupations and leave the county without any protection or any compensation for their property."[5]

If you consider that at the start of this century, white supremacists predicted black people would not survive—that we would either be killed, kill ourselves off, or starve to death—you begin to recognize the genius of who we are. Our people inherited from their African ancestors a deep and abiding faith in the Creator that would be repeatedly drawn on for sustenance. Empowered by their spiritual convictions, they turned weakness into strength and sorrow into joy, making a way when there seemed to be no way. Rather than dwell on what they didn't have, they praised God through prayers and songs for the abundance they were working toward. One spiritual reads: "I'm a-going to eat at the wel-come ta-ble . . . I'm a-going to feast on milk 'n honey . . . some of dese days."

In the meantime, they used another ancestral gift, kinship, a support for one another that formed the basis of the tribal system. Celphofis Robinson, a 100-year-old resident of Oakland, California, who remembers growing up in the Mississippi countryside at the start of the century, said the key word for his people was *sharing*. "Fathers would hunt, big brothers and neighbors and cousins went fishin', and Mama'd send us kids all over the woods to pick blueberries, and hecky . . . we'd a been whupped if we'd come back with just enough for ourselves. Git us buckets full, and when she were finished making preserves or cobblers, whatever she fashioned, us kids would go round the neighborhood, delivering to others the little bit o' something what we had." And so despite the stinging bite of racism, there was a period of relative stability for our people. By 1917, 90 percent of all black children were born into two-parent families.[6]

Later, in the 1920s, when the boll weevils invaded the cotton fields, eliminating thousands of agricultural jobs[7] and propelling our relatives toward Northern cities in search of work, we continued to hold on by using all of our inner resources. During the Great

Depression, many Americans experienced financial ruin, but black industrial workers were hardest hit when they were laid off en masse, the last hired and first fired. Black domestics and service workers also were faced with sudden dismissals.[8] Our response included rent parties, with neighbors and friends cramming little apartments wall to wall, dancing and playing bid whist while everyone donated something. In churches, matrons cooked chicken dinners that fed folks and raised money to care for others. All over, we were organizing relief efforts, filling food baskets, and sponsoring food drives.[9]

Look at our history and you'll often find evidence of the belief that we could shake some good out of the worst troubles. Dr. Wade's maternal grandfather, who lived in Mississippi, was a child of sharecroppers whose life might have remained unremarkable had he not learned to read, write, and do math. He used his knowledge to challenge the landowner who had been cheating his family and was promptly thrown off the farm. Rather than give up, he learned carpentry and started his own contracting business. In turn, Dr. Wade's mother, became a teacher. She and Dr. Wade's father, a realtor, were able to give their seven children college educations.

The hardships and oppression of scarcity deeply affected our people, and one effect was divisions among our men and women. It all started with the threat that white supremacists believed our men posed, owing to the potential for rebellion due to their physical strength. After all, the African people who survived the brutal Middle Passage were among the hardiest, strongest, and most resourceful. The purported sexual prowess of our men was based on a rumor that apparently began with European missionaries who had been sent to Africa hundreds of years before, and caused envy among some white males.[10]

Intimidated by our men, slaveholders made certain our maternal ancestors believed they couldn't count on black men. This was fundamental to the system of bondage. In the infamous and at the time, widely distributed, Lynch Letter, Willie Lynch, a slave owner in the West Indies advocated mind control techniques. He recommended, for instance, torturing and humiliating a black man in front of his wife and children by stripping him naked and tying each of his ankles to wild horses who pulled in opposite directions.[11] Lynch believed punishments such as this reinforced the belief in black women that their men could not protect them. These methods, Lynch advised, would create an atmosphere in which: "You've got a nigger woman out front and the nigger man behind and scared." This way, Lynch concluded, slave owners could sleep soundly, assured of continuing profits.[12]

Inhumane practices such as these dictated that black men had to look the other way no matter how badly their women were treated by authority. Another practice that contributed to early tensions between black men and women was the convention of slaveholders designating black women and their children, not black men, as a family.

For the most part, the only thing white men could offer slave women was disrespect, even if the white man was President Thomas Jefferson. During his lifetime, Jefferson refused to free Hemmings or their children. In some Southern states, it was illegal to publicly identify the white father of a black child.[13]

When slavery ended, black women were portrayed as having low moral character, but the most scathing caricatures and vicious stereotypes were reserved for our men.[14] Propaganda mills worked overtime, portraying them as rapists, unreliable, lazy drunks, and corrupt leaders. Today, in our changing economy, the image of African American men has continued to take a battering as demographic, social, and economic changes have eliminated jobs they have traditionally held. Thousands more have been driven out of the workforce because of discriminatory practices in hiring and firing.

Another significant economic factor pertains to welfare rules that required that recipients have no able-bodied men in their homes. Many unemployed men were forced to leave or pretend they had abandoned their families. This predicament, which author Linda Villarosa describes as emasculating and humiliating, wore away at our relationships. She writes: "Men, especially poor men, felt powerless, unable to fulfill the roles of provider and protector that society expected of them, and women felt unable to help them. Both felt trapped in a cycle of poverty, where, ironically, they were better off apart than together."[15] In recognition of the damage these policies caused, new federal welfare-to-work grants now include fathers in their programs,[16] but of course, the effects of past experiences could not be quickly undone.

On top of all this, news stories are constantly repeating ominous statistics about our men. And in books and movies they're often portrayed as rapists, drug lords, junkies, gang bangers, thieves, and adulterous preachers. Is it any wonder that we are blinded to the good men out there who are willing to transform and work toward lasting love?

One woman we interviewed said she has nothing against black men but added that she has decided to stay away from brothers. "I don't hate them, I just don't date them anymore." Although she'd been in three relationships with white men, she hadn't experienced any more success with them than she had with African American men. What she and so many of us have not realized is that our hidden beliefs lead us to distrust anyone who gets close. Brenda Richardson certainly learned this when she married Mark, who is white, and they began to struggle with their issues, including racial ones. Unless we're healed, we recreate the same scenarios with mates, no matter what their race or gender. Dr. Wade has heard this from lesbian clients as well.

OUR EMOTIONAL LEGACY

Following is a list of the negative phrases we have collected about men from women clients and friends. They demonstrate the kinds of messages many of us have heard about men. Can you think of others?

> The only difference between a man and a dog is a dog's tail is longer.
>
> As soon as you give him what he wants, he'll be gone.
>
> If we had to depend on your daddy, we'd be on the street.
>
> Well, you know how men are.
>
> Don't expect to depend on a man when you grow up.
>
> That man is no good.
>
> Don't pay your daddy no mind, he's drunk.
>
> That man is so cheap, he's got the first dollar he ever earned.
>
> I ain't studying that man.
>
> That is one lazy nigger.
>
> He doesn't contribute one red cent.
>
> He's as dumb as a doornail.
>
> Your daddy don't care about nobody but himself.

He's the biggest liar that ever lived.

Black men prefer white women.

He better not come crawling back here.

Never tell a man everything.

I will leave his black ass in a minute.

I don't need no man to take care of me.

You should always put a little money aside in case you have to leave him.

'Cause a black man will use you, Honey, and bleed you dry.

I can't believe you were dumb enough to trust him.

A man only wants one thing.

White men will treat you better.

If these messages sound familiar, ask yourself who taught them to you, through words or behavior. It may have been a caring father or brother who thought he was acting in your best interest or a father who was so violent or "woman crazy" that you grew up expecting the worst from men. It may have been your mother or grandmother who frightened you about men by saying something such as, "You'll be lucky to get someone half as good as your daddy; they don't make them like that anymore." Or maybe, if your father abandoned you early in life, you know him only through someone's harsh description.

Your mother or the woman who raised you didn't have to verbalize her criticisms for you to have incorporated her man-doubting beliefs. It was enough to observe her behavior and body language. In addition, negative memories of your father can date back to your preconscious memory.

Catherine, a twenty-one-year-old college student, said her mother never said a bad word about her father, even though her parents had been divorced for a number of years. Still, Catherine sensed that her mom was fearful of him, and Catherine came to dread his anger without knowing why. In a meditation, Catherine spontaneously got in touch with a preconscious memory. She felt she was in utero and her father was forcing her mother to have sex. When Catherine told her mother about this, she admitted it was true and said that she'd left Catherine's father when she was eight months' pregnant because he had raped her.

In looking back, you may have developed a better understanding of how experiences that support your scarcity beliefs deeply affect your behavior with possible mates. In researching what makes relationships work, Dr. Gottman underscored the power of thoughts. He found that couples who averaged five times more positive thoughts and interactions than negative ones had a high chance of marital success.[17] Negative experiences and associations are so powerful that relatively few are needed to destroy a relationship, while a relatively high number of positive interactions and thoughts are required to maintain lasting love.

HEALING SCARCITY/EMBRACING ABUNDANCE

Genograms, created in 1978 by psychologist Murray Bowen, are diagrams of a person's family history. We'd like you to build a version which was created by fertility therapist Niravi Payne.[18] Your genogram work will help you become aware of experiences that may have contributed to your scarcity beliefs. Then you'll be better able to understand how these beliefs affect your love life and what you can do to change them.

Three generations of relatives are included in a genogram: yours, your parents, and your grandparents. Don't worry that you don't have enough "real" information, because this process doesn't require documentation. You don't have to track down birth dates, for instance. A genogram is composed of emotional history, the kind of information that you would share with a therapist.

After constructing your genogram, ask your mate, if you have one, to construct one of his own concerning the attitudes he has developed about scarcity. It can be helpful to see how your family's messages dovetail, and they will. Following are step-by-step instructions.

Phase 1: Collecting Information

Begin with a clean notebook or use the journal in which you have recorded your affirmations. A section of this journal will be designated for your genogram work. You will be recording pertinent emotional experiences that shaped the attitudes of your grandmother, your mother, and yourself, looking for family patterns, or relationship styles that repeat themselves.

Your Grandmother

In the "grandmother" section, you will determine whether a grandmother (or any older relative) influenced your scarcity beliefs, either directly or indirectly. You may have known this person personally or only through your mother's stories of her. If you are fortunate enough to have information about both your grandmothers, divide your "grandmother section" into two and include both as you search for your family patterns. For example, in one woman's family, for three generations the women have all picked alcoholics as mates. After an alcoholic pops up in the first generation, there's a 90 percent chance of that recurring. After you've completed your genogram, you'll have a personal understanding of how patterns repeat in families.

If you want more details, try stimulating your memory by going through old family photo albums, or consider asking relatives for more information. Ask questions about your grandmother such as the following:

What events may have contributed to her belief in scarcity, for example: financial ruin, poverty, work that involved being subservient to people who lived comfortably?

Did she marry? More than once?

Were there other men besides her husband in her life?

Did her mate's work cause him to be away a great deal of the time? If so, how did she respond to this?

Were there any major losses or catastrophes in her family?

What was her relationship with her parents? Did they have any addictions?

Were there any troubling childhood experiences concerning men?

What events could have made her believe she'd never have enough of anything, including love?

How did she feel about her spouse? What was their union like?

Who was "in charge" in her household?

How are you or your mother like her?

Your Mother

If you were raised by someone other than your mother, you may want to include both your biological mother and the person who raised you. Record events that you recall, and if necessary, interview other family members for additional information. Your questions can include many of those listed in the section on your grandmother, as well as the following:

> What were the financial and marital circumstances of your grandparents when your mother came along?
>
> What, if any, major addictive behaviors did she exhibit (e.g., food, alcohol, spending, drugs)?
>
> What is your earliest memory of her?
>
> What was her relationship to her father?
>
> How were her love relationships similar to her mother's?
>
> If she had one or more brothers, what was her relationship with them like?
>
> How was her father like her mate?
>
> How have your relationships mirrored those she has had?

Your Father

Explore issues similar to those in the preceding sections, including his relationship with his parents and siblings and what role models he had for how men treat women. If your father was absent, how does that fit into the general pattern in your family? What was he taught about women? What is your earliest memory of him? As you consider your relationship with your father, ask yourself what lasting impression he left you with concerning men. What were some of those experiences?

Your Life

As you record the details of your emotional life, remembering to consider the questions listed in the previous sections, also respond to the following questions: What do you remember your mother saying to you about men? Did she have a favorite saying? What messages did she pass on to you about abundance or scarcity? What was your relationship with your father like? What was the nature of your parents' relationship? How were they getting along when your mother was pregnant with you? What are your earliest memories concerning your father—those heard or experienced? What would you be reluctant to tell a stranger about your father? What is your attitude about men? What scarcity issues do you hope to heal?

Culling "Information Bytes"

Once you have compiled your information, start at the first section, and working your way through to the end with a red marker, circle the four experiences under each section for each relative that most shaped your grandparents, your parents, and your own attitudes about love and scarcity. Now paraphrase each of these sixteen experiences into "information bytes." Let's say your grandmother was married to a man who worked hard but drank heavily, wasted the family's money, and cheated on his wife. His description might be boiled down to "hardworking, extravagant alcoholic/womanizer." If you have only good memories and information about your parents and grandparents, remember that many intact families did get along well but were often scrambling so hard to make their lives work that they couldn't provide the emotional nurturing that the children needed. In that regard, you would have had a scarcity of nurturing or support. It's also important to ask what part of your family story you're leaving out because it's too painful to consider.

One of our abundance group members, Ondine, spoke lovingly about the supportive marriage that her grandmother and grandfather had enjoyed, but when questioned by another member of the group, she began to recall that her grandfather had had several affairs. It was key in understanding how a pattern of never feeling fully loved had been repeated in her family.

When you have at least twelve information bytes connected to scarcity patterns, you're ready to compose your genogram.

Phase 2: Constructing Your Genogram

One of the most attractive aspects of a genogram is its sheer simplicity.
You will need to know only six symbols to put together the emotional
map of your life. These symbols include the following:

☐ male relative   ⊘ deceased female relative

○ female relative   —————— connection by marriage

☑ deceased male relative   ——//—— divorce or separation

KIM'S GENOGRAM

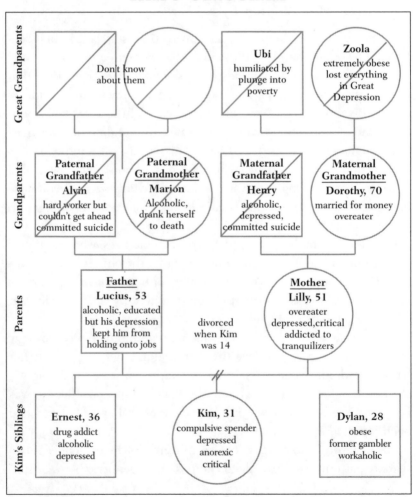

Analysis of Kim's Genogram

Kim, a thirty-one-year-old office manager, began working with Dr. Wade because she was worried about her compulsive overspending and her quickly unraveling relationship with her live-in boyfriend, Leroy, a thirty-one-year-old construction worker who was a recovered marijuana addict. Kim described herself as being overly critical of Leroy, especially now that he had "gotten his act together." Kim was also depressed and had to force herself to eat. For Kim, not eating was life-threatening. She had been struggling with anorexia since high school. The theme running through Kim's life was one of deprivation: not loving herself enough to eat, not having enough money, not feeling enough passion to sustain a relationship she said she wanted.

Kim felt certain that her problems were related to her conflicted relationship with her mother. But even when one family member appears to be causing another's behavior, it's really the cumulative effect of intergenerational patterns that leads to the behaviors.[19] Kim was able to trace her family back to her maternal great grandparents. At 250 pounds and five feet, ten inches, Kim's great grandmother towered over her much smaller husband. Together, they built one of Atlanta's first prosperous black businesses. Unfortunately, they lost everything during the Great Depression and died penniless.

Having seen her parents lose all they had worked for, Kim's maternal grandmother got married for stability—to a local undertaker. But he turned out to be severely depressed, and eventually he committed suicide. Kim's maternal grandmother soothed herself with food, and like her mother, became extremely obese. The family traits of overeating and depression were passed on to Kim's mother, who is one hundred pounds overweight and is extremely critical of others.

On the paternal side of Kim's family tree, her grandmother was an alcoholic who drank herself to death after her husband, Kim's grandfather, committed suicide. The only child of this troubled union was Kim's father, who, genetically predisposed, developed alcoholism. Although highly educated, he was depressed, as was his father, and subsequently was unable to hold a job.

The intergenerational belief on both sides of Kim's family tree was this: Life is unbearable until you find a way to insulate yourself from the pain. The "insulation" on her father's side was alcohol, on her mother's side, food. Both responses showed themselves in Kim's generation: Kim and one sibling had eating disorders (Dylan was a compulsive overeater), Kim spent compulsively, her younger brother was a compulsive gambler, and her older brother abused drugs and alcohol. Recent genetic studies demonstrate a link between all addictive illnesses.

Looking back over her parents' disastrous marriage, Kim said, "Mom was extremely cold toward Daddy, and she put him down all the time about not being able to bring in enough money. She turned on me early on, because she was extremely jealous of my relationship with Daddy. When he got drunk, he taunted her about being fat, and he didn't get along with my brothers either, especially Dylan, because Daddy hated to see his son become overweight. I was the only one he paid attention to. He said I was the only normal one in the family."

Emotionally abandoned by her mother and desperate to keep her father's love, Kim secretly concluded that the real reason she had been rejected by her mother was that she was inadequate. She believed she wasn't smart enough or pretty enough nor could she do enough to warrant her mother's love and care. She concluded that the only way to secure her father's love was to be "skinny enough." She thought she was rebelling against her mother's overeating, but her undereating was the flip side of the same coin, both had eating disorders. In addition, Kim's lack of nurturing caused her to struggle with another ailment that had been passed down through her family and that usually goes hand in hand with addictions: depression. Although Kim refused to drink, she tried to "self-medicate" her despair by spending. With addictions running amuck in her family, she was drawn to Leroy, who smoked marijuana several times a day.

People raised in families in which there are chemical addictions such as drugs or alcohol—or behavioral, such as gambling—are unconsciously attracted to mates with similar issues. One woman, the daughter of an alcoholic, was waiting in line at an automatic teller machine when she felt sexually aroused by the stranger up front, even though his back was turned to her as he used the machine. She only understood her attraction when the man finished and walked past: He had alcohol on his breath. We are drawn to the familiar, so it's no coincidence that when Kim's boyfriend stopped using drugs, she lost interest in him and began to criticize him. Clean and sober, Leroy could no longer be an emotional stand-in for her unreliable, addicted father. She believed men were supposed to be unreliable and addicted. At the same time, her belief that she wouldn't have to feel pain if she could be skinny enough began to surface, and she lost her appetite.

Kim continued to work in therapy to break through her family patterns. One of the affirmations she used repeatedly was: "I am enough, and I deserve to have enough love, money, and food. Life is full of abundance."

After sketching your genogram and adding the information bytes, you will be surprised at the power inherent in the words on the page. Now you can ask the following questions: What scarcity beliefs have been passed down to me? What attitudes about life and relationships were passed on to me? What did my father's behavior have to do with the way I view men? How have I followed in my mother's emotional footsteps with lovers? How have my scarcity beliefs affected my relationships?

Your genogram will offer you a new perspective concerning your life. Keep it handy and take good care of this valuable family record. We will be turning to it for work in upcoming chapters.

Converting Our Childhood Messages

To counteract the effects of damaging scarcity messages, find a favorite photograph of yourself as an infant or a young child. Take it to a copy shop and make at least three copies, one that you can put in a frame beside your bed, another for the dashboard of your car or any other places where you spend time alone, and the final one for your desk or work space. You're going to deliver a series of monologues to yourself to change your family messages and to enable you to stop blaming yourself for acting out the intergenerational patterns you have inherited. Speak lovingly and reassuringly to yourself. When possible, kiss this photo, telling yourself you are loved and that you deserve to have love. End every conversation with yourself by affirming: "God has filled the world with everything I need, and I deserve love in abundance." And you do.

Converting Our Scarcity Beliefs about Food

No one has to tell us we have issues with food. As a group, we tend to weigh more than women of other races. And in the United States, we are certainly among the millions of adults trying to lose weight, one-third of whom take dietary supplements[20]and who spend $33 billion a year.[21] You may have tried diets and already know they don't work. There are three reasons in particular that diets fail: First, they require us to ignore feelings of hunger, but that also means we learn to ignore feelings of fullness.[22] When the diet ends, we're usually out of touch with the sense of when our body needs more food. Second, dieters experience a psychological phenomenon called *reactance*, which refers to the human tendency to want what is prohibited. Finally, researchers have confirmed what dieters have always known: Once dieters slip up, we're more likely to binge,[23] which lands us back where we started. Nine out of ten dieters gain their weight back.[24]

Being overweight is a threat to our health and our looks, and it negatively affects the way we feel about ourselves. If you've tried losing weight but experienced little success, don't give up. You may have scarcity issues concerning food. After thirty-five years of yo-yo diets, fasting, and weight reduction programs, Brenda Richardson began viewing her eating binges as unconscious attempts to stave off feelings of scarcity. She worked at convincing herself that she truly did have everything she needed in abundance, and as she began to heal, she went down two dress sizes, from sixteen to twelve, and for the first time ever, her weight was stabilized. She writes:

> Over the years I had come to understand that all people have some-thing called emotional hunger, which is very different from physical hunger, which generally occurs in the morning, at noon, and in the early evening, and is easy to spot. The emotional hunger was the real reason I was overweight.
>
> Historical context as well as family experiences determine the extent of our emotional hunger. For instance, I knew that many of our slave ancestors had to exist on food that was rationed out, and we were punished by having food withheld. Many of our ancestors were put in a position of having to steal to feed their children.
>
> There's a famous narrative in which a woman tells of a white mistress who planted a piece of candy and dared a slave girl to steal it. When the

girl finally succumbed to her hunger and took the candy, the woman not only whipped her, but in an attempt to hold her down more securely, she placed a rocking chair on the child's head and sat on it as she beat her. This broke the girl's jaw, which never healed. She grew to be a woman whose disfigured, caved-in face terrified children.[25]

I was saddened by this story, but it helped me to consider how sweets and food had come to mean so much to me. My earliest memory concerning food involves an experience that occurred shortly after I began living with my mother again, after a four-year absence, when I was five. I was seated at the dinner table, surrounded by guests, and grew enraged when my mother refused to give me a large serving of food. I can still see myself hurling a lamb chop across the table. This was quite unusual for me, the "good girl" in the family, so I can only imagine that my "hunger" had a lot less to do with food than it did with my need to feel loved. Although my mother was slender, through the years I heard many stories from her about not having enough to eat as a child. Any scarcity beliefs I adopted as a child were reinforced by the scarcity of food in my house. My mother scrimped on food so she could afford to keep up the mortgage on our home. At some point, I began to believe there would never be enough food.

As part of my healing, I began keeping a food journal. The most important entry occurred on my way to my youngest son's basketball game. Although I had just finished a hearty dinner, as I started down the steps that led to the gym, I caught myself thinking that when I went home that night, I was going to build a huge ice cream sundae, and I pictured myself eating it. Right then and there, I stopped in my tracks and wondered what unconscious thoughts had triggered my fantasy, and what I really wanted and needed. As if she'd been waiting for decades to address me, my inner voice answered, "Not enough respect. You're about to go into a gymnasium where most of the other parents are white. You're going to feel left out and alone."

Looking back at all the times in life I had felt rejected or unaccepted, I realized food had been my substitute for the respect and love I was craving. The trick is that no one else can give us that kind of love and nurturing—we only give it to ourselves. Today, whatever the situation, if I feel emotionally hungry, I feed myself what I really want. I envision myself hugging myself, and I tell myself that I am loved and wanted. This visualization has worked wonders.

Except for servings of fruits and vegetables, I soon began to cut each of my meals in half, including fast-food and restaurant servings. For the first few days, I felt ravenous and angry. But after three days, the *power of my visualizations kicked in. Except for my normal need for three main meals, I did not long for food. After three weeks I began to lose weight. Two months later I could wear a dress I hadn't been able to fit in for four years. I loved walking into an abundance meeting, having someone compliment me on a pair of slacks, a suit or blouse, and telling my sista/friends that I hadn't worn this or that piece since my twenty-year-old son was ten. (And no, they don't look mammy made and out of style.) Altogether, I've lost more than twenty pounds.*

For the first time, I'm not dodging cameras and mirrors. Best of all, I feel great because I'm healing from within. It's the perfect eating style for me. Although I do put some thought into what I prepare, I'm too busy to measure fat grams or prepare special meals. And I hate feeling deprived. Last week I bought myself an Almond Joy, and enjoyed it without the guilt, because it took me four days to finish it off, one bite at a time. I never felt the need to gobble it down because I knew I was giving myself enough of what I really needed.

Someone in my abundance group asked if I was suggesting that racism causes many of us to overeat. I told her I certainly couldn't speak for other sisters but that I did know my responses to racism, including my scarcity beliefs, had made me fat. While I couldn't eradicate racism, I could change my response to it.

If you have identified yourself as an overeater or if you have issues with being overweight, the following guidelines may be of help.

Guidelines for Eating Abundantly

1: Identify your earliest memories about food, and consider whether you are using food as a substitute for love.

2: If you plan to cut back on your food, talk this over with your physician. Then for at least a week, record what you eat and what's occurring with you emotionally. When you find yourself fantasizing about overeating, ask yourself what you're worried about not getting enough of. The bottom line is almost always love.

3: Don't skip meals. Eat a nutritious breakfast, which many people eliminate for the calories. Skipping breakfast not only impairs your mental performance, but calories consumed early in the day are less likely to add pounds.[26]

4: If you're cooking, don't "eat from the pot." You want to be able to see exactly what you're eating, which should be approximately half of what you would have eaten in the past. Remember, you're doing this for yourself, so no one wins if you play "tricks." For instance, don't prepare a foot-long hero sandwich and consume half of it; because that would obviously still be too much. When you hear your inner voice saying, "It's not enough," ask yourself what you're really afraid you won't get enough of. Then follow up your answer with the visualization of you hugging yourself and soothing yourself with loving words, such as: "I love you, and I'm going to give you everything you need."

5: If you're worried that you don't even know what a "normal-sized" meal looks like, try a few frozen low-calorie meals. At first you may feel that you're getting ripped off, but this size portion will eventually be enough to satisfy you. Instead of eating from the container, use a pretty plate and place mat, even if you're eating at work.

6: A few minutes before eating, visualize yourself consuming less and feeling satisfied. If you're tempted to eat more than you've put on your plate, repeat this visualization. When you've finished your meal, if your stomach feels stretched and heavy, you'll know you ate too much. Figure out why you overate, and promise yourself that you'll start giving yourself the love you need, rather than the food you don't.

7: If you feel the need for a sweet, know that that's perfectly natural. Take a bite or two of a cookie or candy bar. Enjoy each bite, and then put it away. Or freeze (nonpeanut) M&M candies and eat about five of them at a time; they take longer to melt in your mouth when they're frozen. If you're tempted to eat more, first ask yourself what you're afraid you won't get enough of, then follow up your answer with your loving visualization.

8: To appease your physical hunger, snack lightly on fresh veggies and fruits, thin pretzel sticks, and unbuttered popcorn. Stock your freezer with several half-filled bottles of spring water. (You don't have to keep buying new ones; refill them with filtered tap water.) Wherever you go in the house or out, take one of these bottles along so you can drink these cool treats throughout the day.

9: Whenever you feel an urge to binge or eat a lot of something unhealthy, ask yourself what incident is pressing your scarcity buttons. Most of us have become so conditioned to being the only black person in a room or experiencing racist incidents, such as in stores or at work, that we may shrug off these occurrences, thinking they're no big deal. In fact, these incidents send out scarcity alarms, as do arguments with lovers or relatives or even minor disappointments. Another woman found that she overate when her house felt cold because she was sub-consciously reminded of growing up in a home with little heat, where she felt neglected and unloved. Before you reach for that food, give yourself some loving with the self-love visualization. Filling ourselves with love is the only way we'll ever feel we have enough.

10: Don't scold yourself when you slip up. Reassure yourself that you're learning to give yourself what you really need. And if after a weight drop you plateau, your inner voice may grow loud and insis-tent, suggesting that you're wasting time or that this approach is ridiculous. Continue to soothe yourself with visualizations.

11: Include exercise in your regular routine. It's important for both your physical and your mental health. Before starting, talk with your physician about whether you should be taking vitamins and other nutritional supplements.

12: Finally, check out Overeaters Anonymous for more help and emo-tional and spiritual support in halting overeating.

Converting Other Scarcity Beliefs

Time

The next time you rush to an appointment, speed through a traf-fic light, or feel your adrenaline pumping as you try to meet a deadline (why do you think they're called deadlines?), take a deep breath, then repeat this affirmation: "Thank you, God, for giving me enough time. I have enough time." Repeat this slowly and continuously as you feel your heartbeat slow down and return to normal.

Money

Does your heart accelerate when you click on at an automatic teller machine? When it comes to finances, do you limp from one calamity to the next? Do you indulge in impulse buys, feeling convinced that each item is something you must have or that the price is too good to pass up? If so, write a monthly plan for your spending, and stick to it by repeating (aloud or to yourself) this mantra: "I am worth taking care of, and I buy only what I plan for. God is my source." Say this ten times, whenever necessary. Also, consider how scarcity beliefs about money keep you from saving. You might want to start with something as simple as balancing your checkbook and then begin identifying situations when you're overspending on food, clothes, or other items because of your need to feel loved.

Finally, consider buying *The Basic Money Management Workbook*, which was designed to help readers understand their beliefs and attitudes about money. Written by Glinda Bridgforth, a financial recovery expert who has written about this subject for *Essence* and *Black Enterprise*, the workbook can be ordered via the Internet (www.amazon.com). Or send $25 for the book—this price includes postage and handling fees—to Bridgforth Financial Management Group, 8160 Hansom Dr., Oakland, CA 94605.

Debtors Anonymous is a free twelve-step program that helps those with money issues—check with your local AA chapter for their number.

Spotting Conversion Experiences

Returning to your genogram, consider which negative family patterns have been converted into advantages in your life. Mary Ann, for instance, said her mother often negatively compared her to her father. Although these criticisms hurt her, Mary Ann realizes they also (unwittingly) encouraged her to be like her highly educated father. Working to be "just like him," Mary Ann followed in his footsteps and broke her mother's family pattern in which women did not receive an education. She attended college and eventually earned a doctoral degree.

How have you or one of your ancestors converted a troubling incident into a triumph? Awareness of this conversion experience will put you in touch with some of the abundance that already exists, and also fosters a sense of gratitude for the many gifts that have been passed on to you in your life.

In the next chapter, we examine barriers to self-love. You'll learn that self-love isn't something we should just talk about having; giving ourselves love is something we should focus on *doing*. We demonstrate our self-love by continuing to work at healing.

4

Love Yourself

Sister Spirit Katherine Dunham (b. 1909) was one of the greatest dancers of our time. Raised in Chicago, she eventually attended the University of Chicago, where she studied anthropology. Wanting to learn more about her heritage, she did her academic fieldwork in the Caribbean, studying African-based ritual dance. At a time when so many people, blacks as well as whites, disparaged Africanism, Dunham was celebrating our beauty and uniqueness. Frustrated that so few people were aware that African culture is at the heart of popular culture in the United States, she devoted her life to traveling the world and performing ethnic dances. In learning to love ourselves and love every aspect of our being, we can continue to be inspired by Ms. Dunham.

**Anti-intimacy belief explored in this chapter:
I'm not good enough to be loved.**

Marisa, thirty-two, works as a television reporter. Tall and elegant, she looks like someone who has it made, especially now that she has saved her money and purchased a new condominium. Since moving in last year, she has spent minimal time buying furniture and arranging her belongings. She said, "I don't like rugs or plants, and I haven't put any photos out yet. There are just plain white curtains." The barrenness of Marisa's home was symbolic of her emotional life. She said with a painful smile, "I haven't been on a date since college."

With caramel-colored skin, huge oval eyes, high cheekbones, and her hair pulled away from her oval face in tight braids, Marisa is a picture of African beauty. But she seldom made eye contact when she spoke, and she ignored men who signaled their interest. Looking at her, it seems impossible to believe that Marisa never imagined that a man could be interested in her. She was like so many of us who unintentionally devise ways to keep suitors away, fearing that we'll be hurt. The real problem is that at the core, we don't believe we're worthy of love. Some of our self-protective measures include becoming overweight; developing harsh, critical personalities; being clingy and controlling; spending so recklessly we frighten lovers away; or, like Marisa, donning a cloak of detachment. Even when men manage to battle their way past our defenses, our own belief that we are unlovable can overwhelm our relationships, because once we're adults no one outside of ourselves can convince us that we're lovable.

Long before any of us were born, Alexander Dumas wrote: "Love without esteem cannot go far or reach high. It is an angel with only one wing." One woman who heard that quote just laughed. "Pretty words, and you can believe them if you want. But I know why I don't have anybody in my life. Brothers have been handing me contracts, and I signed 'em without reading. The fine print said, 'I *will* have other women, and I *ain't* gonna marry your butt!'"

Marisa also insisted that lack of self-love had little to do with her being alone. "Of course I love myself. How else could I have come so far on my own? I'm the reporter my news director calls on when she needs someone to cover a complex story. That's hard-won recognition. . . . I'm alone because, until now, finding the right guy hasn't been high on my agenda."

In fact, it wasn't on her agenda at all. During her freshman year at a historically black college, she was voted homecoming queen, but she discouraged romantic overtures by pretending she had a hometown sweetheart. Asked why she would make such an effort to resist men, she paused before saying, "It never seemed I was supposed to have someone. I've imagined myself in a wedding gown, but I can't picture a groom beside me." In Marisa's case, it's easy to understand why.

Self-love is the internalized love and affection that our parents gave us that helps to sustain us through difficult times. In one respect, as children we're like a flower whose well-being is dependent on the quality of the soil in which it grows. Our families were our soil, and our inner life was created from our childhood experiences. But if we had parents who did not grow up feeling valued and loved, it would have been difficult for them to give us what they never experienced. Author Julia Boyd writes: "I once heard a great teacher say, you can teach others only to the extent of your own knowledge."[1] Some of us have been blessed to have received unconditional love in our childhood homes. In the book *Black Women Stirring the Waters,* forty-four California Bay Area women of African descent who have achieved stunning professional and personal success in their lives share details of their loving and supportive parents, most of whom managed to keep their relationships intact, as well as nurturing extended families and teachers.[2] Undoubtedly, the success these women experienced in the larger world, despite enormous obstacles, was in large part due to this early infusion of love. They represent many of us who hail from loving environments. Nurturing childhoods, such as these, can, to some extent, provide insulation from the sting of racism and oppression.

Those of us who did not feel unconditionally loved as children may feel the pain of the neglect as adults. When this wounding occurs, we develop a negative belief: "They don't love me because I'm not good enough." The good news is that once we grow up we can choose to get what we need and we can heal the hurt. That's just what Marisa was doing by joining our San Francisco abundance group.

Sharing details of her childhood, Marisa explained that from the age of three, after her mother was institutionalized for mental illness, she was raised in foster homes. When asked to draw a picture of how her childhood had felt, she fashioned a family of stick figures sitting around a campfire, and she drew herself outside the circle. What a painful image of isolation.

Despite Marisa's protestations that she loves herself because of her professional achievements, her inability to visualize being with someone who loves her is a reflection of her lack of self-love. We can't create for ourselves what we can't imagine. Another member of our abundance group, Eva, who is twenty-eight and a former model, said, "It's hard to imagine that what I want—a loving partner, a fulfilling job, and children—is really possible. I feel like I'm asking for too much."

Eva, and other women in the group who worked with their genograms, found at the root of their scarcity patterns an almost complete absence of self-love. And their love lives reflected that. We're all attracted to the people we think we deserve. To gauge your level of self-love, all you have to do is ask yourself, what have my romantic relationships been like?

If your answer is that you're currently in a committed, mutually satisfying relationship, you rate high on the scale of self-love. If you have a pattern of picking relationships that have been abusive and demeaning, or if you've thought that most of the men who cared about you were "boring" or "losers," that too says a lot about how you feel about yourself. If you haven't been in any committed relationships at all, or if you've convinced yourself that you "shouldn't even bother getting out of the house because there is no one out there," that's a sign that you're creating scarcity for yourself because you feel unworthy of love.

A lot of us haven't viewed loving ourselves as a priority because we've had to focus on surviving. But according to bell hooks, "When we love ourselves, we know that we must do more than survive. We must have the means to live fully. To live fully, black women can no longer deny our need to know love."[3]

Although Marisa realized she needed love, she had difficulty naming qualities that a mate could love in her. She listed "hard worker" and "opinionated," which are good qualities for a resume, but she found it hard to believe a man could find her attractive. When asked why, she paused and finally began to open up.

"When I was little, I prayed for my life to be easier. My white foster family lived in the country, and I had the only black face around. You could see me coming for miles. The children were really racist and tormented me. I hated them . . . not my skin color." She immediately contradicted herself by adding, "I talked my white foster mother into getting me some bleaching cream. I wanted to be lighter so I wouldn't stick out."

She was eventually moved to a nearby city, to a foster home that housed two African American girls who were sisters, but the issue of skin color continued to haunt her. Her new provider, a Barbadian woman called Mama Ethel, had skin that was a deep brown. She too had been wounded, and she rejected herself and Marisa. "The two other girls who lived there were sisters who had long braids and very light skin," Marisa recalled. "Mama Ethel would speak to them in a sugary sweet voice and in the same breath tell me, 'Get your black ass over here.' She said my hair was so coarse it hurt her fingers to touch it."

Marisa said Mama Ethel lavished attention on the other girls' hair and dressed them nicely. "Not me," Marisa said. "She'd say she only needed a minute to press my little bit of scraggly stuff." Marisa's eyes glistened. "Can you imagine anyone being that hateful?"

Unfortunately, we can imagine this. African American women have been raised in a society that venerates a narrow Nordic standard of beauty. Most of us have been involved in experiences that communicated messages that our skin tones are too light or dark, our noses too flat or broad, our lips too wide or thick, our hair too short or thin or kinky or nappy.

Our continuing pain over these experiences led to two incidents in 1998 that have caused an uproar. In one, an African American honors student in North Carolina was banned from participating in a debutante ball hosted by a black sorority because some of its members did not approve of her dreadlocks and wanted her to tie them up, away from her shoulders. The young woman refused to change her hairstyle and accused the sorority of discrimination toward their own racial group.[4]

In the second incident, in Brooklyn, New York, a white teacher read a book (by a black author) to her black and Hispanic third-grade class about an African American girl whose spirit is as indomitable as her "nappy" hair. The teacher reported that some of the parents were so angry about this "negative" description of a black girl's hair that they threatened her life, and she has since quit her job. It's understandable that the parents might have been frustrated with this teacher, no matter how well intentioned, because she obviously didn't know enough about our history to be sensitive to our issues. But this incident went way beyond any opportunity for dialogue between parents and a teacher of another race.

Carolivia Herron, the author of the book in question, *Nappy Hair*, said although she was initially shocked by the incident, she had second thoughts. "Well of course, a pain that has been in people for 200 years doesn't go away in 20 or 30 years. That is not enough time to erase 200 years of the pain of believing ourselves ugly because our hair was not straight like the hair of the slave owners."[5]

Writing for the *New York Times*, author Jill Nelson suggested that the brouhaha was an example of how barriers to self-love sometimes can also be "perpetuated not by the white community but by the black one." She concluded that "too many African Americans have internalized and passed down these beliefs, as if proximity to whiteness inherently enhances our worth."[6]

Nelson touched on our central issue as black women: If we are to create the love and abundance we desire, we must learn to love ourselves even after centuries of being told we are worthless. Fortunately, a growing number of us, including journalist Katti Gray, have come to believe that "nappy" is not a dirty word.[7] Many women point out that nappy simply describes the tightly curled hair that is predominantly a characteristic of people of African descent, and not as Webster's Dictionary suggests, a derogatory or contemptuous term for black hair.[8] That attitude is obviously shared by patrons of the Oakland beauty salon, Oh, My Nappy Hair!, where so-called "nap specialists" arrange dos ranging from Nubian knots to glossy styles achieved with chemical relaxers. Perhaps one sign that sisters are becoming more relaxed about our tresses is that a second Oh, My Nappy Hair! is thriving in Los Angeles, and in Sacramento, a grooming and hair center is named K.I.N.K.S. These are just a few of the businesses across the country whose names challenge the long-standing conflict that has existed about our hair.

Unfortunately, even the most fashionable tresses, whether straight or nappy, won't alleviate the shame so many of us feel about our features, and the problem is that shame blocks self-love. Many of us keep our shame a secret, convincing ourselves that we've grown out of that "stuff," but then something like *Nappy Hair* surfaces and all hell breaks loose.

We assume we've gotten over it because, like most people, we don't really understand how shame lingers. It is often confused with guilt, but whereas guilt makes us feel we've *done* something wrong, shame makes us feel that we *are* wrong. Like a burning lump of coal that's too hot to handle, shame is passed on from person to person. That's why Mama Ethel told Marisa she only needed a minute to press her "scraggly" hair. In truth, Mama Ethel felt that her own deep brown skin and African features were flawed, and so she hurt Marisa. The cycle continued, and Marisa was forced to internalize Mama

Ethel's shame. That is exactly why so many of us still feel that *we* are wrong.

The bitter irony is that our demeaned features are greatly admired in the Motherland. Sisters who have visited African countries often come back beaming after being told repeatedly by strangers that they are beautiful. But that's certainly not what most of us were raised on. In our abundance group, when women began sharing hurtful experiences that arise from their features, it became obvious that it would have been almost impossible for them to have developed a deep sense of self-love.

Anyone who says "light-skinned" sisters have it easier is perpetuating one more divisive myth. Eva, a tall, elegant Vanessa Williams look-alike, who has sandy brown hair and blue eyes, is a former model. She is the product of an interracial marriage; her father was Jamaican, her mother, Swedish American. When Eva was an infant, her father was imprisoned for immigration problems and was deported, and her mother divorced him, because, she told Eva, he was lazy. At the age of nine, Eva found her mother in bed with another woman. "She has since told me she is bisexual." Eva felt confused because her mother was furious about being "caught" and she also made Eva feel ashamed about what she had witnessed. Additionally, Eva was also humiliated by her father's imprisonment and disappearance, which her mother also told her to keep secret. Making matters more complicated, she and her mother moved to sixteen different predominately white cities before Eva was eighteen.

"I was always the new girl in town, the girl with the big lips and a flat nose and wild hair. My mother never discussed race, no matter how often I brought it up." When she made a point of spending time with other African American women, she was often rejected and branded a "high yellow bitch." Becoming a successful model didn't increase Eva's self-love. When she fell in love, it was with a man who not only had the same name as her father but was an illegal immigrant at risk for deportation.

Another woman in our abundance group, whose story was introduced in chapter 2, is Mary Ann, a religious scholar of forty-one. With richly toned brown skin, a slender build, and a face that could grace a painting of a Somalian queen, she is quite lovely, but her color-struck mother preferred Mary Ann's two almond-toned sisters. Throughout

Mary Ann's childhood, her mother encouraged her sisters, but not Mary Ann. Her scornful response to Mary Ann's ideas would be, "Just get off your high horse." She wasn't intentionally cruel; she was repeating what she had learned in her childhood home.

Though our parents may have provided models of achievement, they were often unable to teach us how to love ourselves. Many parents were so caught up in simply trying to provide for us that they equated material support with love. In Toni Morrison's novel *Sula,* a character asks her mother, "Did you ever love us?" The mother's bitter response says it all: "You settin' here with your healthy-ass self and ax me did I love you? Them big old eyes in your head would a been two holes full of maggots if I hadn't."[9]

This is the kind of attitude that left many of us with the assumption that the only way we could be good to ourselves was by indulging in expensive clothes, jewelry, or cars. Theses external fixes masked our feelings of pain and shame. There was a sense that at least if we didn't feel good we could look good. Unfortunately, once the momentary thrill of the new items wears off, we find this "self-loving" is self-defeating, and we feel worse.

Tonya, thirty-eight, a petite Jazzercise instructor who described herself as a "compulsive clothing shopper," was constantly in financial crisis; her telephone was disconnected, credit card representatives called her at her job demanding payment, and one night when she was supposed to be entertaining her honey's parents, she had to cancel because her electricity had been shut off. Not surprisingly, she had little success in maintaining a relationship; her financial problems drove away anyone who got close to her.

After working with Dr. Wade, Tonya was able to trace her need for buying pretty clothes to childhood experiences that left her feeling unloved. Born into a Guyanese family, Tonya was the only sibling with light skin. Her father, a black nationalist, had rejected her and sometimes even denied he was related to her. As an adult, Tonya spent her money on pretty clothes in a failed attempt to make herself feel the love and acceptance she never received from her father.

The black community seldom discusses the wound caused by black parents who choose favorite children and reject others on the basis of physical features. Being the least loved sibling is not something a child easily gets over. Researchers have found that when a "color complex" is unresolved in families, children absorb the damaging feelings as part of their identities.[10] Those of us who felt excluded from a close relationship with a parent may go through life desperately seeking that parent's love and recognition.[11] As adults we search for lovers (or food or anything) to fill that empty space.

Rejected by her father, Tonya believed she was unworthy of anyone's love. She has never been in a committed relationship, nor is she close to her siblings. Parental partiality often destroys closeness between siblings and divides families. Children seldom blame their parents, but instead turn against one another. Even if the family is split down the middle, with one parent choosing one child, and the other parent, the other child, each sibling feels deprived of love by the parent who rejected her.[12] The chosen child certainly doesn't get off scott free. When these lighter skinned sisters become adults, they often feel men are attracted to them only because of the way they look, not for the person they really are.

As the sibling with longer, thicker hair, Brenda Richardson felt guilty that her mother obviously preferred her to her sister, whose hair was described by their mother as "the bad stuff" she'd inherited from their father. Their mother wasn't intentionally hurting them; she'd grown up in a family where the parents had picked favorite children, and this was all she knew. Also, Brenda's mother loved and admired her own mother, who had long black hair. Now that she had a daughter with fairly long hair, she devoted time to "oiling" the girl's scalp with a foul-smelling mixture of Dixie Peach and Glover's Scalp Mange, which was supposed to speed up further growth. As a "prank" (which was actually passive-aggressive anger), Brenda cut off her braids. Her mother responded as if someone had died, and Brenda felt guilty about hurting the person she most loved. Years later, on her forty-ninth birthday, in a healthy act of emotional liberation, Brenda had her hair cut short.

Marisa too has worked to break free of childhood shadows. Last month she looked up a male college classmate who had been generous with his feelings and time. After graduation, he had let her know he wanted to be part of her life. But on the day he was to help her move to a new city, she arrived an hour and a half late. "When I got there, he'd given up and left. For years I just thought of him as some crappy guy. Now that I've been engaged in this healing work, I see that I was late that day because I acted out my fear of having someone get close to me. Every time he looked at me, I imagined he was seeing me the way Aunt Ethel saw me."

Through the years, this man kept in touch through Christmas cards and by calling her for lunch whenever he was in town. But she'd never explained her actions or given him the green light that she was available to be in a relationship. Now, she felt she had changed. After making a date to see him, Marisa shared her new awareness about that long-ago day. "He was very receptive," she told the group, "and thanked me for my candor. I don't know what will happen with us. But it wasn't his reaction that was as important as the process of putting myself out there, taking a chance because I believe that someone can love me."

Learning to become our own ally is a goal for all of us. That "little voice" that told Marisa that someone who could care about her was "crappy" was actually the voice of her own shame. Dr. Wade calls it "the enemy within." It is often what we hear when we look in the mirror, and it speaks to us in contemptuous ways: I might as well stop flirting; he won't be interested in someone who looks like me. I don't want him to take a picture; I never look good in photographs. If I took this weave off my head, he'd never ask me out again.

Obviously, this isn't the way we'd speak to someone we love. It's anything but a loving voice. This enemy within not only is made up of the voice of the person who initially humiliated us which we've internalized. It can also be traced back to our ancestors. Their self-love sustained a crushing blow when they were enslaved. To rebuild our self-love, we need to identify the antecedents of our current feelings.

OUR HISTORY:
THE STRUGGLE TO MAINTAIN
SELF-LOVE

The very nature of slavery is that it dishonors one group and gives honor to another.[13] Landowners knew they couldn't enslave our people by violence alone, so they tried to break our spirits. They believed that the best slaves were docile and had to have a deep sense of personal inferiority.[14] "Seasoning slaves" was a process of physical and emotional torture considered so crucial to running a plantation that whites traded information on the most effective methods.

Some of our people were beaten if they used the words "I think," because they were not supposed to be capable of normal thought processes. Some were forced to wear heavy masks that covered their faces if they "misbehaved." It could get so hot inside these masks that when they were taken off, the skin would come off with it. Toni Morrison has said of this device: "What is interesting is that these things were not restraining tools, like in the torture chamber. . . . humiliation was the key to what the experience was like."[15] In fact, humiliation was a seasoning strategy.

This dehumanization process wasn't limited to adults. Our sense of self-love is derived from having nurturing parents who are there for us. Women in bondage often labored with their infants tied to their backs. But inevitably, their babies grew too heavy for the mothers to carry them and still work at a pace fast enough to escape the lash. Toddlers were often left with other young children in a barn presided over by slaves too young or too feeble for agricultural work. Some toddlers fed themselves by dipping their faces and hands in a trough that had been filled with slop, and sometimes pigs and chickens ate alongside them.

Once our ancestors were considered old enough to work (at about the age of six), they were continually in danger of being whipped with braided leather straps that cut deeply into the flesh. Slaves were beaten for "disobeying" and for any actions construed as being "uppity." These beatings were generally postponed until other slaves could be gathered to bear witness. The so-called transgressor was generally stripped, then tied to a tree or hung by the thumbs. Pregnant women were not spared. They were forced to lie face down in a depression that had been dug in the ground while they were being whipped.[16] When beatings were considered insufficient punishment for the "crime," salt was rubbed into wounds or the bleeding skin was covered with molasses to attract biting insects.[17]

More subtle seasoning practices included dressing our people in rags or clothing made from an unattractive, rough fabric called "negro cloth"; if they were not barefoot, their feet were shod in ill-fitting "negro shoes." But degradation went far beyond what we wore. Although our great grandparents dressed and bathed whites, prepared their food and nursed their babies, many white people insisted on not being "touched" by us and said we were filthy and had an odor that not even soap and water could eradicate.

Degradation worked in strange ways. Mixed-race children of slaveholders were often victimized by the wives of plantation owners. Still, these "whiter-looking" black people were deemed by whites to be prettier, cleaner, and smarter, and often they were assigned "easier" work. Sold at special auctions, they drew higher bids. This also gave rise to a class of free blacks, for some were recognized by their white fathers, sent abroad to be educated, and on their return sometimes given land and, sadly, slaves.[18]

This behavior drove wedges among our people, and that was the point. In pamphlets that offered slaveholders advice on how to "manage" their captives, one key strategy that was recommended was to keep us at one another's throats over our physical features. Willie Lynch, the slaveholder we discussed earlier, recommended that plantation owners use envy to control their slaves, pitting the light against the dark, and those with "coarse" hair against those with "finely textured" hair.[19] It was a strategy that worked to some extent.

After emancipation, some light-skinned blacks associated only with one another. They established churches, social organizations, preparatory schools, and colleges that accepted only blacks who had hair silky enough to run a fine-tooth comb through or skin so light that blue veins could be seen at the wrist. This exclusivity didn't make lighter-skinned African Americans feel any less ashamed of who they were; remember the pain of Eva, whose story we told earlier.

The idea behind the dehumanizing treatment of course was to destroy our spirits. Thank God, those tactics failed. We may have been bowed, but we as a people were not broken. That fact alone, in the face of this well-planned campaign, makes us realize that it isn't just romanticizing when we describe our ancestors as superhuman. It was the more-than-human aspect of our ancestors that gave them an indomitable will to survive.

Psychiatrist Victor Frankl, who had been a Jewish prisoner in a Nazi war camp, observed that the people who lived through the monstrous hardships of the Holocaust were those who felt they had a reason to live, and often that reason was their religious faith.[20] Undoubtedly, a similar faith sustained our people through the black holocaust. Throughout various African cultures, there is a deeply held belief that the Spirit forms an intrinsic aspect of every human being. This view, that all human beings are embodiments of the divine, was also shared by psychiatrist Carl Jung, who believed that if we want to live our destiny, we must tap into, connect with, and integrate the energy that is within us.[21]

In Africa our ancestors had long tapped into that divine energy, "working the spirit" through their bodies in ceremonies that involved rhythm, music, and movement. Once in their new lands, they often melded these traditions with the religions of their oppressors, creating forms of worship that included Cuban Santeria, Brazilian Candomblé, Revival Zion in Jamaica, and the Black Church in the United States. These religious practices shared a common goal: survival and triumph over the brutality of slavery. Theologian Joseph M. Murphy explains that throughout the African diaspora, religious traditions allowed our ancestors to manifest "a real and irreducible force."[22]

For this reason, our people were able to trust that the slaveholders could not break their spirits: They could not be separated from God who is Spirit, is Love, is Light within. It's no coincidence that one of the most joyful songs our people created, proclaimed this message: "This little light of mine, I'm gonna let it shine." It was faith that sustained our dignity.

If we could go back in time and listen in, at the end of the day, to the talk at a slave quarter, we might see signs of our humanity being nourished in many forms: praying and singing, reading when possible, but also laughing. Lookouts were posted outside doors, so slaves could be warned if any whites came along. And inside those huts, there our people would be, many considered by their "masters" as their most humble step-and-fetch-it servants, laughing up a storm, mimicking those very "masters," howling at how ridiculous the "mistress" or "master" had behaved. Our ancestors knew their physical survival depended on pretending to submit to whites, but out in the slave quarter, they knew they could drop their veil of duplicity. They were loyal to one another, and they developed a biting contempt for a black person who crossed the line and became what we would later refer to as an "Uncle Tom." Just to underscore how beliefs travel through the generations, to this day we reserve a particular disdain for black people who are labeled as traitors. And no matter how high up we may go, there is no position that makes us feel more isolated than being accused by our own of having "sold out": Witness the ostracism of Supreme Court Justice Clarence Thomas.

Still looking in on that slave quarter, we would see our ancestors using the little time they had for their own domestic chores, such as making a quilt, doing laundry, preparing food for the next morning, or packing more mud and grass into their chimneys. They might have been singing, maybe a spiritual, to release pent-up emotions. In another crowded hut, someone might be spinning a tale about turtles and hares. Perhaps we would see an adult pause long enough to whisper in a child's ear, "Yous a fine girl, and yous is gonna make it. Things is gonna git better, jest wait and see."

For a long while, things did not get better. In fact, after Reconstruction, the assault on our humanity escalated. Violence against black people became so rampant that a congressional committee was convened to investigate. Defeated and vengeful white Southerners created a society that aimed at punishing former slaves. Jim Crow tactics included "colored only" vending machines, filthy rest rooms and drinking fountains, and run-down and underfunded schools. In courtrooms, we were sworn in on separate Bibles.[23]

Not only were our people forced to ride in the backs of buses, but when traveling by train, on occasions when there were whites riding in the same railroad car, some of us, including the future federal judge Constance Baker Motley,[24] had to sit behind screens because our very presence was considered so objectionable. While white proprietors encouraged us to shop at their stores, many would not allow us to squeeze a piece of fruit to test it for ripeness or to try on clothing or shoes. We weren't allowed inside white-owned restaurants, and we had to wait at the back door to buy take-out food.

In the United States, our fortification against this hateful storm was the black church, which was at the center of our communities. Historian Lerone Bennett, Jr. explained that these institutions seeded and reseeded the fields of black being. He writes that "even the conservative churches taught black power, robing their servants in gowns and titles of authority, teaching them how to speak, how to challenge, how to maneuver, giving them, all the while, the only sense of power available for them." He further points out that black churches collected substantial sums of money, which, in many cases, financed the first black banks and insurance companies.[25]

It was also in the black church and fledgling businesses, as well as in our neighborhoods, that the titles given to us by whites—*Auntie* and *Boy*—were dispensed with; we referred to one another as *Miss* or *Mrs.* or *Mr.* or even *Sister* or *Brother.* This was a tradition so deeply ingrained in our behavior that even today, in the South, many of our young people still punctuate sentences addressed to grown-ups with "yes, Ma'am" and "yes, Sir." (Some of us still find ourselves cringing when white children or service workers casually refer to us by our first names, unwittingly tapping into our collective memory bank.) The titles of respect that we used with one another allowed our people to hold their heads high.

Those of us who were not raised in the South had different kinds of experiences that caused us to feel isolated and humiliated. Genny, forty-six, a newspaper editorial writer, was the only black girl in a predominately white girls' school in the Midwest during the 1950s. She recalled the most popular girl in class standing at the front of the room to hand out invitations, "calling out everyone's name but mine."

More recently, Rita, a literary agent, celebrated her first big commission by touring France's wine country. While there, she ran into an American on a tour bus, who said, in a loud whisper, "What the hell is a nigger doin' way out here?"

In 1990, Condoleezza Rice, working as President Bush's Soviet affairs specialist, was returning from a summit meeting with Soviet leader Mikhail Gorbachev when, at San Fransisco International Airport, she was shoved by a white Secret Service agent, who told her to get back behind the ropes. He viewed her as a threat to security.

After years of negative conditioning, we need simply look around the boardroom or courtroom or university classroom or the neighborhood where we are the only or the first or one of a handful, and the old familiar sense of isolation is resurrected.

In the sixties, we fought back with slogans such as "Black is Beautiful" and "I'm Black and I'm Proud!" to encourage a more positive sense of self. This movement has expanded to include more positive role models for our children. Magazines such as *Essence, Ebony, Emerge, Heart & Soul, Black Elegance,* and *Black Enterprise* are chock-full of

African Americans of every possible shape and shade, who represent our physical beauty as well as professional achievements. On television and in the movies, celebrities such as Oprah, Maya, Vanessa, Halle, Naomi, Brandy, Latifah, Whitney, Whoopi, Della, and Venus and Serena reflect our rainbow varieties. Of course, not all of our public role models are entertainers or athletes. During President Clinton's impeachment trial viewers were treated to a sighting of a legal star: Cheryl Mills, 33, a Phi Beta Kappa graduate of the University of Virginia, who completed Stanford Law School in 1990,[26] was one of only three attorneys chosen by the President to defend his political life.

Two years earlier, in November of 1997, television viewers following the much heralded birth of the McCaughey septuplets in Des Moines Iowa, were somewhat startled to realize that both of the highly trained perinatologists who shepherded the record-setting pregnancy were two African American women. The day after the momentous birth of the seven live babies, Doctors Paula Mahone, 40, and Karen Drake, 39, were honored by a group of minority students carrying a newly minted certificate that read: "In history, 'Blacks' are known as slaves . . . But thank God, today you made it possible for minorities to make history around the world, indicating that it's not the color of your skin that's important, but the effort that one puts forth as a human being, to be all that one can be."[27]

Attorney Mills and Drs. Mahone and Drake remain connected to the community. Mills is co-founder of an organization that helps impoverished students attend college,[28] and the physicians are informal mentors to several minority teenagers whose babies they have delivered.[29]

While these positive changes serve as a soothing external balm that helps us to survive, many of us still require healing and a deep transformation that begins with an internal shift. As women of African descent, we face a special challenge: We must learn to love ourselves in a world that says we are unlovable. This difficulty is addressed in the film *Beloved*, when Baby Suggs, played by Beah Richards, stands in a forest clearing preaching to her black neighbors:

> *Here in this here place, we flesh, flesh that weeps, laughs; flesh that dances on bare feet in grass. Love it, love it hard. Yonder they do not love your flesh. They despise it. They don't love your eyes, they'd just as soon pick 'em out. No more do they love the skin on your back. Yonder*

they flay it. And O my people they do not love your hands. Those they only use, tie, bind, cut off and leave empty. Love your hands! Love them. Raise them up and kiss them. Touch others with them, pat them together, stroke them on your face 'cause they don't love that either. You got to love it, you![30]

Expressing painful historical memories and recognizing the effect they still have on our lives is an important step toward loving ourselves completely.

OUR EMOTIONAL INHERITANCE

Hoping to stir your memories so you can examine the ways in which your self-love was diminished by shame, we have included a list of taunts used by whites during slavery. Eventually, however, other African Americans wielded hurtful taunts that few of us escaped. It's important to say them aloud and, when applicable, to recall situations in which they were used.

"You're pretty . . . you must have some Indian [or white] blood in you."

"Act your age and not your color."

"Don't blame me, you got that kinky hair from your daddy [or mother]."

"Light skin black people can't dance."

"Blue-gummed."

"You think you're white."

"Flat-nosed."

"You're too dark to wear bright colors."

"Light-skinned blacks are stuck-up."

"If snow was black, you'd be a walking blizzard."

"Your hair's like Brillo."

"If you're yellow, you're a lucky fellow. If you're brown, stick around. But if you're black, get back."

"You proper talking, high yellow bitch."

"Black bitch."

"Nigger."

"Don't bring me no nappy-headed grandbabies."

"She's got good hair."

"I can't go out in the rain [or swim] because my hair will go back."

"Tarbaby."

"I've got some Hopi Indian blood; that is, I'm hoping I'm anything but black."

"Smart black people are uppity."

Reading through these insulting words and phrases may have unearthed memories concerning incidents in which you were made to feel ashamed of who you are. Most African American women have a story to tell. Following are some samples.

Hair stories

Jill, twenty-nine, said, "My hair [which is silky and light brown] made me my grandmother's favorite. I felt terrible for my sisters, so ashamed. Now, I keep it short, and it turns me off when men suggest I let it get long."

Loretta, fifty-four, recalled, "When I was little, about every month my mother would spend all day Saturday shampooing and straightening my hair. Until it was done, we couldn't answer the door if somebody knocked, because folks outside my family couldn't see me like that. I had a lot of hair, so I'd spend the day by the stove, wincing when the hot comb touched my damp roots and the steam burned my scalp."

Deedee, twenty-nine, said, "I would search the back pages of *Ebony* looking for the latest hair grow potion. You've seen that model with the long hair that hung over one of her shoulders. None of that stuff ever grew my hair, not on my head . . . but I did have bushy eyebrows . . . . Seriously, though, I had some rough times with the kids teasing me about my no-grow hair."

Skin Stories

Jackie, forty-seven, told us, "By the time I went to Howard, there were a lot of other brown-skinned sisters attending. But that didn't change the brothers' dating habits. I swear, I could have gone to parties wrapped in nothing but thousand-dollar bills, and the brothers would have knocked me over to stampede toward some high yella girl surrounded by barbed wire with a sign around her neck that said "I've got crabs."

Amy, thirty-four, said, "When I was only thirteen, living in Florida, I was raped by a white baseball player. When he climaxed, he kept calling me a black bitch. He was arrested and prosecuted, but sometimes I still hear his words in my head."

Evelyn, thirty-two, said, "I *know* the reason I don't have a man is because I'm dark. Whatever. I say fuck 'em."

Rose Emma concluded, "In the sixties, I went through an ultra-militant stage. You know, chanting 'Kill Whitey' and all that. One day I read about a famous black photographer who was looking for models. I was so excited about meeting him, but when I went in for the interview, right in front of all these other women, he said really loudly, 'Sorry, but light-skinned people need not apply.' I slunk out of there. We always find ways to discriminate against one another."

Sharing stories such as these is important because when we become aware of our feelings, we can acknowledge them to ourselves and others, and take care of ourselves when we hurt. Once the members of our abundance group became more conscious of their emotions, they began to notice that our meetings were one of the few places where they could let down their guard. Marisa said, "The self I present to the white world is always on guard." She was describing the hypervigilance that many of us feel interacting in the larger world. We've learned to maintain this guard to protect ourselves from further humiliation, but this coping mechanism can lead to more isolation.

Marisa said her background, being raised in the foster care system, "was so close to the negative stereotype that many whites have about us, I realize I made an incredible effort to let my white graduate school colleagues and now my coworkers assume that I'd grown up in a close and loving middle-class family."

Other women in the group agreed that they had unconsciously grown so preoccupied with trying to maintain a certain image—spending too much money on buying the "right" clothes, for example, or modulating their voices—that they hadn't owned up to the terrible pain of their childhood experiences. Consider your current life and how you handle feelings of isolation in the larger world. It can take a heavy toll. Leanita McClain, the black journalist who served on the editorial board of the *Chicago Tribune*, committed suicide in 1984. Author Bebe Moore Campbell has used McClain's story to assess the cost of being a black woman in a white-normed environment. She writes: "Black women consciously choose their speech, their laughter, their walk, their mode of dress and car. They trim and straighten their hair. . . . They learn to wear a mask."

Do you sometimes feel as if you are wearing a mask? If so, what are you doing to keep in touch with the real you? The fact is that for hundreds of years our people were in proximity to whites only when they were serving them. Change occurred only because we forced our way in. So it's not surprising that you might not feel welcome and relaxed in the larger society.

As a child, if you integrated a white school or attended one that was predominately white, how did your parents prepare you for the experience? Many of us were told to hold our heads high and work our hardest. But because our parents weren't emotionally prepared for integration, they sometimes sent us out the door with the same shaming messages they had experienced. Some of the comments we've heard repeated include: "Don't be acting like a baboon, getting all up in those white girls' faces." "Her parents aren't going to want her bringing home some black girl." "Why would you want to join them for scout meetings? They don't want you there." The natural responses to this kind of shaming include humiliation and anger and, underneath it all, a deep sadness.

Another "layer" of shame can be created by family secrets. During slavery, keeping secrets could mean the difference between life and death, bondage and freedom. But even now, when this defensive style is no longer necessary, it is a pattern that many of us have never broken. Perhaps you were warned by one of your parents not to discuss "things that are nobody's business but our own." Did your parents keep secrets from one another?

Consider, also, secrets concerning births, paternity, and informal adoption. Clients have told Dr. Wade about anger and resentment in their childhood homes concerning "sisters" or "brothers" who had features different from the rest of the family. There are stories of big sisters who turned out to be mothers and fathers who actually were stepfathers. What were your family secrets? They can stretch across generations, affecting many lives.

Karen, forty-four, a businesswoman, was struggling to heal her behavior in relationships. She had always felt emotionally distant from her lovers, her daughter, and her girlfriends. It wasn't until she happened to learn, long after her marriage had ended and her daughter had grown up, that the woman who had raised her was not her mother at all. Her biological mother was passed off as her paternal aunt who lived only a few miles away, a woman she had not even liked and who had died a few years earlier. Karen was furious about having lived so close to her biological mother without ever having a meaningful conversation with her. But it was also a relief for her to learn the truth. She realized that sitting on this secret for four decades had made the woman who raised her so tense they had never shared moments of real intimacy. It was the very same pattern Karen had been acting out in relationships, and she became actively engaged in healing.

As we said earlier, emotional freedom is something we grant ourselves. That's what Mary Ann learned. Each week, she and the new man in her life, who lived in another town, had been speaking on the phone. At the end of one of these conversations, he said, "I look forward to talking to you next week."

When she hung up, her interior critical voice went to work. "Why did he specifically say next week? Did he have a hot date planned with someone else?" Knowing her inner voice could be either her enemy or her ally, Mary Ann decided to tackle this negative message with something more loving. She told herself, "He enjoys your conversations, and just because he said next week doesn't mean you aren't free to call him again this week."

A few days later, she did just that—it was an unusual move for her. Having had such a difficult relationship with her mother, she was fearful of rejection. But she took the chance anyway. When her friend answered, he was friendly but said, "I've got company. Sorry, I can't talk." And the conversation was brought to a quick end. By now, her internal voice was running wild. "You should never have called him. He tried to dump you last week and you didn't get the hint. You'd better forget about him."

We're proud to say that Mary Ann took charge of that voice and arm-wrestled it into submission. Talking to herself in the most loving way, she calmed her fears. Later that week, when her friend called back, she didn't sound resentful because she didn't feel that way.

He began the conversation with, "Sorry I couldn't talk the other day, it's been crazy here, and . . ."

A relationship that could have been torpedoed remains afloat and hopeful because Mary Ann told herself that she was worthy and that she was fun to talk to. By becoming aware of her innermost thoughts and feelings, she learned what we all must: If we believe we are lovable and treat ourselves lovingly, it makes everything else easier.

HEALING SHAME/EMBRACING SELF-LOVE

The Welcoming

This is an exercise that puts you in touch with a level of anger you may not have known you felt. You'll be using a pillow as a stand-in for a person or people who may have made you feel ashamed, separate, and isolated. You'll also want to get a long-handled wooden spoon, tennis racket, or rolled-up towel; then sit back, close your eyes, and take deep cleansing breaths as you begin the visualization:

See yourself as one of your African ancestors—your wrists and ankles in chains—being led off a ship that has just arrived in the "New" World. Imagine also seeing a cruel captain raising his whip about to strike you, when you notice a crowd of people running toward you. As they draw closer, you see the faces of people who have loved and cared for you, individuals you recognize because of their goodness and inner strength. These people force the captain to undo your chains. See yourself and your allies confronting the captain and his crew—they have the faces of racist people you have encountered, people who have humiliated you. They turn and run, but you and your allies quickly gain on them.

Now open your eyes, pick up the wooden spoon, tennis racket, or rolled-up towel, and beat the daylights out of the pillow. Speak out loud, yelling and cursing if you like, telling those people that you're not going to take it anymore. Call them by name if you know them, tell them you have a right to love yourself, and feel pride in who you are. Keep hitting and tell them aloud of the pain you have suffered. When you can't beat the pillow anymore, sit back and close your eyes again, breathe deeply, and experience your feelings. After a pause:

See yourself surrounded by your allies, who are cheering for you. They're saying, "Welcome." "We love you." "We're so proud of you." "We're blessed to know you." Memorize these voices so you can hear them later, as you move about in the larger world. Feel the warmth of the kisses and embraces. They carry you off on their shoulders. Feel the sense of truly belonging.

Use this exercise at least once a day for five days, and again every time you experience a shaming, racist incident.

Letter Writing

Write two letters, one that only you will see and another that you might choose to mail. In the first letter, let it rip. Tell the significant adult who made you feel uncomfortable about your looks what he or she did and how the pain has affected you. The purpose of this letter is to release your hurt and to let the hurting little girl in you finally have a voice. The value of this exercise is that rather than get angry at ourselves or those who get close to us, we're expressing the anger directly at those who hurt us. This is not the time to be understanding; save that for letter no. 2.

In the second letter, express your experiences in moderate and loving tones. Use language such as "I feel," rather than blaming words such as "you should have . . . " or "you never. . . . " Simply describe your childhood experiences and how you felt when they occurred. The idea is to let this person know what you felt as a result of family patterns and how they've affected your life in both positive and negative ways. We suggest that you begin on a positive note and end that way also. It doesn't matter if you are writing to someone who has passed on; write these letters anyway.

Pillow Talk

As soon as possible after writing your letter, find a private space and set up a cushion to use as a stand-in for that hurtful adult from your past. Tell this "person" how he or she hurt you. The beauty of this Gestalt psychology–based exercise is that your unconscious doesn't care if this is actually the person from your past; it just wants relief from this unfinished business. Don't be afraid to speak up. Remind yourself that you're no longer protecting the shameful secret of your abuse, neglect, or other trauma you may have suffered.

Talking to Your Hair

Do you feel residual shame about the length or texture of your hair? Do you hate the word *kinky* or *nappy*? Whatever your feelings about your hair, don't put yourself down. Rather, be gentle with yourself. And whether you wear your hair natural or straightened, make peace with your choices by letting go of shame. As Carolivia Herron, the author of *Nappy Hair,* has suggested: "Of course there is no direct correlation between politics and hair. People can have Afros and be absolutely worthless or have straight hair and be the rock of salvation. Many people just want variations in their hairstyle."[31]

If you feel discomfort with your hair, write about it in your journal or in a letter to the person who criticized your hair. Standing in front of a mirror say: "I love you, you nappy, kinky, wavy, thick, bountiful, powerful, beautiful hair. You are one of my best friends. Thank you!" You might feel silly when you speak this way. But repeating loving words to and about your hair will penetrate your subconscious and help you to love your hair. Use this approach with any of your physical features that you connect to shaming experiences—including features that may have been passed on from Native American or European American ancestors.

In the next chapter, we examine another barrier to self-love, the emotional and physical abandonment many of us experienced in childhood.

5

Open Your Heart
to Your Man

Sister Spirit Margaret Murray Washington (1861–1925) worked her way through Fisk University and opened her heart to her future husband, Booker T. Washington, the great American inventor and founder of Tuskegee Institute. Sister Washington, a noted organizer and activist in her own right, was key in helping her husband build Tuskegee into a vital center of education. She also knew how to stand by her man, publicly supporting some of Washington's most controversial positions. In allowing ourselves to become emotionally vulnerable with our mates, let us be guided by the story of Sister Washington, a vital force in her community and in the life of one of our country's greatest heroes.

**Anti-intimacy belief explored in this chapter:
Those I love will leave me.**

Diane and Ondine are two women who were raised in strikingly different environments, Diane in Oakland in a two-parent household, and Ondine in Haiti, with neither her mother nor her father. But decades later, as these two women worked to change their emotionally empty lives in abundance group meetings, they realized that, in truth, both of them had been abandoned.

Abandonment goes beyond the long-term or intermittent absence of a parent because of death, separation, or divorce. It also includes the emotional alienation caused by a parent who, although physically present, was distant, cold, or abusive. The inability to support a child may be due to mental illness, substance abuse, being overburdened with work or child care obligations, or a dysfunctional family history. Unfortunately, women who were abandoned in childhood, by one or both parents, are often attracted to mates who end up deserting them physically or emotionally.

Diane, a forty-one-year-old hairstylist, had recently divorced her husband of twenty-one years, despite the fact that he was an excellent provider who bought the family a large house, luxury automobiles, and so much gold jewelry that Diane's customers call her "Princess Di." A petite woman who seems taller in her designer heels, Diane said, "People thought I was crazy for leaving Ernest, but he was verbally and physically abusive. He used words and his fists to beat me down." Throwing up her hands in frustration, she said, "Now I'm alone and lonely."

So is Ondine, thirty-five, a surgeon. She traced a finger along the hem of her pleated skirt and lowered her head, which was covered in a close-cropped natural. Speaking in a lilting Haitian accent, she said, "I hate being alone too. It petrifies me, so I settle for men who have nothing, not even a table to sit at. I was married to a man who turned out to be a drug abuser, but I kept telling myself that at least he wouldn't leave me. And I stayed until I couldn't take anymore. My last boyfriend was so unreliable, I never knew when he was coming home."

Both women had chosen men who are narcissists: people so deeply hurt in childhood that they unconsciously devote all their energy to looking out for themselves. Narcissistic lovers often shock us by their callousness. No matter how kind or loving we may be to them, they are often capable of incredibly cruel and thoughtless acts. These personality types are seldom attracted to narcissistic women, but they seem to have radar for women who were abandoned during childhood and who will do anything to keep their mates from leaving.

This point was made by one of Dr. Wade's male clients, Monty, a classic narcissist. During a therapy session, he said, "I've never been with a woman who was like me. I look for givers, and then I take and take until she gets sick of it, then I move on to the other woman I've had waiting in the wings."

Monty spoke from a hurt born out of a double abandonment. His father was a compulsive gambler who left the family for another woman and never returned home. His mother reacted by leaving him with his grandmother for six months so she could "have some fun." Monty was able to begin healing only when he recognized his losses and the pain and anger he had buried, as well as his profound fear that if he allowed a woman to get close he would face abandonment again.

He wept bitterly over the hurt he had sustained and the hurt he had dished out to women who had loved him and placed their faith in him. A devout Christian, he said, "Lord Jesus, please take this selfishness out of my heart. I don't want to be like this." He eventually married and became the stable and loving man his father had never been.

The women in the group discussed their experiences with narcissistic men, recalling times when they'd been left waiting by the phone or had walked in on a lover in bed with another woman. The other women began nodding their heads—they'd been there—but it wasn't until they started to explore their childhood losses that they could begin to understand how their abandonment issues led them unconsciously to re-create wounding emotional events in their present lives.

When it was Ondine's turn to speak of her childhood losses, she said, "My parents were unwed teenagers, and my birth was considered a disgrace. When my mother became pregnant with me, my father's parents, who were well off, sent him to a university in Chicago to escape the scandal. My mother stayed in Haiti until I was six. By then she had married someone else, and they had a three-year-old son. My mother and her husband took my brother with them to New York and left me behind with my grandmother, who loved me very much.

In Chicago, Ondine's father earned a college degree, and he sent her occasional gifts. From New York, her mother sent a small part of her salary back to the island for Ondine's support. She didn't see her mother again for six years. Although she saw her father only twice during childhood, he insisted she send him copies of her report cards and schoolwork, and he wrote back offering critical feedback on her work.

Her father's emphasis on education, her only link with him, spurred Ondine on to win top honors in grade school, and at sixteen she immigrated to Chicago, where she lived with him and his new wife, a woman who resented Ondine and manufactured excuses for fighting with her, then literally put her out. This compounded Ondine's sense of abandonment. At seventeen, she moved in with a cousin who lived nearby. Despite these disruptions and having had an inadequate secondary school education, Ondine remained a stellar student. She won a scholarship to an Ivy League college and eventually became a physician.

Women like Ondine, who have been stunningly successful, don't necessarily look wounded. Society has a tendency to assume that since so many children suffer losses and seem to get by, they're not sustaining any lasting damage. And many of us try to convince ourselves that we're not hurt. Ondine learned to deal with the absence of her parents by making excuses for them, rationalizing her loss. She said, "My mother left because she had to find a way to support me. My father's parents forced him to leave." In all the years of growing up without her parents, Ondine had never characterized her experience as abandonment, nor had she allowed herself to feel her longing for her parents' love and support. "It was just fine," she said. "My grandmother loved me enough to take both their places."

Whether they're in a Caribbean island or a small town in the South, many black parents have found it necessary or expedient to leave their families behind to create opportunities for themselves as well as their children. While many of us understand why our parents decided to leave, it's important to keep in mind that a child's natural needs don't disappear because a parent offers a good rationale. Just because we understand why it happened doesn't mean we aren't hurt. If someone steps on your foot by accident and breaks it, you may understand it was an accident, but that foot is still broken and it hurts.

Those of us who have never met one or both of our parents or who have had minimal contact with them can still miss them. As humans, we're emotionally wired to have two parents. All we have to do is look around to see children who are loved and nurtured by a mother and a father. We have a natural desire to understand and know those who gave rise to us. Whether or not we've had the experience of two loving parents, we feel the absence in our lives in the same way an amputee feels phantom pain in a missing limb. Even if the missing parent returns to our lives at some juncture, the wound has already been inflicted. This doesn't mean we can't overcome the loss. We can, but only by consciously working to clean out and heal the wound, not by covering up the hurt.

Most of the time, however, we try to absolve our parents without ever working through the losses, because we love them, want to protect them, and want to deny the suffering that was so difficult for us. We tend to be particularly forgiving of those who provided financial support, because we know of so many more who simply walked away and never looked back. But learning to look realistically at a parent's behavior is a major part of healing. If we can't admit the ways in which they failed us, we can't free ourselves of the secret hurt and anger that bogs us down, or make the necessary corrections in our own behavior.

In our community, this challenge can be a serious problem. Many of us grew up knowing we could play the dozens all we wanted, but when it came to someone talking about our families, especially our mamas, those were serious fighting words.

The reluctance we might feel about discussing disappointments is driven by the sense that we'll overshadow the good our parents brought to our lives and the lessons we learned from them. We remember all those mornings when we saw either our mothers or fathers, or both, or other providers, get up tired and drag themselves to work because they had to feed and clothe us. We hesitate, because we remember times when there wasn't enough chicken or rice or greens to go around, and they pretended they weren't hungry, telling us to "go ahead, Baby, and eat your fill." And we can't forget that when our parents went out into the world so they could support us, they often had to tolerate the most hostile environments. More than any other gift, our parents gave us lessons in survival, and for that we are filled with a special gratitude.

Often we were blessed to have loving relatives step in and try to fill the spaces caused by our parental losses. Ondine's grandmother was so devoted to her that "she used to dress me up like a doll, and if she prepared something for dinner and I didn't like it, she'd cook something else for me." The problem is that even if we tell ourselves otherwise, no one else can make us feel whole and loved the way two nurturing parents can.

Since her mother provided financial support, Ondine convinced herself that she hadn't been hurt by her parents' picking up and leaving her for years, but secretly she believed that anyone she loved would leave her. This was why she was drawn to unreliable men. She created relationships in which she overcompensated, helping her lovers to pull their lives together; some were men who initially didn't have a piece of furniture to sit on and who later cheated on her with other women, took large sums of money from her, and then left. After she realized how the men she'd chosen had replicated her experiences with her parents, Ondine later admitted, "I grew up hungry for a traditional family."

"I *did* grow up in a traditional family," Diane said when it was her turn to discuss her childhood. She also pointed out that the marriage she left behind also looked traditional. "But that's just a word, like a street number painted on the front of a house. It's what's inside that counts, and if it's not healthy it ain't all that." Diane's father, a factory worker, was also a church deacon, and her mother stayed at home to care for their six children. Both were known throughout their community for their kindness and generosity, especially when it came to "lending out" their kids to the neighbors.

"Someone would say, 'I need to get my garden dug,' and before they could finish the sentence, Daddy would volunteer one of us kids," Diane recalled. "He never asked whether I wanted to do these chores. I usually volunteered so I could protect my brothers and sisters. Over the years I did hundreds of chores for other people. My folks didn't think of kids as real people. When we had company for dinner, we had to wait until all our guests had eaten, and then we had whatever was left over. We weren't rich, but Daddy was a good provider, and I know he loved me, because I ran to hug him every night when he came home from work."

This was a misinterpretation. What Diane meant was that she knew she loved *him*. Her father showed his family love by providing for them, but the truth is, he took advantage of his children and treated them as if they had no feelings. Because she hadn't confronted her feelings, she married a man who treated her as callously as her parents had and then some. Like her father, her husband was a good provider, but that didn't mean he loved her.

Another version of acting out unresolved abandonment occurs when we behave in a way that pushes a mate to leave. Early in her career, Dr. Wade worked with a young couple, Henry and Gladys. Gladys had lost her father early in life to leukemia, and Henry's mother had died while giving birth to him. Both were desperate not to be left behind again by someone they loved.

Tall and handsome, Henry was a waiter who received lots of attention from other women, but he'd been in love with Gladys, a receptionist, since high school, even though her anger was open and palpable. Henry had his faults, such as having trouble expressing his feelings, but for years he was willing to accept Gladys's overt hostility. He thought his wife was moody and difficult, but what he didn't understand was that, subconsciously, Gladys didn't want him to get close enough to hurt her and leave, the way her father had.

Finally, Henry couldn't take any more of her coldness and lashing out, and he suggested a separation. Gladys sought help from the community clinic where Dr. Wade worked. During that first appointment, Gladys criticized Henry and went into detail about his faults and shortcomings, blaming him for all the problems in their marriage. She truly couldn't see her part in their conflicts. As they continued to work in therapy, Gladys realized she'd systematically been pushing Henry away. Inadvertently, she had created the very thing she was most afraid of. Fortunately for this couple and their children, they stuck it out, and with a lot of therapy, they have created a loving and supportive marriage.

People of all races and ethnicities wrestle with abandonment issues. Every immigrant story includes the traumas of family disruptions and losses, as well as the hostility faced on arrival in a new land. But for our people, "forced immigrants" who were stripped of all supports and who endured the lingering problems of racism and oppression, the experience of loss has been compounded.

OUR HISTORY: OUR HEARTS' LOSSES

It's easier to put our losses into perspective when we consider that family was—and still is—of utmost importance throughout Africa. Then our ancestors were kidnapped from their homeland. After emancipation, we worked to pull our families back together, only to have them shattered anew.

What is not widely known is that for a while, at the end of the eighteenth century, it looked as if the separations that occurred with slavery would come to an end. In Virginia, Maryland, and Delaware, tobacco planting had begun to wear out the soil, and farmers turned to planting grains, which did not require large numbers of agricultural workers. Many landowners began to free their slaves. But then, in 1793, Eli Whitney invented the cotton gin, which cleaned cotton fast and profitably. A huge labor force was needed to grow and harvest the crop. Once again, slave labor paved the road to huge profits.[1] Eventually 75 percent of the world's cotton would come from the South. This potential for profit sparked a massive number of black family separations. One of every three slaves would be sold off.[2]

Since the importation of slaves into the United States had been outlawed in 1808, slavers met the new demand for captives with two equally brutal approaches: They created "slave farms" in which people of African descent were born and bred.[3] And they organized slave coffles, marches that became a familiar sight as captives were forced out of areas in which they were no longer needed into states in the deep south—"Cotton Country." Newly purchased human beings were chained together, creating long lines of captives that stretched as far as the eye could see. They traveled through blistering heat and freezing cold, sleeping in woods and fields,[4] the men and children half-naked, women with their breasts exposed, most of them shoeless, and many dying along the way.

Former bondwoman Sis Shackelford of Virginia recalled what it was like to see a coffle just before the captives were marched off. "Everybody in the villages come out, especially the wives and sweethearts and mothers, to see their sold-off children for the last time. And when they start the chain a-clanking and step off down the line, they all just sing and shout and make all the noises they can, trying to hide the sorrow in their hearts and cover up the cries and moaning of them they were leaving behind. Oh, Lord!"[5]

Yes, Lord indeed, for who else might our ancestors have turned to? In what is perhaps one of the most haunting of all spirituals, they addressed their grief: "Some-times I feel like a moth-er-less chile. Some-times I feel like a moth-er-less, chile. Sometimes I feel like I'm al-mos' gone."

If there was ever proof that their losses were never forgotten, it was the frenzied search for relatives that began right after emancipation. In addition to paying for ads in the classified sections of newspapers, people took to the road. Witnesses recall that throughout the South, major thoroughfares were clogged with African Americans searching for their loved ones.[6]

Historians Darlene Clark Hine and Kathleen Thompson write: "The first summer of freedom was a time of searching. Black women traveled from town to town, from farm to plantation, looking for their children. 'They had a passion,' said one officer of the newly formed Freedman's Bureau, 'not so much for wandering as for getting together. Every mother's son seemed to be in search of his mother; every mother in search of her children.'"[7] Unfortunately, countless numbers of our people never saw their loved ones again.

During Reconstruction, there was a relatively short period of stability, but the black family structure was further strained during the great black migration, which began at the turn of the twentieth century. Millions of single black men, fathers, and then, increasingly, mothers left their children with relatives in the poverty of the South to head for the North and higher-paying jobs. While many new arrivals eventually gained an economic toehold and sent for their family members, others were swallowed by the inner city, their home ties shattered. In Jamaica, where chronic unemployment has tended to marginalize unskilled workers, many families are also fragmented, and women head a significant number of households.[8]

Orlando Patterson, a professor at Harvard, argues that high paternal abandonment rates are connected to the legacy of slavers' breaking up families. He said, "In no part of the world do you get this phenomenon except among ex-slave populations in the New World."[9] Most of these men don't simply pick up and leave because they're uncaring. In addition to our history of forced separations, economic factors must be taken into account. Men feel like fathers when they can provide for their children, but discrimination has led to unconscionably high levels of unemployment and underemployment among our people.[10] All of this has translated into high levels of physical abandonment. According to census reports, 64 percent of African American children are raised without one or both biological parents.[11]

There are no statistics to indicate how many more of us had parents who lived with us but were so caught up in the complexities of their own struggles that they left us feeling emotionally unsupported. Dr. Martin Luther King, Jr. was troubled that so many black parents were forced to ignore their children because they had to hold down two jobs. He wrote: "With the long distances ghetto parents must travel to work and the emotional exhaustion that comes from the daily struggle to survive in a hostile world, they are left with too little time or energy to attend to the emotional needs of their growing children."[12]

OUR EMOTIONAL INHERITANCE

With our history it's easy to see how fear of abandonment and loss plays a major part in our lives. It's a catch-22: Our history has led many of us to believe that we're unlovable and that we shouldn't let our lovers in close because they will leave us or let us down, yet because of childhood losses, many of us are drawn to lovers who will do just that. The only way out is healing, and that includes allowing ourselves to experience our feelings. This may sound obvious, but the truth is, children who have been emotionally or physically abandoned develop a coping mechanism that allows them to ignore or misinterpret the way they feel.

Perhaps during your childhood, your feelings were discounted by someone who made remarks such as "Don't cry" or "It's nothing" or "I'll only be gone for a while, what's the big deal?" When we're taught to deny hurt feelings, we become disconnected from them—in essence, abandoning ourselves. That means we're not able to stand up for ourselves and say, "I deserve healthy love." Five personality types often emerge from abandonment experiences. Can you see yourself in any of these?

Ms. Responsibility: Hiding our feelings of neediness, we make ourselves indispensable. We're the ones who care for the aging parent; we're the parent who alone nurtures the children. We're the "glue" that keeps the family together, while working full-time. The one feeling we're definitely in touch with is resentment. We allow others to make demands on us until we reach the breaking point. Then we lash out or become physically ill from the pressure that we put on ourselves.

Ms. Victim: Fearful of another desertion, we want to be as "good" as we can be, and that may mean fixing him the best possible meals, keeping his house spotless, providing sex wherever and whenever he wants it. We constantly ask for reassurance that he loves us. When we don't get sufficient proof that he cares, we manipulate and cry in an attempt to get our needs met. When they're not met, we get angry.

Ms. Love 'em and Leave 'em: Rather than suffer through another loss, we never get fully emotionally involved with anyone, so it's easy for us to pull up stakes the first time our love interest commits any infraction. We are sisters who may have multiple lovers or boyfriends, and we are constantly on the move; that way, we never have to be left behind.

Ms. "I'm Giving Up on Love": You almost can't blame us. Seems we've had the worst "luck" with love, so we've decided to just give up: spend our money on vacations instead of new outfits, stop worrying about our figures, and "enjoy" life. The only problem is that we're lonely, and we're secretly terrified of having any more situations in which another person walks away.

Ms. Mistress: We gravitate toward married men, because like the missing parent in our childhood, they're completely unavailable. If we find a guy who does leave his wife, and perhaps his children, then we're always terrified he'll dump us too. But if he's like most men who cheat, he continues to string us along. Then we feel like little girls, all dressed up and waiting by the window, hoping Daddy will show.

If you saw yourself in any of these profiles, it might help to know that these behaviors are mechanisms that we use to protect ourselves from further pain. The problem is that these coping styles don't leave any room for us to love ourselves or receive love from our mates. In fact these behaviors create the deprivation that makes us feel so sad and angry.

The good news is that when these patterns are transformed through healing, particular strengths are uncovered that can help us create high self-esteem and great relationships. With transformation, the following can happen:

The transformed "Ms Responsibility" can become a great facilitator. Instead of trying to run the household singlehandedly, she helps coordinate tasks. Rather than taking on way too much, she learns to ask for help.

The transformed Ms. Victim can be especially compassionate. When her partner comes home after a terrible day, she can listen without being judgmental. She has learned to give and receive in equal parts.

The transformed Ms. Love 'em and Leave 'em can be shoulder to shoulder with her mate, an equal to turn to for support and advice. She has learned not to take off and dump her mate the first time there's a challenge to be faced.

The transformed Ms. "I'm Giving Up on Love" knows how to live well or enjoy life. She and her partner can create a life of fun and adventure. She has stopped pushing away the people she loves.

The transformed Ms. Mistress can be an attentive partner who is sensitive to her lover and shows him she appreciates him. She has learned she deserves love and constancy.

You've obviously decided that you want to make a change in your life. It is that very resolve that will take you to a higher place. Everything you have learned about yourself in this and previous chapters is turning you into a healthier, more attractive being.

HEALING LOSS AND OPENING OUR HEARTS

Taking Emotional Inventory

Anyone who has been abandoned and abused will have some feelings that are close to the surface and others that are deeply buried. The object of this exercise is to begin to experience emotional responses

that, in the past, you would have tried to ignore. This is a way to practice seeing people as they truly are and not as stand-ins for someone
from the past.[13] The five steps are as follows:

Identify a reaction: The event may be something as significant as
your partner getting fired from work or as commonplace as dis-
covering the guy you've been eyeing from across the classroom is
not interested. In the past, you might have walked away and said
it didn't matter. But now you ask yourself how you really feel.

Experience the emotion: Don't brush it off. Relive the situation in
your mind so you can reexperience those feelings. We've included a
list of negative and positive emotions that you'll want to familiarize
yourself with.[14] Do you feel numb, angry, sad, hateful, lonely, hurt,
bored, betrayed, frustrated, inferior, suspicious, repulsed, shy, confused, rejected, unfulfilled, weak, guilty, shameful, or empty? Or do
you have a positive feeling, such as triumph, hope, affection, joy,
love, a sense of community, relief, involvement, contentment,
equality, trust, attraction, curiosity, clarity, support, satisfaction,
strength, innocence, pride, contentment, or fulfillment?

Connect your current feelings to a situation from your early childhood. When did you feel this way as a child?

Observe how you reacted to the current situation. If you feel you
overreacted or underreacted to the situation, decide how you would
like to respond the next time this or a similar situation arises.

Mentally picture yourself using the new response. This mental
rehearsal makes it easier to use this response when you need it.

To demonstrate the effectiveness of this process, we've included
the story of a couple. Lee, a fifty-year-old clerical worker, was locked
in conflict with her husband, William, fifty-one, a fireman, over the
purchase of a car. She wanted to buy a second new car because when
William took their grandchildren on camping trips, he drove their
new van, leaving Lee with their older, less attractive car.

Lee initially insisted that all she felt was angry, "because William
is kind of tight," she said. But when she pictured herself driving the
old car, and looked through the list of emotions, she realized that she

was also experiencing shame. "It's old and I have this feeling that people are thinking I'm a loser." Connecting the feeling of shame to a childhood experience, she said, "I used to have to wear hand-me-downs, and I got teased a lot."

Without any prompting, she said, "I've been taking out my anger about that stuff on William, haven't I?" Then her face brightened, as she added, "I wanted that car so I could impress other people. I think I better learn a different way to take care of myself."

When asked what that "different way" might be, Lee said sadly, "I've got to find a way to love myself more."

This was a major breakthrough for Lee. We trust that there will be many such epiphanies in your life. In the coming days, as you continue to repeat this emotional investigation and become more aware of your feelings, you will find it easier to communicate your needs.

Reparenting Yourself

Sitting comfortably and holding a pillow, pretend that you are, first, one parent, and later, the other parent (if applicable) who abandoned you. Gently stroking the pillow, which represents you as a child, speak the healing words you need to hear from your parent. Have your mom or dad apologize for hurting and abandoning you and acknowledge your feelings and how the loss affected you. Finally, have this parent describe aloud your attributes and talk about how lucky he or she is to have had you. Sit quietly, stroking that pillow (yourself), taking in the apology and basking in the parental approval. Many initially find it difficult to come up with loving messages, but keep practicing so that you have a nurturing voice that will speak to you when you need it.

Honoring Those Who Came before Us

Scholar, medicine man, and shaman (or high priest) Malidoma Patrice Somé, who was born in Burkina Faso (formerly the Upper Volta) in West Africa, has observed that much of the unhappiness in industrialized societies relates to a disconnection from ancestors. He wrote that "ancestors have an intimate and absolutely vital connection with the world of the living. They are always available to guide, to teach, to nurture."[15] Dr. Somé (pronounced So-mā) also believes that the best way to move forward is first to reconnect with the past.

We suggest you create a place for honoring your ancestors. Designate a space with a table, desk, or ledge that you can think of as your ancestors' shrine or altar. (Some people who feel uncomfortable with the idea of shrines commune with their ancestors while taking walks, jogging, or meditating.) If you decide to create an altar, you can use this space to do your visualizations and any inner work you do. It doesn't matter how large or fancy this spot might be. You can set up a bargain-store coffee table under a bedroom window or an antique table near a fireplace. What's important is that you begin to think of this as a place of solace, even if you just sit there after a stressful day and do absolutely nothing except breathe.

There are no hard and fast rules about the objects you place in this space. You might want to cover your table with a favorite cloth. It might include a photo of one or more of your grandparents, a Bible, or a copy of your genogram. Keep two candles here to represent the spirits of your unknown ancestors. You may want to give these ancestors names.

Dr. Somé says he has included on his shrine stones to represent his ancestors, as well as their photos, African masks, soil, and water in a container he considers special.[16]

You may want to write a letter to a relative from the past or speak aloud, telling him or her about your life today and some of the challenges that you have faced. Articulate what you most want to learn from the past.

Having this place of comfort will be tremendously helpful for you as you work through the next chapter, which focuses on anger. If repressed or expressed in an unhealthy manner, anger can destroy our health as well as our love relationships.

6

We Can Be *Good* and Angry

Sister Spirit Fannie Lou Hamer (1917–1977) was raised in Indianola, Mississippi, where she picked cotton and worked for nearly two decades as a sharecropper. Her life changed in 1962, when her unsuccessful effort to vote angered some local whites, who tried keeping her "in her place" with economic retaliation and physical violence. Saying she had grown "sick and tired of being sick and tired," she turned the anger she felt over her mistreatment into fuel for change and became a civil rights activist. In 1964, the world spotlight focused on Hamer at the Democratic National Convention. Although her efforts to be seated with the all-white state delegation were spurned, she spoke with passion and eloquence about having been arrested and beaten. It was a speech that is considered one of the most significant of the Civil Rights Movement. As we, too, learn to use our anger in a way that can enrich our lives, let us remember Hamer, an embodiment of righteous defiance.

> **Anti-intimacy belief explored in this chapter:**
> **It's not safe for me to face my anger.**

The young woman, a domestic worker, told Dr. B.: "I've never been angry in my whole life." Pretty and plump, her face framed by an Anita Baker haircut, Claritha, twenty-four, was a single mother of two who was referred for pro bono therapy by her clergyman.

Claritha had every reason to be angry. A horrendous incident had prompted the recommendation for therapy. She and her children had been alone in the small apartment they shared with her mother and her mother's boyfriend, when two men with guns kicked in the front door. They demanded that Claritha lead them to where her mother's boyfriend kept his drug stash. "Every time I told them I didn't know, and I didn't, he slapped me and pushed the heat [the gun] up against my head. My kids were screaming. These guys dumped drawers and pulled the insides out of closets. I was begging them, Please don't hurt my kids, Please don't hurt me. I'm all they got."

Overcoming her initial shock, Claritha directed the men to a place in the house where she'd seen her mother's boyfriend hovering. A floorboard was pried up, a bag was unearthed, and just as suddenly, the men were gone.

"I made my kids pray with me. We thanked God for sparing our lives. If I did feel any anger, Jesus cleansed me of it, and I forgave those men. I've never really been an angry person." Unfortunately, Claritha could continue her therapeutic appointments only sporadically. She had been trying to make a life with her boyfriend, a former prison inmate who, like her, was a born-again Christian. But the sheer weight of poverty and oppression, and her own buried rage, bore down on her so heavily, she had little energy for healing or for sustaining a relationship.

During her initial appointments, Claritha insisted that her faith in God could keep her from getting angry. She was forgetting that even Jesus expressed anger, such as the time he drove the money changers from the temple. But Claritha maintained that she not only didn't resent her assailants, but wasn't angry at employers who occasionally tried to cheat her out of money and certainly not at her father, who deserted the family. Most of all, she contended, she was not angry with her mother, a hardworking woman who also worked as a domestic.

In many homes, there are such strong taboos against any show of anger that we've lost the ability to recognize it when we feel it. Even when we sense our own anger, we might work hard to suppress or deny it. But just because you may not allow yourself to feel angry doesn't mean you're not, and anger isn't necessarily bad. It's an important emotion that, if appropriately expressed, helps us stand up for ourselves, and it can create intimacy. Unfortunately for Claritha, she had learned it wasn't safe to face her anger. Dr. Wade soon learned what experiences had convinced her to keep her anger underground.

From the age of six, Claritha took care of four younger siblings. Understandably, her mother returned home from work exhausted, "and she didn't want to hear nothing about no problems or she'd whup all our butts." When bad news was unavoidable, "I felt so bad telling her," she said.

Her experience of raising her siblings is by no means unique. Today, working mothers are the societal norm, but because there have always been black families who struggled financially, working mothers are not new in our communities. In many of our families, everyone is expected to pitch in and help out. This has given rise to many "parental children," kids who have had to take on parenting responsibilities. In healthy families, there are boundaries concerning children's responsibilities; while they certainly pitch in, they still have time to be children. But in families in which the parents are absent or compromised, an older sibling essentially becomes the parent, and everyone pays a high price. The mother loses her deep maternal connection to the younger kids, the parental child is without a parent, and usually this child is without friends, because she's too busy caretaking to hang out with her peers.[1]

Trained to be the "defender of the home," parental kids often grow into adults who are reluctant to complain about sacrificing their childhoods and later their needs. Claritha said, "My mother was out there every day, just like I am for my kids. I don't fault her for nothing."

It's important to distinguish between anger and rage. Anger is specific and has to do with a particular event. Something external occurs, you don't like it, and you feel angry. Despite her denial that she felt any anger toward her attackers, Claritha was angry, but because she had never been allowed to express her feelings, she was also enraged.

Rage is long-term fury that builds up inside because of a prohibition against expressing one's feelings. When anger has been forced beneath the surface, it can suddenly explode, much like the lava lake inside a volcano. Both rage and inappropriate expressions of anger can wreck relationships. Let's consider two different types of rageful personalities.

Sandra, thirty-six, an attorney, was invited to her best friend's house, where she was being fixed up with a guy that was supposedly perfect for her. Things seemed to be going well until a discussion about O.J. and Nicole came up. Just as this new guy was trying to make a point, Sandra blurted out, "I don't give a fuck what the statistics say!" Sandra later said, "I just get so passionate about some things." When we're rageful, we can't easily explain our behavior; it seems to come out of nowhere and is usually disproportionate to the stimulus. Understandably, other people don't want to be around us because they don't know when we're going to go off on them.

Not everyone who is full of rage explodes. Some, like Claritha, who was raised in a home in which there was no room for her feelings, learn to mask their rage. Deserted by her father, forced to become the parental child, and beaten, she was unconsciously determined to keep her rage from boiling over. She must have intuitively realized that the family would fall apart if she rebelled against her overwhelming responsibilities. Claritha simply couldn't bear another loss, and she sacrificed her needs instead.

So much of Claritha's energy was tied up in keeping her feelings beneath the surface that she didn't have any energy left to demand full payment from her employers, making it impossible for her to afford to move someplace where she and her offspring could be safe. All she could do was pray that her boyfriend could one day make a better life for them. She was waiting to be rescued.

In therapy, she used a rage-release exercise and started to express her feelings. Using a cushion as a stand-in for her mother, she cried, saying, "I didn't have no business trying to run no family. I was just a kid." But she stopped abruptly. When asked why, Claritha explained, "It just don't feel right. It's disrespectful." Unable to face the depth of her rage and the pain it masked, Claritha discontinued her therapy.

It is not unusual for clients to pull out of therapy when they reach a point of acknowledging their anger. Expressing these feelings can be particularly difficult for those of us raised to view ourselves as nurturers or those of us who grew up in homes where we were told that only "low-class" folks show their anger, while "refined" folks are models of decorum.

Ondine, the Haitian sister whose story was introduced earlier, had been taught manners and decorum by her paternal grandmother, who for decades maintained her dignity despite her husband's adulterous behavior. After Ondine joined our abundance group, she finally reached a point where she could say aloud, "I'm aware of being really angry with men." The fact that her anger was out in the open was a healthy sign. Still, she resisted the idea that her anger had anything to do with her father's abandonment and refusal to provide any financial support.

As long as her anger toward her father remained unexpressed, it would be difficult for Ondine to break her pattern of getting involved in one-sided relationships, giving her all to these men, and getting nothing or very little in return. We call this "settling for crumbs." Ondine insisted that all she needed was to choose different men, but she couldn't choose differently until she was able to hold her father accountable and say "I deserved more!"

Ondine, an Ivy League–trained surgeon, and Claritha, who was unable to finish high school and had two unplanned pregnancies before she was eighteen, couldn't have had lives that were more different, yet they offered the same explanation for why they couldn't express their anger toward their parents. For both of them it was a matter of being disrespectful. Many of us are in the same predicament. Though we may adore our parents, our bonds with them may be so tenuous we can't even admit to ourselves that we're angry for fear of breaking the bond completely and irreparably.

Another important factor in suppressing our rage is that only decades ago the slightest show of anger could have cost us our lives or, even worse, the lives of our children. Today, many of us still plaster on a smile out of fear that we'll be seen as one more angry sister. Toni Morrison has said, "If we're not totally understanding and smiling, suddenly we're demons."[2]

Perhaps the most persistent image of a rageful sister is the vaudevillian Amos 'n Andy character, Sapphire, a black woman who rolls her eyes, with hands on her hips and elbows jutting out like swords, while she dogs her man. We decided to turn that image on its head to help you better understand anger and how it can negatively affect your relationships. We have created an informative self-test called the "Sapphire Quotient."

THE SAPPHIRE QUOTIENT

The following quiz is designed to help you understand your anger. You'll find that some of the answers will seem equally desirable. Choose the one that seems best to reflect your personality. Don't search for the most politically correct response. Ask yourself, "What have I done in the past?" or "What would I be apt to do?"

1. This was supposed to have been the night when he met your parents. But by now, Mama and Daddy are long gone, and so's the food and the candlelight. Brother man pulled another no-show. But now that he's walking through the front door, you

   A. Hide your tears, you've been so worried, wondering if he was alive or dead.

   B. Yell and tell him to get his raggedy butt out of your house.

   C. Tell him you're very angry and hurt and want to know what's going on.

   D. Don't say a word; you're not talking to him tonight, maybe not for weeks.

2. Your teenager, still reeling from your divorce and obviously jealous of the new man in your life, gets all up in your face when you call him on his behavior. Your man has been sitting quietly until now, when he angrily grabs your son by the shoulder. You

   A. Let him go ahead and give that boy a good beating; he's been asking for it.

   B. Tell your man, "Oh no, he's my baby, so you can just sit on down."

   C. Insist they lower their voices, the whole neighborhood will hear them.

   D. Suggest that everyone take time out so you can all cool down and talk about it later.

3. Your guy called to say something's come up—he'll explain later—but in the meantime, he can't see you tonight. Later, out with your friends, you peep him walking into a restaurant with some woman whose skirt hugs every well-rounded curve—this sister's got back! He looks shocked when he sees you, and you

   A. Go home and wait till later to tell him you're angry and hurting.

    B. Narrow your eyes and grab his arm; no hoochie girl's gonna take your man.

    C. Smile, despite a sudden migraine. You can't stand when sisters act ghetto.

    D. Pretend you don't see him, and you and your friends indulge in a huge meal.

4. He's married! You've just found out. How could he have lied to you after you opened your heart and your bed? You

    A. Contact his pastor and his wife; let him find out how it feels to suffer.

    B. Admit you can't live without him, especially since he's promising to leave her.

    C. Recognize you're in a crisis and call a therapist.

    D. Calm down after he apologizes and gives you a platinum American Express card.

5. You've tried convincing him to take this opportunity—an offer to move from security guard to security chief. But he doesn't want it, says he's a simple man and that you'll have to deal with that or walk. You

    A. Decide not to give up on him yet; you'll find a way to convince him.

    B. Clean your house; it's already spotless, but cleaning helps you think.

    C. Consider whether you can accept him unconditionally, and let him decide whether to take the job.

    D. Sit down and read the Bible; as a Christian you try to keep the peace.

6. Your honey's niece, a charming young woman who has always admired the two of you, has asked that you both host her wedding reception. Her parents have passed away. She says she'll foot the bill herself; she only needs you two to handle details. Knowing your guy often lets details slip through the cracks, you

    A. Would feel guilty about letting her down, so you handle all the tasks.

    B. Make a list for him and continue to remind him of his responsibilities.

C. Ask him what he'd like to handle; if he does nothing, do what's realistic for you and let the rest go.

D. Tell him it's his niece and if he wants to screw up her reception, so be it.

7. Your husband of several years, who is struggling with depression, has lost interest in eating healthy meals, no longer exercises, and smokes several cigars a day, all which are jeopardizing his health. You

A. Keep telling him how frightened you are by his behavior.

B. Sign him up at a gym and insist he see a psychologist.

C. Become so depressed that only shopping can relieve your anxiety.

D. Share your concerns with him and ask him to have a medical workup so his doctor can advise him.

8. You and your honey have been arguing, and now he's trying to make his point. Since you are in complete disagreement, you

A. Are so anxious to speak you keep interrupting.

B. Listen until he's finished and ask questions to make sure you understand him.

C. Quietly sit there while building your defense in your head.

D. Storm from the room.

Now that you have completed the Sapphire Quotient test, you can add up your score. Begin by jotting down the number of the question and the letter of the answer you've chosen. Then compare your responses to the "healthy responses" key, giving yourself twenty-five points for each correct answer:

	Healthy Responses
1.	1. C
2.	2. D
3.	3. A
4.	4. C
5.	5. C
6.	6. C
7.	7. D
8.	8. B

If you scored 150 to 200 points, you're excellent at handling your anger in a relationship, or at least you know what kind of behavior is loving and supportive, even if you don't use that knowledge yourself. If you scored 150 or below, there's a good chance that you learned it wasn't safe to feel your anger, or you may be turning your anger against yourself and those close to you.

The truth is, no matter what your score, you're a winner because you're working to change for the better. We suggest you keep reading; finding out why the other answers are wrong will help you learn more about the "dos" and "don'ts" of a sound relationship.

1. The brother's a no-show.
   A: Worry: If someone humiliates you by not showing up, are you really going to worry that he might have been killed, or would you be *hoping* he was? Since women are often reluctant to confront men, we've learned how to worry. Worry is often displaced anger.
   B: Send him packing: You'd be giving yourself an opportunity to express your anger, but that would put you back where you started, alone.
   C: Talk it out: correct. Here's how: Start by telling him how you feel. For instance, "I felt scared and hurt when you didn't show up, and I'm very angry. Mom and Dad were here, and I wanted them to love you as much as I do. It's not okay with me for you not to show up. Why weren't you here? I'd like to work with you on changing this pattern. Will you work with me?"
   D: Refuse to speak: This only leaves the anger welling up inside you, and nothing is resolved. The icy silence also creates an atmosphere so unwelcoming he doesn't want to be there and neither do you.

2. He's about to hit your son.
   A. Let him beat your son: Hitting children (or anyone) is always wrong; in addition, this sets up a situation in which your mate and your son would become enemies.
   B. Order your mate to sit down: If you want your lover to be an equal partner, you can't treat him in a controlling way.
   C. Tell them to lower their voices: Telling your mate and your son to lower their voices is also controlling behavior.

D. Suggest a time out: correct. After about twenty minutes, when everyone feels calmer, each person should have a chance to speak about what he feel and needs, without being interrupted.

3. He's out with another woman.

A. Talk it out later: correct. The first thing you can do for yourself is acknowledge your feelings to yourself or a supportive friend. Later, with your mate, talk it over. By now you know how: Acknowledge your feelings, and ask for what you want, perhaps for him to join you in couples therapy. This is a serious problem that is damaging to your self-esteem. If he won't seek help, you deserve more and need to leave and get more. Either way, you need therapy to help you find out why you've picked a man who's unfaithful.

B. Grab his arm: Confronting him in public would only lead to more humiliation.

C. Smile, despite a headache: Headaches often occur when the anger inside us mounts like hot steam in a pressure cooker that has no release valve. Rather than expressing our feelings, we make ourselves sick.

D. Enjoy a big meal: Indulging in food is a popular way for stuffing down anger. Your feelings go unexpressed, and you may be ruining your health, not to mention your figure.

4. He's married!

A. Call his wife: Acting out your anger by intentionally hurting someone else would be wrong.

B. Continue the affair: Having an affair with someone you know is married is the height of self-destruction; you're telling yourself that you deserve only crumbs of love.

C. Call a therapist: correct. You'll want to explore the questions: "Why was I willing to engage in a relationship in which I received so little in return? What makes me believe I deserve so little?"

D. Take the credit card: A married man offering you a platinum credit card might sound pretty good, but what's the hidden cost to you?

5. He doesn't want a promotion.

A. Change his mind: We have no right to try to determine someone else's course in life. Even if you succeeded at pressuring him into what you want him to do, he'd be resentful.

B. Clean your house: This would be avoiding your feelings. We've all had mothers, grandmothers, or aunts who cleaned house so they could avoid their anger. One client called his mother a "vacuumaholic." Whenever you stuff your anger down, you're hurting yourself.

C. Search your own heart: correct. Unconditional love requires that we accept our mates for who they are and what makes them happy, not what makes us happy when they do it our way.

D. Read your Bible: You're avoiding the issue and sending a bitter unspoken message to your partner: "I'm turning to God to find the patience to tolerate your lazy butt."

6. His niece wants help with her wedding.

A. Handle all the details yourself: Taking care of everything sends a signal that you believe you can't count on him. Remember, you create your own reality from your beliefs. Besides, you'll feel angry and resentful if you handle everything.

B. Remind him of his responsibilities: Constantly reminding a man of his responsibilities is nagging, which is hostile behavior. It's akin to jabbing him repeatedly with a stick.

C. Let him choose his assignments, then move on. If he doesn't take on any chores, you can do what you feel comfortable with. Let his niece know which tasks you've chosen to handle, and let her work out the rest with your husband, if the two of them choose to. Don't put yourself in the middle.

D. Tell him to deal with his own failures: This is obviously hostile behavior; you would be putting him down.

7. He's jeopardizing his health.

A. Continue to remind him of your concerns: Telling him what to do is controlling, and, again, nagging is a form of attack.

B. Set up his health regimen: Signing him up for exercise and insisting on therapy is angry, controlling behavior.

C. Shop till you drop: This is another way of avoiding your feelings.

D. Ask him to have his doctor advise him: correct. Tell him you love him and that's why you're asking him to take responsibility for his health.

8. You're arguing and he presents his view.

A. Interrupt your partner: This is disrespectful, and it escalates a disagreement.

B. Listen, then ask clarifying questions: correct. Ask clarifying questions, such as, "Are you saying that you don't feel loved when I tell you what to do?"

C. Pretend to listen: Constructing a rebuttal and not listening is a way of shutting your partner out, and you'll never understand what he's trying to say.

D. Walk out: Storming from a room cuts off any possibility of working things out. If you need a cooldown period, say so and state when you'll be back.

We hope that working through this test has demonstrated for you that although anger can be driven underground, it can never be successfully hidden. It can show up as arched eyebrows, as clenched jaws, or in an overly bright smile that looks more like a grimace. People don't even have to see an angry person to pick up on his or her anger. Rage might be heard as we "crack" gum in the middle of a quiet theater or blast loud music from the open window of our cars. Suppressed, anger can hurt us and the people we care about. After looking at our history, however, it's easy to understand why our ancestors believed it wasn't safe to vent their anger.

OUR HISTORY: COVERT ANGER

Although slaveholders portrayed our ancestors as happy and docile, they knew that keeping slaves was a risky business. There was always the potential for armed rebellion. Through the centuries, on board slave ships (as in the famous Amistad uprising) and on plantations in the Caribbean, South America, and North America, African people risked their lives, and often lost them, because they simply wouldn't take it any more. The most widespread rebellion of all occurred in Haiti in 1791, when one hundred thousand slaves burned fourteen hundred sugar and coffee plantations, all the while hacking their white oppressors to death and, when possible, throwing them live into the blaze.[3]

The rebels in Haiti were eventually led by Toussaint-L'Ouverture, a man who, by all accounts, had been a "model slave." But the fury of this fifty-year-old gray-haired, barefoot coachman fed the flames of rebellion. In two years he led his men to defeat the English and Spanish armies, unified Haiti, and held his own against Napoleon. Although Toussaint-L'Ouverture was arrested, transported to France, and died in prison, his successor, Jean-Jacques Dessalines, another former slave, led the rebels in killing sixty thousand French soldiers. In 1803, the rebels declared Haiti a new republic. Lerone Bennett, Jr. explains that their victory "electrified the world and sent shivers down the backs of American slaveholders."[4]

There was good reason for their fear. Before slavery ended in the United States, there were more than two hundred fifty uprisings and major conspiracies.[5] The largest slave revolt occurred in Virginia, in 1831, led by Nat Turner, a mystic and bondman. He and about sixty followers killed fifty-one white people. Turner was captured and hanged, as were many other black people, some of whom were only loosely suspected of being associated with him. The Southern states reacted by passing stricter laws to tighten their hold on our people.[6]

Laws, however, couldn't stop the daily acts of sabotage that occurred on every plantation. Newspapers from this period are filled with accounts of unexplained arsons and poisonings.[7] In addition, our people frequently ran away, despite terrible punishments. Recaptured slaves were sometimes punished by having iron collars with bells fitted around their necks so they could be heard wherever they went or by having their toes chopped off, or even by death. Still, many of our people continued to break out, a direct refutation to slaveholders' claims that captives were happy with their existence. White physicians eventually coined the word *drapetomania*, which meant "an insane desire to run away." They said we were crazy for trying to be free. They didn't realize anger fueled our ancestors' feet.

The race toward freedom was a torturous journey, with dogs often hard on the heels of the escapee. Traveling alone or carrying a child through routes that included rivers and dark forests, runaway slaves followed the "drinking gourd" (the Big Dipper) or looked for quilts hung on lines, which were often encoded by our people with secret messages, a hidden language that guided some to the clandestine houses. The escapees traveled on what was known as the Underground Railroad.[8] Free blacks as well as whites who provided food, clothes, and shelter were known as "station masters"; they risked their lives to help slaves, despite harsh laws. In fact, the largest number of successful escapes occurred after the passage of the repressive Fugitive Slave Act. For many rescuers, this was a way of expressing their anger, as well as their moral and political abhorrence of the system.[9] The best-known conductor of all was sister Harriet Tubman, herself an escaped slave, who, fueled by her anger, made as many as fifteen trips into the South to rescue more than two hundred slaves and deliver them to freedom, all of this despite the $40,000 bounty on her head.[10]

Tubman succeeded where most failed. Successful escapes were rare for a number of reasons: Slaves were generally unaware of the geography, the places of refuge were few and far between, and their brown skin made the escapees highly visible.[11] Also, slaveholders paid through the nose for the return of runaways, so they could maintain their image of invincibility among their other captives. Many a bounty hunter earned a profitable living tracking our people down. Even when our ancestors made it to the North, they weren't necessarily safe. Slaveholders placed ads offering rewards for runaways, unashamedly describing them by the disfiguring features they had "earned" for running away in the past: ears or fingers cut off, facial burns, permanently raised welts crossing legs and arms, and backs covered in gashes so deep a man could lay a finger in them.

Even that didn't stop our people. More ingenious escapes involved hiding in a trunk and being shipped to the North and, in another case, a fair-skinned woman's passing as a white man and traveling by train with a slave attendant, who was actually her husband.

Driven by hunger and fatigue, most runaways returned to their plantations,[12] especially women who were grief-stricken over leaving their families.[13] In some areas, returning meant being taken to the workhouse, where "gentlemen" could pay someone else to beat their slaves for them and avoid having their clothes stained with the blood of our people.[14]

Our ancestors may have comforted themselves by recalling biblical figures who eventually triumphed over adversity. One of their "battle songs" is familiar to many of us: "Josh-ua fit de bat-tle of Jer-i-cho, Jer-i-cho, Jer-i-cho; Josh-ua fit de bat-tle of Jer-i-cho, an' de walls come tum-blin' down."

Music could only momentarily cool their rage, and some realized they needed to be angry to survive. Mothers taught their daughters never to simply submit to a white man. A woman recalled her mother's warning: "I'll kill you, Gal, if you don't stand up for yourself . . . . Fight, and if you can't fight, kick; if you can't kick, then bite."[15] But there seldom was open retaliation, even for the black servant whose eye was poked out with a fork by her white "mistress," who was angry that the potato she had been served was insufficiently cooked. Many (but certainly not all) slave women hid behind a mask of docility and found quieter ways to settle the score. Some put ground glass in the gravies they served whites; others spit in their food.

After emancipation, anger was kept at a simmering point as black children grew up realizing their parents were powerless in the face of white hostility and violence. It was inevitable that conflicts would occur between mothers and fathers about how to raise children and what to teach them about their anger. Author Zora Neale Hurston recalled that her parents had differing views. While her mother thought it was important not to break her daughter's will, her father felt "it did not do for Negroes to have too much spirit. He was always threatening to break mine or kill me in the attempt." He predicted that Hurston's "sassy mouth" would attract white posses with ropes and guns, and that she would be hung.[16]

Decades later, in the 1960s, when young civil rights protestors took to lunch counters and initiated voter registration drives and protests, their parents' warnings echoed those of Hurston's father. In many instances, their predictions came true. Some white people fought our liberation attempts with firebombings and assassinations, knowing they would likely get away with it. Sam Bowers, the Imperial Wizard of the Mississippi White Knights, recently convicted of ordering the death in 1966 of civil rights leader Vernon Dahmer, is said to have assured a fellow Klansman: "No jury in the state of Mississippi is going to convict a white man for killing a black person."[17]

These attitudes so enraged our people that they took to the streets in mass demonstrations. In the sixties, thousands of young black people, sometimes hand in hand with white students and eventually joined by people of all ages, were empowered by the stirring speeches of leaders such as Dr. Martin Luther King, Jr. Though they were pelted with racial epithets and subjected to physical violence, they managed to respond with nonviolence. But that doesn't mean that they weren't angry. Anger is vital energy that needs direction.[18] Their anger gave them the strength to challenge the prevailing system. Through courage and determination, these demonstrators showed the world that God was on their side just as surely as when Joshua fought the battle of Jericho.

When riots broke out, beginning in 1964 and continuing for the next three summers—in areas such as Watts, Newark, and Detroit—crowds often burned and looted everything in sight. This chaos was to our detriment, because many of the businesses affected were never rebuilt. But the rage of our people had finally boiled over. For those who understood America's history, violence seemed unavoidable.

Although there have been substantive changes, our wounds have never healed because they're constantly reopened. In a *Dateline* television segment, two producers, a white woman and a black woman, dressed similarly and armed with hidden cameras, shopped at various department stores. Even when the black woman was the first to approach a makeup counter or clothing rack, she was usually ignored or there was a long delay before she was acknowledged by salesclerks. On the other hand, the white shopper often had the attention of two salesclerks at a time, in some instances while the black producer, who arrived first, was still waiting.[19]

There have been various similar hidden-camera reports by the TV networks demonstrating that people of African descent face discrimination in so many aspects of their lives, such as in receiving mortgage loans, applying for jobs, and renting and buying homes; despite these reports, most whites don't believe this discrimination takes place, which only increases the frustration. According to a national survey, an estimated 80 percent of African Americans are united in the belief that they lack equal opportunity for good jobs, education, and housing, while a majority of white people insist that equal opportunities do exist for African Americans.[20]

This denial by white people is one reason that, in the workplace, our feelings often fester concerning racial slights or exclusionary practices. So many of us have had our complaints met with a white supervisor asking, "How do you know he treated you this way because of prejudice?" So many of us have grown frustrated with having to present proof, or risk being branded as overly sensitive, that we just shrug our shoulders and try to put such incidents out of our minds, rather than listen to white managers suggest that we are overreacting. We are left "between a rock and a hard place." Researchers have found that the risk of high blood pressure among African Americans appears to be mitigated when we challenge unfair treatment.

Researchers from the Harvard School of Public Health in Boston and the Kaiser Foundation Research Institute of Oakland, California found in a study of more than 4,000 men and women that black professionals who were aware of discrimination[21] and who challenged unjust treatment appeared to be at lower risk for high blood pressure than blue-collar workers who were less aware of discriminatory acts and less likely to challenge them.[22] These results showed that even when we become so conditioned to racism that we aren't consciously aware of it, we're still deeply affected. Researchers have found that, in addition to responding to physical threats, people also get angry when they feel their self-esteem or dignity is compromised, when they've been treated unfairly or unjustly, when they have been insulted or demeaned, or when their goals have been thwarted.[23]

The researchers may not have realized that their description of what makes people angry characterizes how people feel in racist situations. Making matters even worse, many black women also have to put up with sexual innuendos and worse from coworkers. More often than not, they keep mum about this too. Dr. Gail Elizabeth Wyatt found that fewer black women than white women who experienced sexual harassment at work took action.[24]

Sometimes we're caught off guard when anger seems to suddenly boil over in the workplace, which is often a hotbed of unexpressed racial tension. Witness the furor in Washington D.C., in January of 1999, that was sparked when one of the mayor's white aides used the word "niggardly" (a synonym for "miserly" which has Scandinavian origins and which is centuries older than the racial slur). The aide, David Howard, apparently said, "I will have to be niggardly with this fund because it's not going to be a lot of money." One of his black coworkers thought Howard had used the word "Nigger." Howard tried to explain the misunderstanding, but soon rumors of hurt feelings had reached Mayor Anthony Williams' office. Howard offered his resignation, and the mayor immediately accepted. This touched off a firestorm of discourse around the country, with white as well as black language purists arguing that "niggardly" is a perfectly acceptable word;[25] while on the other side, some of the mayor's African American constituents in man-on-the-street interviews, denounced use of the word because it sounds insensitive. When Howard was reinstated by the mayor, the issue seemed to be shelved, and journalists rushed off in pursuit of the next hot story. Few seemed interested in exploring the history and beliefs that had made Howard's black co-workers react so strongly in the first place. That subject, the sudden absence of cameras seemed to imply, is an old story. Once again, the anger was pushed just beneath the surface.

The biggest problem with these dispiriting situations is what happens in our bodies when we get angry. We physiologically prepare for action with something called the fight-or-flight response: Sugar pours into our nervous system to give us more energy. The nourishment is circulated throughout our body as our heart accelerates. In addition, more adrenaline is secreted, and our pupils become dilated for improved vision. If there's no discharge of this buildup, our body stays in a chronic state of preparedness, our heart beating rapidly, blood pressure up,[26] and muscles tensed. No wonder chronic anger creates so much physical damage, setting us up for headaches, respiratory and skin disorders, arthritis, emotional disturbances, and high blood pressure. In fact, while 25 percent of Americans in general will eventually experience hypertension—chronically high blood pressure— that figure is 35 percent among black Americans. And the ailment is more often fatal for us, accounting for 20 percent of the deaths among our population, twice the figure for white people.[27]

In an attempt to understand this dilemma, researchers studied groups of black people in the United States, Jamaica and Nigeria (rates of hypertension in rural Nigerians are among the lowest in the world). Jamaican and American black people in the study shared an average of seventy-five percent of their genetic heritage with the Nigerians. What they didn't have in common were high measures of hypertension. Rates of high blood pressure were seven percent among Nigerians, with slightly increased rates in urban areas; 26 percent among Jamaicans and 33 percent of the black Americans suffered from hypertension or were on medication to lower their blood pressure. Forty to 50 percent of the increased risk for black Americans could be attributed to many being overweight, lack of exercise and poor eating habits. But Africans who have moved to Europe in past decades also have higher blood pressure than whites who live there. Researchers noted that "there is little dispute that blacks in North America and Europe face a unique kind of stress—racial discrimination."[28] Not surprisingly, conscious and unconscious rage damages our relationships as well as our health.

OUR EMOTIONAL LEGACY

As you consider how the ancestral belief "It's not safe for me to face my anger" affected your life, you'll want to take out your genogram. Have there been major losses in your family because someone expressed anger inappropriately? Or have there been losses because someone repressed her anger and failed to act or protect when necessary? Who had a reputation for being very angry? Why do you think that person was so enraged? Look also for any patterns of anger going underground. Remember that any loss triggers anger; it's one of the stages of grief.

In her genogram, Helen, thirty-six, tracked a pattern of overt anger that stopped in her father's life and then went underground. Despite the social prohibitions of the 1950s, her paternal grandfather flaunted his relationship with a mistress. His wife, Helen's grandmother, responded by setting the farmhouse on fire and killing herself. Helen's father, as a result of his mother's lethal rage, understandably was terrified of anger. He was viewed as a "sweet-natured" man who channeled his energy into his work. In reality, his anger toward his father for precipitating his mother's breakdown, and toward his mother for abandoning him, was suppressed through his workaholism. Although Helen's father was able to provide his family with a comfortable lifestyle, he was away from home so often that Helen and her mother had to fend for themselves.

Helen's mother, who also hid her rage, had a "victim" personality, blaming her problems on everyone else and expecting others to care for her. Helen discovered she emulated this victim style; she became financially dependent on a man who was also a workaholic. An important aspect of her healing involved getting in touch with her own rage, which seemed to surface as she spoke to her boyfriend with steely contempt.

As you look over your genogram, recall how your parents dealt with their anger toward each other. Were there long stretches of frigid silence? Did they rage at one another? Was there violence? Were there sarcastic put-downs? How did you respond to what you experienced? Does your story echo their relationship? Some women who saw lots of anger respond by never allowing themselves to feel or express anger, yet they end up choosing mates who blow up. The family pattern of rage repeats itself even though the woman isn't displaying overt anger.

If you were beaten by your parents, you may have a history of violent relationships. The "whippings" many of us experienced are connected to the slavery experience. Our ancestors harshly disciplined their children to teach them quickly the dos and don'ts of plantation life, before a slaveholder taught them in a more brutal fashion. In addition, some parents emulated the brutality of the slavers through a process psychologists call "identification with the aggressor." The pattern has continued: Corporal punishment occurred in many of our homes, as well as in the homes of families of all races whose intergenerational history includes major losses. It's important to remember that the problem of corporal punishment is not limited to black families. Like all of the difficulties we discuss in this book, this is a human problem; corporal punishment, in particular, is a worldwide human rights issue. A number of European countries, including Denmark, Finland, Norway, Sweden, Austria, Cyprus, Croatia, and Latvia, have deemed it necessary to ban this punishment outright. [29] Although this and other issues we raise are not limited to our people, our work involves narrowing the focus, with an eye on how we have been shaped by our unique history. Many of us suffered fierce beatings from our parents, and often this brutal treatment was accompanied by threats such as, "Stop crying or I'll give you something to really cry about" or " I brought you into this world, I'll take you out." Beating us was also one of the ways many parents released their rage at the brutal, racist treatment they themselves received.

If you were physically abused as a child, it's important to consider how many men you've been with who have been violent. One sister, Jackie, a vice president at a major bank, remembers being in the fifth grade, when a white teacher accused her of stealing $20 from her purse. Even though Jackie's father received word that she was exonerated, he beat Jackie. "He said even by being accused, I had disgraced his name," Jackie lamented. "Now I know he beat me because he couldn't express his anger toward the white school authorities." Jackie grew up to be charming and extremely caring and considerate to others. But she betrayed herself by hooking up with a violent man. Her first boyfriend, to whom she eventually became engaged, was so brutal that during a tense moment, he broke her nose with a punch to the face.

Jackie's childhood abuse and her choice of an abusive mate were not coincidental, according to Dr. Wyatt, who reports that women who were physically "disciplined" by their parents are more likely to get in relationships in which their partners throw, smash, hit, or kick things or physically attack their partners. Dr. Wyatt also found a higher incidence of unplanned pregnancies among women who had been beaten as children.[30] Being beaten made us feel unloved and unlovable, ashamed and angry, and as if we had no rights.

In addition to allowing our anger to betray us in our choice of mates, we may also turn our anger against ourselves by drinking, smoking, overspending, engaging in unprotected sex with risky partners, or overeating. One psychologist, Michelle Joy Levine, the author of *I Wish I Were Thin, I Wish I Were Fat,* has found that many of her overweight clients eat to fill a hunger born from anger. The very act of chewing, she explains, "can be related to intense oral sadistic rage towards another. This primitive fantasy reflects the desire to destroy by ripping, tearing apart, and then completely devouring, the person who is hated."[31] Consider Levine's theory the next time you're eating. Who would you like to rip to shreds?

Becoming aware of your anger can change your life for the better. That's certainly what happened with sister Tina Turner, who reflected on her abusive relationship with her former husband, Ike, in her autobiography, *I Tina*. As his beatings became more intense, she was paralyzed by fear. It wasn't until she caught Ike in bed with another woman, and tried to commit suicide, that Turner woke up to her rage. Only then did she have the courage to leave and start a new life, which has included an even more successful career and a caring mate.

Helen, who emulated her mother's "victim" personality, has also made changes in her life. She has moved out of the apartment she shared with her boyfriend and has started paying her own bills. "Being alone and enjoying it is a whole new experience for me," she told the group. No longer censoring her anger, she is finding the strength to take care of herself, reclaiming the power she had been assigning to others.

HEALING OUR ANGER

Expressing Anger About Racism

We have every right to feel angry about both the history of abuse and contemporary discrimination that we have suffered as people of African descent. Yet we must keep the energy of this anger moving in a positive direction, or it can turn in on us and contribute to feelings of shame and low self-esteem, and cause us to behave self-destructively. However, if the anger is inappropriately turned outward, we can hurt those close to us and push love away.

The righteous anger we feel concerning mistreatment can lead us to work for legislative and judicial relief. In 1997, a thousand black farmers filed a class-action discrimination lawsuit against the Government. Black farmers said they were routinely denied federal aid through programs designed to help farmers (and sometimes the refusals included overt racial remarks) while aid was almost automatically given to white farmers. Over the years, the number of black farmers has dwindled from fourteen percent to one percent of the nation's farmers. Not surprisingly, many of the individuals involved in the suit are furious about the debts they incurred from high interest commercial loans, and the loss, in many cases, of their family land and their livelihoods. In 1999, the federal government responded to their claims with tax-free settlements of up to $50,000, forgiveness of any federal debts, and a change in policies to insure that future denials are given for legitimate reasons. While many of the litigants say the money is too little too late, most praised the government for trying to redress a wrong.[32] The successful outcome of their suit was a reminder that anger can be a powerful force when appropriately channeled.

Remember that it's important to talk about your anger, check it out with your mate, sista/friends, coworkers, or the members of your abundance group. When we're stuck in anger, we can't fully taste, our intuition flattens out, and above all we can't feel love. By understanding and expressing anger, we keep it moving toward positive change. Anger is too expensive for any of us to hold on to for very long. There's an old Buddhist saying that the worst curse you can put on anyone is "May you be angry for the rest of your life."

Examining Your Family of Origin

Gather some family photos that date as far back as possible, so you can reflect on anger in your family and how it affected your life. Once you start looking at old photos from the standpoint of understanding family patterns, you'll begin to see your family in a new light. Candid photos are just that: They reveal the truth. Here are some pointers on detecting your family's hidden anger:

1: Place several family photos from your childhood side by side. Note patterns, such as who generally stands close together; look for repeated groupings (such as you always standing alongside a favorite sister). Is there a family member who's usually outside the group, or one who's usually in the middle? What might that indicate to you?

2: Notice whether your parents stand close together or often leave a space between them. If your mother or father was a single parent, what does that parent's posture and body language say about how he or she feels about being alone? Notice your parents' hands. Are they balled into fists, clenched tightly in their laps? What about their heads? Are they tilted away or toward each other? What might that indicate? Is he or she standing rigidly? Compare the relationship you've just "seen" with what you notice in photos of your own romantic relationships. What patterns have you repeated?

3: How do you fit into the picture? Are you generally a sibling who was hugged and embraced by other members of the family? Do you often look uncomfortable? Why? Cover up the mouths and noses of various people, including yourself. Look only at the eyes, and ask yourself what each individual is feeling. What memories and emotions surface as you look into these images?

4: Does anyone look genuinely happy? How about you? Recall circumstances during the time when the photos were taken. Was it a happy or dissatisfying time for you? Did your face or anything about you reflect your true emotions? Is there a point in time when you began to look more angry or withdrawn? What had occurred?

5:   Now look at more recent photos of yourself with your mate or in previous relationships. Is there a great deal of space separating you from your partner? In most of the photos, are you leaning hungrily into a male, or are you, perhaps, the one others are leaning on? Despite physical closeness, do you or the partners seem to have their heads tilted away from you? Does your partner seem angry? Do you? Were your needs being met in this relationship? How does your satisfaction or dissatisfaction show up in the photo? Is there a discrepancy between the smile on your face and the way you were feeling inside? What conclusions do you draw from this?

6:   Finally, look at the members of your family of origin and state aloud how your family's anger affected each. Speaking to the photo, tell them how their anger affected you.

The previous step can be enormously effective. Staring into a photo taken of her and her big sister, Brenda Richardson apologized to Tamra, who was the family scapegoat. Rather than owning up to how angry everyone in her family had been, family members pointed the finger at Tamra, who eventually died a lonely, miserable death as a mental patient. After weeping over the photo, Brenda promised her deceased sister she wasn't going to let her "continue taking the rap." She told her she was angry, too, and that she was going to let herself feel it. To whom do you need to speak in your family photos?

Taking Your Anger to the Source

Recalling a time when you felt very angry with a lover, use a cushion to represent that person and tell him how he hurt you. Detail one event in particular, and describe how you felt. Don't hold back; really get it out. When you really feel in touch with your feelings, continue looking at the cushion, and say aloud, "Now I'm taking the anger back to where it belongs." Direct your anger to the adult from your childhood who made you feel bad in a similar way. Unleash your anger. Remind yourself that no one can get hurt with this method and that you only stand to gain. If you're unable to truly sense your rage, repeat the exercise every day until you feel your rage surfacing, then continue the exercise until you feel it dissipating.

Also, if you are currently in a relationship, this exercise works wonderfully when you have a bone to pick with your mate. Before discussing the issue, pour your rage into a letter or into your pillow work, then take your anger back to the original source. You will find that by the time you approach your mate about the problem, you are much cooler headed, and the two of you will have a better chance at finding a solution. This exercise can be a lifesaver and a love saver!

Keeping an Anger Journal[33]

Remember that it's always healthy to confront racist behavior, but when that's not practical or possible, begin recording racist incidents in your journal (if you can't bring yourself to write, stand in front of a mirror and verbalize your anger). Fold a page in thirds lengthwise, and over the left column, write at the top "Incident"; in the middle column, write "Actual reaction"; and on the right, write "What I wanted to say." This journal should be kept someplace safe, so you'll feel confident that you can record your true feelings. Keeping this journal is a self-loving act. It keeps you from dumping your anger on someone you love. Rather than stockpiling your anger, you're releasing it through writing. If you're unable to record the experience at the time it occurs, as soon as possible recollect your feelings and get them off your chest. Be sure also to call a friend or support group member to tell her what you're writing in your journal.

If you happen to be someplace where you can't open your journal but you know you need to "get it out," improvise. Brenda Lane Richardson stopped at a café for breakfast and asked a white waitress if she could seat herself. The woman held her hand about five inches from Richardson's face, like a rebuking traffic guard, and said in a loud voice, "Wait!" Although this woman's embarrassed coworkers quickly rushed over to apologize and smooth over the damage, Brenda was understandably furious. She wasn't willing to let this waitress have the last word, nor did she want to make a scene. Instead, right after she was seated, she wrote on paper napkins what she wanted to say to this waitress. By the time her food was delivered, she felt not only a sense of relief but elation. She was able to eat abundantly, consuming only half of the pancakes and eggs she had been served, and not taking out her anger on her body by overeating.

Using Bodywork

Consider having a trained bodyworker (someone trained in Reichian therapy, Rolfing, or Heller work), a masseuse, acupuncturist, acupressurist, or chiropractor assist you in releasing toxic energies from your body.

In the next chapter, we discuss how relationships are affected by depression, which is anger and frozen emotional energy turned inward and against the self.

7

You're Not Evil, but You Might Be Depressed

Sister Spirit Sojourner Truth (1797–1883) was born into slavery and had no formal education, but her intelligence lit a fire in the abolitionist movement. After she escaped in 1827, she became a noted speaker. Her most famous speech, "Ain't I a Woman?" was an early attempt to call attention to stereotypes of black women, including one that dictates that we are so strong that we don't experience emotional pain. In our journey to connect with our true selves, accepting our vulnerabilities and naming the sorrows that cause us to feel depressed, we are empowered by the story of Sojourner Truth.

**Anti-intimacy belief explored in this chapter:
No matter what I do, it won't make a difference.**

Weeks earlier, Lattice, a thirty-eight-year-old interior designer, and her live-in fiance, Willie, thirty-two and a former football player, had set up an appointment to begin couples therapy. But on the morning of their first appointment, Willie was fifteen minutes late. Rushing in, he explained that their four-year-old son had not been "in the mood" to attend preschool. Lattice, who is thin and angular, rolled her eyes, loudly sucked her teeth, and folded her arms across her breasts. Though she hadn't said a word, she was clearly fed up.

Willie, whose once muscular body had softened, tried to explain the predicament that had caused him to be late. "The boy refused to go, so finally, I had to . . . " Before he could finish the sentence, Lattice said, in a voice filled with contempt, "take him to your mama's house." She continued by mumbling something under her breath, which she refused to repeat aloud, but which Willie interpreted. "She said that now my mama can spoil another boy to death. Lattice thinks my mother coddled me and that's why I don't have a job. But taking care of our son is my job now. I'm a househusband."

With an edge to her voice, Lattice said, "How can he be a househusband? We're not married, the boy he's supposedly at home with is in preschool, and the house he's caring for is cleaned by a housekeeper." She looked toward Dr. Wade as if appealing for understanding, "What kind of *househusband* is still asleep when the woman heads off to work? I have to practically pull him out of bed. Then, when I get home, he's eaten everything in the refrigerator. He doesn't work because he's lazy."

Dr. Wade set rules for their therapeutic sessions: Each person was to (1) refrain from interrupting the other, (2) speak directly to the other (rather than about him or her), and (3) use "I feel" or "I need" messages, as opposed to using blaming, "you, you, you" messages and insulting words such as *lazy*. She explained that describing our men as lazy perpetuates one of the most damaging lies slaveholders ever told about us. The truth is that we have always stressed the work ethnic. Hard work has killed a great number of our people, including our men.[1]

The mood was lightened as Dr. Wade repeated one of her favorite quotes about the "lazy black man" stereotype. Her *Essence* colleague, Dr. Gwendolyn Goldsby Grant, had once said, "Didn't nobody go all the way to Africa to kidnap some *lazy* people to pick cotton." Dr. Grant used humor to remind sisters that what we see "on the street corners of America is a used-up labor force, suffering from chronic unemployment and without hope."[2]

It is that sense of hopelessness, the belief that no matter what we do it won't make a difference, that leaves so many of our people filled with despair. Many of us have been raised to believe that we must be strong, even if that means suppressing our emotions and pretending we have put childhood hurts "behind us" and "moved on." There's a high price for this subterfuge. It leaves us feeling trapped in a downward spiral: The more we despair, the more ashamed we become because of our despair and the more we try to numb ourselves to the pain. All of this can wreak havoc on our lives and relationships.

When Dr. Wade asked Willie to tell Lattice how it made him feel when she described him as lazy, he bristled and said sarcastically, "Happy, actually, because at least when you insult me, I know I have your attention. That's the first time in twenty-four hours. I spent all day Sunday [yesterday] feeling like I was talking to a wall."

As he spoke to Lattice, she seemed to disappear from the room, folding her feet beneath her long brown silk skirt, tucking her chin into her chest, and rounding her shoulders. Urged to express her feelings, she said in a flat, emotionless voice, "I feel nothing. The situation's hopeless. I can't put him out because our son loves *him*, not me. Willie says it's because I'm evil. But the truth is, I'm the only grown-up in the house. Willie won't work, so I have to—all the time. I know I lost my last assistant because of my temper. I'm exhausted, yet I can't sleep. I wake up worrying about our bills, and if I dare make a move while I'm lying there, he wants to have sex." She spit out the word *sex* as if it were a dreaded disease. With a deep sigh, she concluded, "My life has always been hard, and I guess it always will be."

Without realizing it, Lattice had described many of the symptoms of depression: a sense of emptiness, hopelessness, fatigue, insomnia, loss of interest in sex or other normally enjoyable activities. Her pessimistic thinking and constant criticism of Willie sounded like an audiotape of "disaffirmations," a nonstop barrage of negative beliefs and sayings; this kind of thinking is also a symptom of depression. Other symptoms include over- or undereating, oversleeping, loss of energy, lethargy, frequent crying, forgetfulness, thoughts of suicide, feelings of worthlessness, and irritability.

Lattice said that even when she could sleep all through the night, she still had to drag herself out of bed. "Then I have to talk myself through the rest of the day. It's hard to work because even bright colors look gray. I hate to eat, so I'm skin and bones, and I don't even enjoy playing with Willie Junior, our son. I'm so miserable."

The distress she had been experiencing for months was quite different from having the blues. From time to time, everyone feels down.

This is a normal response to life's blips, such as being chewed out by a boss or having a disagreement with a friend. There is also situational depression, which can be quite severe, resulting from traumatic life events such as the illness or death of a loved one, the loss of a job, or a financial setback. An unresolved, situational depression can become chronic with symptoms that persist. Lattice was suffering from chronic long-term depression, and initially it wasn't clear why.

As she continued her therapeutic work, she recalled crying repeatedly as a teenager over songstress Nina Simone's "The Other Woman," a song about the loneliness of two women who share the same man. Lattice's father had left the family for another woman. "My mother never talked about what my father did. She was still in love with him and put her life on hold, waiting for him to come back to us. After he left us, he came back for one night and that's when she got pregnant with my brother. Mom always thought Daddy would come back, after she'd had the son he'd always wanted. But Daddy never returned. I blamed myself, and so did my mother. She used to say that everything changed between her and my father after she had me. There was no one I could talk to. Mom didn't like me to mention him." Burdened by the thought that her very birth had cost her mother her happiness and caused her to lose her own father, Lattice became depressed.

The term *depression* tends to be confusing. In years past, mental health professionals tried to distinguish between *major depression,* which was attributed to a chemical imbalance and treated with drugs, and *minor depression,* which was linked to childhood trauma and treated with talk therapy. In recent years, however, the effectiveness of drugs such as Prozac have turned those classifications inside out. These new drugs are most effective in treating minor depression, which had been thought to have no biological basis.[3] In addition, both psychotherapy and an improved health regimen often reduce the symptoms of both minor and major depression.

For our purposes, it's enough to say that some forms of depression are more severe than others. These are marked by what we call *vegetative signs,* that is, profound physical changes such as weight loss, weight gain, prolonged insomnia, and any severe physical disorder in the wake of those symptoms. Most serious of all is someone who has not just thought of suicide but who has formulated a plan ("I'm going to keep saving these pills until I have enough to kill myself.") Despite the potential severity, depression remains one of the most treatable emotional disorders. We'll learn shortly how Lattice dealt with her depression.

Concerning the causes of depression, it is known that children who experience parental abandonment become depressed. Researchers have found that infants separated from their mothers produce lower levels of serotonin, a brain chemical that in short supply is connected to chronic long-term depression.[4] Depression can start out as emotion that cannot be expressed in a healthy way about a situation we feel powerless to change. The unexpressed feelings, especially anger, are trapped inside us and create a sense of helplessness, which breeds a sense of hopelessness. Since emotions are energy in motion, when we hold down or ignore our feelings, we become depressed; our energy is "pressed down."

Dr. Nancy Boyd-Franklin has written: "One of the most devastating outcomes of the legacy of slavery and oppression is the feeling of powerlessness and rage that many Black people experience."[5] Given our history of racism and oppression, and the violence so many of us encounter, it's not surprising that the National Black Woman's Health Project reports that more than half of us live in emotional distress.[6] That figure is much higher than the estimate of 9 percent for U.S. women in general who are depressed at any given time and the estimate of 20 to 25 percent who will suffer some of its symptoms at some point in their lives.[7] Unfortunately, health care providers often misdiagnose us, and we seldom recognize the symptoms in ourselves. Only 7 percent of us receive treatment for the ailment.[8] Misunderstandings surrounding African Americans and depression have led to at least five myths that deeply affect the way we view one another, our relationships, and ourselves.

One of the most hurtful and damaging stereotypes, which we call Myth No. 1, is that black women are evil or just plain angry. Few people understand something essential about us: Rather than taking to our beds when we feel down, we usually continue working until we're ready to drop, becoming increasingly irritable. The reason for that is connected to our history. Black women in captivity were expected to do "men's" work, such as driving mules, carrying heavy loads, and pounding stakes into hard soil; then, at the end of a long day, they went home and started "women's" chores: cooking, cleaning, and nurturing their families.

If these women had told slaveholders they were too sad to get up and go to the fields, they would have been punished severely. Today, we hold the chains and whips ourselves, driving ourselves at breakneck speed. For instance, when Brenda Richardson gave birth to her daughter, she insisted on leaving the hospital seven hours later. Once home, she strapped her infant into a carrier and walked a mile to her oldest son's school, refusing a ride from her husband and some of his parishioners. When she arrived at school, her son's teacher was momentarily speechless, then said, "Didn't you just give birth?" Brenda Richardson kept this schedule going for two days. Then Dr. Wade arrived with turkey dinner and a good bottle of brandy. She hung a sign on Brenda Richardson's front door instructing others not to knock, and she urged the new mother to bed. It was only then, in the safety of her sista/friend's company, that Brenda Richardson broke down and sobbed, admitting she was tired to the bone.

Many of us mask our depression with this attitude of infallibility. The deep feelings of grief continue unabated because they don't fit into our schedule. So we get mad because we tell ourselves we can't feel sad. When people see that many of us are hyperirritable, which is a symptom of depression, they mistakenly call us evil. In fact, many of us really are depressed and exhausted.

Diane, a thirty-eight-year-old public-utilities executive who spends much of her time away from work assisting in a Black Muslim outreach program for youth, has a reputation as "one evil, castrating sister." In truth, she is sad. Her father abandoned the family when she was only six years old, when her mother was pregnant with her ninth child. For years their home was in turmoil, and life outside wasn't much better. One of few African Americans in Cleveland's predominately Italian neighborhood, Diane was ridiculed by her schoolmates about her features. She learned to fight back with lightning-fast verbal counterattacks.

As an adult, Diane spends days shut down and barely speaking, then suddenly emerges from her dark cloud and charms everyone's socks off. Her moods seem to control whatever environment she enters. With her sweeping knowledge of the world, she can put a man down so badly he needs assistance getting up. One brother said an encounter with her was like "dipping my balls in acid." Still, others admire her devotion to working with youth, her elegance, and her curvaceous figure. So despite her reputation, lots of brothers want to know her better, but unfortunately they don't stick around long. On one evening at the movies, when Diane grew irritated with a couple sitting behind her who had been whispering, she jerked around and said in a loud voice in the middle of the quiet theater, "Shut the fuck up!"

Most people don't understand those of us who act this way, nor do we understand our actions. In truth, rageful outbursts, like Diane's, are an unconscious way for depressed people to release adrenaline. These explosions speed up the autonomic nervous system and the production of endorphins, which have an intoxicating effect.[9] The relief is short-lived, however. Diane's depression deepened as she became increasingly isolated: Isolation feeds depression.

Whether shut down and unhappy or smiling and cheerful, we are often in denial about feeling low because we believe we must be strong. In an attempt to prepare us for this world, many of our mothers taught us by example that responsibility meant ignoring our pain. It is this relentless denial of emotions that promotes our depression.

"Some of us even have an aversion to actresses who play roles in which they are very emotional," noted Karen, a twenty-one-year-old English major who attends a historically black college. "The other day, some of us cut classes to play bid whist, and someone had on a soap opera. It featured a black actress playing an innocent and trusting character who cries when she's sad. A lot of the women at the table started yelling to just turn her off. One woman said she couldn't stand her because she 'acts white.' What she meant was weak, and for us that's a no-no." Statistics bear her out. According to a 1996 survey, 63 percent of us view depression as a personal weakness.[10]

Many of us feel far more comfortable saying we are down with a cold than simply saying, "I feel down." A mounting body of evidence suggests that depression actually worsens an illness,[11] which may explain why that little "cold" may hang on for weeks. Shivering and taking to our beds, we shelter our despair behind bottles of NyQuil and Vicks VapoRub.

As for Lattice and Willie, they were both depressed. Although they had worked with another therapist in the past, they were hearing this interpretation for the first time. Their former therapist had encouraged Lattice to leave Willie. The therapist, who is white, failed to recognize his depression. It was possible that she was projecting her own unconscious racism concerning a black man not working, assuming he was "just lazy" or incorrigible.

Misunderstandings weigh our relationships down. One falsehood, which we call Myth No. 2, is that black men and women can't get along. We are not denying that there is an underlying tension between African American men and women, which absolutely stems from our history, but it's important also to recognize that depression forms a big piece of the puzzle.

Our history of oppression left so many of us depressed from one generation to the next that we lacked the resources to nurture ourselves, never mind one another. Although some of us take care of our mates to the exclusion of our own needs, we eventually wind up so depleted, and consequently angry, that our relationships suffer. We continue the heartbreaking cycle of running from our needs because they reawaken the vulnerability we felt when we were hurt as children. As a result, we avoid feeling vulnerable. But true intimacy, which calls for sharing our deepest feelings, requires vulnerability.

During her healing work, Lattice discovered that her hyperirritability and her acting out intensified when she felt frightened. For example, before an interview with some white executives who were considering her firm for their chain of hotels, Lattice lit into Willie with blistering criticism. Three primary threads tie our depression together: fear that we will never be able to overcome the racism and oppression around us, grief over the many painful losses our people endured over the centuries, and the unhealed wounds from our childhoods. Lattice's fear of losing business owing to racism was turned on her mate. She told him, "Since I'm carrying the load in this family, you'd better pray that I get this business or we'll wind up in the streets." It was only later that evening when her interview was over (and had gone well) that she made the connection between her attack on Willie and her own anxieties and fears.

Her rageful behavior had nothing to do with how much she adored Willie. When they first met, he was at the peak of his football career, enjoying great success, and he reminded her of her smooth-talking daddy, who, throughout her childhood, occasionally stopped by with lavish gifts. Willie had wooed Lattice with gifts and luxurious vacations, and he could make her laugh just as her father had.

Her mother's personality couldn't have been more different. After working all day and sometimes having to fight off the "roving hands" of her white supervisor, she came home feeling emotionally shut down and miserable. You'll recall Lattice's angry remark to Willie that she was the "only grown-up" in her house. As she looked over her genogram, she found she had replicated her family belief that "women are wiser, less frivolous, and men can't be counted on." Lattice's deepening depression was, in part, a kind of mourning over the joy she'd been forced to give up, after she and Willie had a child, when she attempted to imitate her mother's model of a "responsible black woman." She hadn't yet learned that she could establish her own way of being a responsible adult, a way that could include joy.

Lattice's mother had been depressed too. Typically depression shows up in families one generation after another. In addition to genetic predispositions, a depressed caretaker functions poorly, and her children grow up feeling unloved and unworthy. Lattice's mother, caught up in trying to cope with the hostile larger environment, keep food on the table, and grieve the loss of her husband, didn't have the energy to nurture her children. They had to survive on minuscule rations of love and support.

Lattice's brother, infuriated by the abandonment of both his parents, took his anger out on his big sister. "He called me all sorts of names, and most of them had to do with the way I looked, big butt, big nose, he never let up." On one occasion, Lattice earned top student honors in her little town, and the mayor asked her to make a speech for Founder's Day. "My brother convinced me that I was so ugly I'd disgrace him by appearing in public." She gave in and refused to speak. By then, her depression had gained a solid hold.

Willie's distress also dates back to childhood. Lattice didn't see that side of him until his team released him as he grew older. Despite Lattice's warnings, he had not prepared for the future. Right after his last game, his hidden pain began to surface.

Raised by controlling, angry parents, Willie suffered through their conflict-ridden marriage. His father achieved success after fighting discriminatory practices for decades and finally purchasing a major car dealership. His lifetime of battles had bruised him, and Willie became the target for his rage and underlying fear that Willie might not make it as a black man in a harsh world. Taunting his son, he told him he would be a failure because his mother treated him like a "sissy." It's no coincidence that although Willie would later meet many women, he loved only Lattice, who eventually taunted him with words that were hauntingly similar to his father's.

Willie's mother showed great devotion to him, insisting that his suits be custom-made and his shoes dyed to match. As he grew older, he escorted his mother to big parties and on cruises. A lot of people call this kind of maternal adoration for a son "pampering," and this has led to what we call Myth No. 3, which suggests that many black mothers "raise" their daughters and "spoil" their sons. Spoiling means treating someone "too well." Willie's mother actually abused him. When a woman doesn't have an appropriate adult partnership and turns her son into a "little husband," it's considered emotional incest. Willie became the person his mother lived for, and it was his job to take care of her emotional needs, so there was no room for his feelings. There was no one to nurture this little boy. Boys in these situations often grow up to be enraged, depressed, and emotionally distant men. With no room to vent his fury at either of his parents, Willie packed it away in cold storage, sowing the seeds for his depression.

That hurt little boy grew up to be a narcissist who was obsessed with love from his fans. Their cheers and praise temporarily enhanced his self-worth. But when Willie was released from his contract, his sense of esteem plummeted. He had no inner resources, and he didn't have the energy to pursue another career. He began sleeping more and tried to ward off his feelings of hopelessness by constantly demanding sex from Lattice. Struggling with her own disappointment and her own issues, she refused closeness of any kind. He covered up his sagging ego and pain with alcohol.

The tendency for people to relieve their "bad moods" with alcohol or drugs has given rise to Myth No. 4, the belief that self-medicating relieves sorrow. In reality, depression that is "treated" with alcohol or drugs can surface as inappropriate rage. In addition, alcohol, other addictive substances, and any addictive behavior (overspending, sexaholism, workaholism) contribute to long-term, ever-worsening problems. Willie's "two or three beers a night" caused him to sleep more; alcohol is a depressant. This made it more difficult for him to get up and search for work.

His increasing inability to provide for the family put Lattice in touch with her childhood memories of her father's lack of support, which in turn fed her depression and rage. She was convinced she had nothing to live for. In therapy, Willie was startled by Lattice's admission that several times in the past she had considered suicide.

The widespread belief that black women are so strong that we don't commit suicide is Myth No. 5. The suicides of well-known stars, such as Dorothy Dandridge, singer Phyllis Hyman, and, more recently basketball star Katrina Price, have done little to dispel this myth. It is true that our suicide rates are lower than among other demographic groups. But what are never included in the statistics on suicide are the thousands of sisters who kill themselves with drugs, alcohol, food, outright neglect,[12] or "accidents," as well as those who attempt suicide but who, fortunately, fail.

Decades ago, after being dumped by an older man who had served as a stand-in for the father she had lost but never mourned, Brenda Richardson attempted suicide by swallowing dozens of sleeping pills. She survived the attempt because of an elderly black woman, who happened to be passing through the park after a long day of domestic work. She dragged Brenda from the car she'd been sitting in and summoned an ambulance. Holding her in her arms, this woman, whom Brenda would later call "Aunt Bea," told her she had no right to presume that God didn't have something better planned on this earth for her. Brenda had managed to hide her despair from everyone else around her. The shame that so many of us feel about being depressed convinces us our sorrow must be hidden at any cost.

Basketball star Katrina Price hid her despondency from friends and teammates in the American Basketball League's Philadelphia Rage. To many, she seemed to have a bright future ahead of her: High school salutatorian, the 23-year-old Texas native graduated from college cum laude with a degree in education. But when the league for which she played suddenly folded, the idea of never being able to redeem what had been a disappointing rookie year, may have been too much for her. A friend said when she asked Price how she felt about the league's closure, Price refused to talk about it. But early one morning in 1999, she called one of her sisters to say she was deeply depressed. Seeming more composed after a long conversation, she said she was going back to bed. An hour later she was dead, found by another sister with a shotgun lying beneath her body. Police believe the fatal shot was self-inflicted.[13] Surely family, friends, and admirers can't help but wonder how differently this would have all turned out if, earlier on, Price had been able to tell others of her mounting despair.

Before she began working with Dr. Wade, Lattice who had been contemplating suicide said, "Thoughts about ending it all usually came to me when I was driving. I thought it would be easy, traveling at 65 miles an hour, to just let go of the wheel." Fortunately, the effects of her therapy were kicking in. A report by the National Institute of Mental Health found that psychotherapy can relieve depression within sixteen weeks.[14] Four weeks into her couples work with Dr. Wade, Lattice reported feeling more optimistic.

Since Willie and Lattice appeared to be suffering from moderate as opposed to severe depression, Dr. Wade advised they start a health regimen that included regular aerobic exercise; abstinence from alcohol, caffeine, and nicotine; therapeutic doses of St. John's wort, a natural mood elevator; amino acid supplements; and B vitamins to boost their energy and metabolic rate. She also advised them to eat three balanced meals a day with small healthy snacks between meals, so that their blood sugar levels would remain even. Slumps in blood sugar level exacerbate depression. If neither of them had shown any change in their condition, Dr. Wade would have considered recommending a referral for antidepressant medication. But in the next couple of months, Lattice in particular improved.

At one point, when recalling the day her dad packed his suitcase and left the family, Lattice cried for the first time in more than twenty years. Also, she and Willie began jogging together in the evenings. Aerobic exercise has been found to induce many of the biochemical benefits of drug therapy.[15]

They also faced the family disease of alcohol abuse. Participation in 12-Step Programs formed an important part of their treatment. Willie attended Alcoholics Anonymous meetings; Lattice attended Al-Anon, a program for family members of someone with addiction problems.

Willie, however, was determined not to "let his guard down." Like many men, he felt it was unmanly to show his feelings. Throughout their initial sessions, he used humor and snide remarks to ward off any sadness. It would be weeks before his wall came crumbling down.

On this particular occasion, Dr. Wade asked Willie to work with her at recreating a memory from childhood involving his father. He agreed, at first wearing an amused grin. But several minutes into the exercise, something changed. Willie recalled that at about the age of seven, he ran to the door to greet his father to show off a new blue velvet suit. His father's response was to laugh and tell him he looked like Shirley Temple. Dr. Wade encouraged him to stand and demonstrate his father's behavior and his size, but Willie insisted on sitting. "He was big, like me," he said.

Dr. Wade stood up, towering over him. "Did he seem this much taller?"

Willie faltered and, no longer smiling, muttered, "Seemed like it."

"Please tell me what your father said and show me how he said it," she went on.

Willie said in a bored voice, "Boy, you look like a clown. Take that suit off, or I'll rip it off you. What are you doing, looking for mommy? Come here, you sissy." Willie's voice now seemed faint for such a big man.

Dr. Wade encouraged Willie: "Tell your father what you wanted to say but couldn't when you were little."

Speaking softly, Willie looked up, saying to his phantom father, "Go to hell."

Dr. Wade coaxed, "Come on, you took a lot from him and never got to express your feelings. This is your chance to let it out."

"I'm not an angry kind of guy."

"Who told you you couldn't be?"

"I told myself."

"What would your dad have done if you'd yelled back?" she asked.

"Oh, he told me. He used to say he'd give me an ass bruising."

"Then he was a bully, too. And he still is. Your son spends a lot of time with him. What would you say to your father if he called your boy a sissy?"

Willie came to life, jumping up and roaring, "Stay away from my son. You son of a bitch! You used me. You treated me like shit. You called me Little Lord Fauntleroy. Teased me for pissing in my pants. Why didn't you stop Mom from dressing me in those outfits? All I heard from you is that I wouldn't amount to shit. And you were right! You were right, you bastard!"

He was weeping now, his sobs so powerful they sounded like a sudden thunderstorm. Dr. Wade asked Lattice, who had been sitting upright, "Is there anything you can do to comfort him?" Lattice crossed the room and wrapped her long arms around his shoulders. "You're not a failure," she said. "You're not. You're the bravest man I've ever known. I love you. I love you." She stroked his cheeks, kissed his face, and looked at him as if seeing him for the first time. Dr. Wade used this period of detente to teach them to take turns comforting one another.

Lattice later said, "I didn't realize he was hurting the way I was. He just always looked so big and strong." Both of them had buried their own grief, hidden even from themselves. Willie couldn't possibly have told Lattice he was wounded because he didn't know it himself.

They required several more months of work, as they learned to communicate, problem-solve, tap into long-buried memories and feelings, and to come to grips with their family histories. But that session marked a turning point in their lives. Their depression continued to thaw, and they actually felt sadder for a while. Once feelings of depression become "overt" and easily recognized, the pain is no longer frozen inside. It hurts to feel the pain, but that is the course of healing.

Since that time, Lattice and Willie have married and moved to Seattle, where Lattice heads a team of interior designers, leaving more time for her own needs. As for Willie, it's obvious that his ability to work had been compromised by his depression. Now that his symptoms are relieved, he works hard as a high school football coach. He likes the cheers when his team wins, but most of all he appreciates the pride Lattice takes in him. They should be proud. They are the first members of their families to explore the real origins of their pain and to confront their despair, which dates back hundreds of years.

OUR HISTORY/OUR COLLECTIVE SORROW

Our individual experiences stand in sharp relief to those of our ancestors. But because we inherited their grief, it's important to continue looking into our historical legacy and understand how it has molded us. As we have seen, many events throughout our history caused our ancestors to feel hurt and angry, but it was the sense of helplessness that caused their depression. For more than a century, every time it seemed there was a chance for life to get better, something occurred to crush their dreams.

For instance, the greatest hope for black people was that one day freedom would come. But after emancipation, our ancestors went out into the world without food or provisions and certainly not with the forty acres and a mule that some political leaders had promised. Thousands of our people starved or froze to death, and others were murdered by vengeful white Southerners. One of the spirituals that our people sang reflects the despondency they surely felt: "Nobody knows the trouble I've seen. Nobody knows but Jesus. Nobody knows the trouble I've seen. Glory, hallelujah. Sometime I'm up, sometime I'm down, oh, yes, Lord, sometime I'm almost to the ground. Oh, yes, Lord."

Many black people viewed President Lincoln as our ally, but it turned out that he didn't think much more of us than our enemies did; he had one of his administrators check out the feasibility of shipping our people out of the country. Before Lincoln could make a decision about our exportation, he was assassinated.[16] Many former slaves, not knowing his true feelings, grieved his death.

"At least we're free," our ancestors must have said, but white Southerners, determined to keep black people as slaves in all but name, enacted laws called Black Codes. These laws prohibited African Americans from having guns or making "insulting gestures." The penalty for marrying someone white was lifetime imprisonment. Men found guilty of any number of trumped-up charges were sometimes auctioned off to white landowners, usually the "vagrant's" former slaveholder for unpaid labor.[17] African Americans could be tried and convicted for "crimes" that included looking whites directly in the eye or failing to move off the sidewalk fast enough when someone white approached, and they could be sentenced to months of unpaid labor on plantations owned by wealthy whites.

But even provisional freedom allowed our ancestors to dream, and many former bondwomen looked forward to staying home to care for their infants and homes while their husbands worked the fields and older children attended school. Many whites called this the height of laziness. Soon a sharecropping system evolved, which provided the only way for most black families to survive, requiring the entire family to work.

The Reconstruction period lasted from 1867 to 1877, after passage of the thirteenth, fourteenth, and fifteenth amendments granted black people political power and social freedoms. Backed up by

Northern military troops, black men were allowed to vote. Our people became representatives in every Southern legislature; and there were black lieutenant governors, treasurers, and secretaries of state. Although many white Southerners labeled this a period of rampant corruption, in reality, in a state such as Mississippi, Reconstruction governments were more compassionate and democratic than any previous ones. As historian David Oshinsky explains, under this new political leadership money was raised to build hospitals and expand state asylums, racist laws were abolished, and free schooling was provided for children, regardless of race. It appeared that real change was going to occur for the first time since slavery had been instituted.[18]

Any hopes African Americans had of a changing society were destroyed, however, by whites' fears and rage. In 1877, when federal troops were withdrawn from the South, the Jim Crow era began. Black political liberty was crushed, and white terrorist groups unleashed their fury as thousands of our people were tortured, murdered, and raped.

Since there were no longer dollar amounts placed on our heads, African Americans were viewed by many whites as less than worthless. Our people were the victims of thousands of public hangings, which were referred to by some whites as "Negro barbecues." These events often drew celebratory crowds, brought by special excursion trains, and when the hanging ended, some whites pumped bullets into the dangling bodies; carved off fingers, toes, and ears for souvenirs; and burned our people to a crisp. Families brought along picnics to watch the hangings. Occasionally, classes were interrupted so schoolchildren could attend. Professional photographers took pictures that they sold as postcards that commemorated the events.[19]

Helpless to take action against their oppressors at the turn of the century, our people created a music born of their frustration and anger. They called it the blues. It draws on a combination of spirituals, African-inspired field hollers, work songs, and the ring shout, a ritual dance for honoring ancestors. Blues vocalists such as Bessie Smith (1894-1937), expressed the despair, anxiety, and hope of thousands of women whose men had gone North in search of work, leaving them behind. The world seemed to listen and care: The first of Smith's many hit records, "Down Hearted Blues," sold 750,000 copies. The blues has been hailed as the mother of rock 'n' roll, but it was altogether different; it was not only sassy and brazen but raucously funny and often touchingly sad. It was about resiliency, not despair.[20]

The genius of the blues is that the singer expresses misery, and listeners achieve catharsis. Some of the most powerful songs serve as dramatic catalysts, moving people to laugh or dance—just get something going. It's said that when blues singer Blind Willie Johnson (1900–1950) sang "If I Had My Way I'd Tear the Building Down" to a crowd in front of the New Orleans customhouse, he was arrested for inciting a riot.[21] Sigmund Freud may have developed psychoanalysis, but African Americans created musical therapy. The blues can help you cope with grief and party at the same time. But the truth be told, not all the singing in the world could prepare our people for the disappointments ahead.

As millions of black Americans began heading North for better jobs, one family member usually went first to pave the way for the others. These separations further weakened our families, which were already beginning to break down from the weight of oppression.[22] Stunned by the virulent racism of the North, our people found that the slaveowners' propaganda campaign had been highly effective. Racism had become so entrenched that no matter where they went from New York to California, it was like jumping from the frying pan into the fire. Then the Great Depression hit, and black people, who had been last hired, were the first fired.

During World War II we lost a great many black GI's in the armed services. Those whose bodies were shipped to Arlington National Cemetary were buried in a segregated section. Still, there was widespread hope among our people that our sacrifices would be rewarded with racial equality. But after having been cheered in the streets of European capitals, black soldiers returned home to racism at its most absurd heights: In the United States, Nazi prisoners of war were transported in all-white train sections; black vets were relegated to substandard "coloreds" sections.[23] Returning vets also faced race riots and other mob violence. Hopes of real freedom were dashed. Playwright August Wilson said the dreams of black Americans were replaced with a "deprivation of possibilities."[24]

Decades later, many of the children of these returning vets, benefiting from the gains of the Civil Rights Movement, swelled the ranks of a burgeoning black professional class, and this time it must have seemed certain that life for African Americans would continue to improve. But as the economy shifted, jobs disappeared in the inner cities, and the demand rose for technically trained workers.

University of San Francisco Professor Yvonne Moss explained that desegregation dismantled the insulating layer provided by black institutions. Schools where black teachers had instilled pride in their students, as well as clinics and social service agencies in our communities, disappeared. The broader nonsegregated service providers failed to step in, and many African American social services fell through the gap. Social services that were administered were often delivered in inherently racist ways.

Many African Americans, educated at substandard, underfunded urban schools, found themselves unprepared to meet the demands of available jobs, and joblessness rose to new heights among our people. Even those who realized the American dream began to understand that no matter how hard we worked, we were not going to be fully accepted by the larger society.

It should not be surprising that many of us feel a deep sense of isolation and despair. Our ancestors believed life would be better in northern cities, and in many ways they were right. But few took into account what it would be like to live in a hostile world, removed from the comfort of tightly knit communities where adults were called Miss or Mrs. or Mr., where the church was the center of hope and the source of social life, and where someone came by to check on you if you hadn't been seen that day or because they wanted to drop off some fish they had caught that morning.

This isn't a fantasy world. Ask an elderly member of our community, and she'll regale you with her memories. A study was conducted in 1913 that confirms this. African Americans who had settled in Harlem reported that down South they visited friends at least once a week for listening to music, singing, and chatting. In the North they had fewer friends and were suspicious of their environment, including their neighbors. Down South, they'd answered the doorbell with "Come in." In the North, the response was "Who's there?"[25] Social historian Donna L. Franklin writes: "In short, blacks exchanged the intimacy of small-town and rural community life for the detached and impersonal social relations of the city."[26] Black marriages also lasted longer in the South than in Northern cities.[27]

That more cushioned "down South" environment dated back to Africa, where members of tribes looked out for one another. For a while, after coming North, our people replicated these lifestyles in urban neighborhoods such as Bedford-Stuyvesant in New York and the Fillmore district of San Francisco. If you were a kid jumping double Dutch or sitting on the stoop, heaven help you if any adult passed by and heard you swearing. She was expected to chastise you. But those communities are gone, destroyed by "urban renewal," desegregation, black middle-class flight, and the drug culture. Even in the South, most of the old neighborhoods are gone.

With the poverty rate among black Americans having declined (down 26.5 percent in 1998), owing to a strengthening economy,[28] there has been a cautious sense of optimism. But for many of us, this optimism is tempered by rollbacks in affirmative action policies and what that might bode for our future. From the late seventies until recently, it seemed that race-conscious selection policies in America's most elite colleges and universities would continue to feed the growing pool of black professionals. A 1998 study published by Princeton University Press found that black graduates of select institutions create "the backbone of the emergent black middle class." The survey found that these students not only earn advanced degrees at rates identical to those of their white classmates, but are slightly more likely than their white peers to earn degrees in law, business, and medicine. Furthermore, they become more involved than their white classmates in civic activities. Unfortunately, white people, and a notable scattering of black people, have successfully pushed for affirmative action rollbacks in California and Texas, and similar policy reversals are being pushed in other states. Advocates of race-conscious admissions policies fear that changes will eventually decimate the black leadership and professional pool.[29]

Against this social-historical backdrop, many of us have felt hopeless. But if ever there was a need to work toward abundance, it is now. Now is the time for us to join together and respond to the Creator's promise, perhaps with these words: "God, we know that you help those who help themselves, and that's what we are doing. We're also praying and seeking. So please open the gate, because we are knocking. We're asking for help in healing so we can transform our lives and fulfill our need for love."

Sister Harriet Tubman led our people through dark forests, dogs at their heels, some parents with babies on their backs. One woman, working alone, led hundreds to freedom. But we don't have to go it alone. The darkness doesn't have to be unrelenting. Our inner radiance, which is God, can shine collectively, creating a floodlight that reveals undiscovered routes.

OUR EMOTIONAL LEGACY

Now that you're acquainted with the symptoms of depression and the factors that create it, consider whether you're struggling with this condition. If so, how might it be affecting your life and your relationships? Do you have memories that suggest that your depression started during your childhood? How might it have affected you at home, in school, and in other areas of your life? What about as a teenager? What events can you recall that mark the onset of these feelings? Start listening in on your thoughts. Are you caught in a cycle of negative thoughts, such as "I'll never get ahead," or "there are no men out there," and so on? Confront any signs of depression. As soon as you hear yourself saying or thinking these negative messages, think to yourself or say aloud, when possible, "Cancel that thought!" Then turn the negative into a positive, declaring, for instance, "I am worthy, and I accept into my life the mate God has prepared for me." Remember that persistent repetition alters our subconscious beliefs.

You can also take out your genogram and look for depression among the people who raised you. Is there anyone in your family who drank heavily or relied on other addictive behaviors to medicate depression? Also, remember that depression in black women is more likely to manifest as irritability and lashing out. Women you thought of as "evil" may have been filled with despair. Now you can consider which factors have caused your relatives to be depressed. What about your parents? If your mother or the woman who raised you was depressed, how do you think that affected the way she raised you? Finally, it can be helpful to consider how your personality and behavior evolved in response to your depression.

HEALING DEPRESSION

Suicide Prevention

If you're deeply depressed, consider whether you've been contemplating suicide. You may have a plan in mind, or you may not be consciously aware of having suicidal thoughts. These unconscious thoughts may have left you with a preoccupation with death and dying. For example, have you been making final arrangements, such as drawing up a will or giving away items that you love? Have you developed an interest in books, news stories, or movies with death or suicide themes? Do you admire people who have committed suicide and wish you had the "courage" to do it yourself?

One of Dr. Wade's clients described a scene in a New York subway station when a man stood dangerously close to the platform edge. She said, "I'm not thinking of killing myself, but I could have walked right up alongside him, waited for the train, and jumped." She eventually admitted she was having suicide fantasies.

If any of this mirrors your behavior, it's crucial that you avoid alcohol or mood-altering drugs, which can impair your judgment. If you're not already working with a mental health professional, we urge you to call the toll-free Lifeline Suicide Prevention Hotline (1-800-310–1160) any time of the day or night. Local listings for crisis lines and other emergency numbers can generally be found at the front of phone directories. Please remember that God loves you and wants you to choose life.

Coping with Depression

If you are depressed, we urge you to seek help from a licensed mental health practitioner. Keep in mind that free or low-cost counseling is available through county facilities and teaching hospitals. Also, consider working with a holistic physician who can help relieve your symptoms with natural remedies or, if necessary, drug therapies. If you don't exercise regularly, be sure to ask your doctor about beginning an aerobic exercise routine, which can be tremendously helpful in lifting your spirits.

Journal Writing

One of the most important steps in healing depression is listening to your feelings. We can do this by journaling. To begin, spend ten minutes every evening writing (if you feel uncomfortable writing, speak into the mirror). Begin with the words: "This is what I feel today," so you can tune into what you're feeling and put some motion into your emotions. After you've finished describing your feelings, write: "This is what I need to take care of my feelings." The need for a hug, a kiss, or a listening ear becomes apparent, so you can do something about it. This work also involves changing your belief system. The belief "I am lovable" gains momentum when you take the time to love and nurture yourself. The belief that "I deserve love" penetrates into your subconscious when you treat yourself lovingly. Here's how a typical day of journaling and self-care could look.

You come home feeling drained, scold and criticize your kids, feel remorse that you've done so, grab a container of ice cream from the freezer, and go to your room, saying, "I don't want anyone to bother me." Before you take that first spoonful, you remember your journal and put the ice cream aside for a minute. You start writing down your feelings. The first words that come out are of anger and frustration. "I'm so tired of having to work so hard. This is sickening. Why did my boss think she had the right to question my decision? I know what I'm doing."

You then ask yourself, "What is my fear in this situation?" As you continue writing, you realize you are afraid that if your boss is questioning you, she may view you as incompetent, and you may be a victim of your company's next downsizing. You write, "Typical, last hired first fired." As you continue writing about the fear and what might happen to you and your family if you lose your job, you realize how alone you feel, and a deep wave of sadness washes over you. You feel your anger and harshness melting, like the ice cream you've left on your dresser.

It dawns on you that you wish someone would hold you. If you live with a mate or children, now's the time to put your journal aside and share your feelings, no matter how difficult or out of character that may be. After apologizing for lashing out at your family members, share your feelings and tell them what happened to contribute to your mood. Ask them for the hugs you need. And by the way, put that ice cream back in the freezer.

If you live alone, call a good friend and share what you're feeling; if you can't meet, just soak in the comfort of a caring voice. Remember, you can also put this book down for a minute and wrap your beautiful arms around yourself, saying, "I know you're feeling sad and scared, and that's okay. I'm going to take good care of you."

A warm shower or hot bubble bath, rubbing your feet and hands with lotion, a cup of herbal tea—any of these nurturing acts will send a strong message to the sad, lonely little girl inside of you that you're going to provide the nurturing and love that you need. Repeat your affirmations as you take care of yourself. "I am worthy and deserving. I am taking care of myself."

Journaling on a regular basis in conjunction with other interventions we have suggested will go a long way toward alleviating your depression. However, there's no substitute for support. Remember that depression and isolation go hand in hand. That means healing with friends or creating or joining a support group. We'll tell you more about how to form one in Part III.

Musically Lightening Your Load

If you haven't already done so, consider investing in or borrowing from your public library classic blues tapes or CDs. Not only do they make you want to get up and shake your booty, but you'll find yourself laughing and singing along.

If you enjoy gospel, there's also a workout with a distinctively spiritual style. Ange Buckingham, creator of the popular Gospel Moves aerobics in West Hollywood, California, has put together an audiotape of gospel music that can help you create inspired workouts. For more information, call 213-368-9564 or write to Sister Buckingham, c/o Gospel Aerobic Revue Workout, P.O. Box 36B46, Los Angeles, CA 90030.

Also, keeping in mind that aerobic workouts have been found to relieve the symptoms of depression, find out if anyone is teaching a samba dancercize class in your area, and devote time to learning some new steps. Samba, the African-inspired dance created by enslaved people in Brazil, is said to generate such energy that it's impossible to engage in it and feel unhappy. As you sway your hips and move to the beat, you'll feel a special pride in the creative talents and energies that our people have demonstrated.

Don't rule out funkerobic classes, which seem to be popping up at gyms and workout centers around the country. A lot of sisters unfamiliar with the urban music scene disdain hip-hop music because they're offended by some of the sexist and homophobic lyrics. They might be surprised to learn "it ain't all that." Over the years, many hip-hop artists have emerged who eschew put-downs. If you find a funkerobic teacher who is sensitive to these issues, you can start your mornings or end your workdays by dancing to a funk beat that's laced with cool wit and often brilliant rhymes. After all, rap lyrics were a creative response to the crack epidemic that ravaged our neighborhoods during the eighties and to the growing number of young black men who were being imprisoned.[30] These young hip-hop artists are following in the footsteps of our ancestors, releasing their frustration, anger, and depression by creating astute and innovative music.

Letting Your "Little Light" Shine

We join Susan Taylor, Iyanla Vanzant, and Oprah Winfrey in encouraging you to make meditation a part of your daily life. Meditating daily will help you feel energized as your inner spirit connects with the spirit of the universe. You will also feel relaxed and cleansed in a way that you never have before. The following meditation is designed to help you connect with the divine light that sustained our ancestors and that lives within us all, and it will quiet your mind, emotions, and body to allow you to gain inner peace. You may want to record your voice reading the words, perhaps backgrounded by soothing music (or see our resource list on page 223, to order a taped version). Schedule about ten minutes a day for this ongoing practice. Doing it first thing in the morning sets a great tone for the day.

Sit in a comfortable position, arms and legs uncrossed, spine straight, and breathing deeply, (or take a walk as you) say to yourself the following: "I am light, I am energy. Thank you, God, for your light and energy." Picture the brightest possible light flowing down through the top of your head, through your body as if it were a crystal tube, to the bottom of your feet. The light pours out through your feet like roots and connects you to Mother Earth. Keep breathing slow deep breaths. If there's any part of your body that feels tight, concentrate light in this area, gently relaxing to a deeper and deeper state. Let stillness drift over you as you renew yourself with the energy of this light. Speak your prayers while bathing in this light, and say aloud what you need to get through the day, for example, "an attitude of abundance" or "peace of mind." Then continue to relax and let go. Let any thoughts that enter your mind simply pass on through. Picture the light getting brighter and expanding until it forms a nine-foot-wide shield around you. For as long as possible, enjoy the pleasant sensations created by this radiance. When you are ready, bring yourself, very gently, back to the present. Practice this exercise in the morning, and when you write in your journal in the evening, be sure to thank God for fulfilling the request you made during your meditative and prayer time.

Strengthening Our Love Relationships

As you learned from this chapter, the depression and anger resulting from our history and daily incidents of racism, can make our relationships more fragile. Although an in-depth discussion, particularly of clinical implications, is clearly outside the scope of this work, we offer you four tools for strengthening love relationships, whether you're in one now or are preparing for one in the future.

Because our relationships have been vulnerable to the whims of others or events that were out of our control, many of us have gone into unions without a clear intention concerning the purpose or goal of the union. To solidify your relationship, you and your mate should write a vision statement. One couple, Maya and Jamal, wrote this:

> To communicate openly and freely with each other, with as much love and humor as possible. To grow spiritually, contributing to our own, each other's, and our shared spiritual love. To deepen our relationship through greater intimacy, playfulness, appreciating and enjoying one another. To stay connected to like-minded friends and family. To take and give heart in our commitment to improving and serving

*others. To become better and better compensated in our chosen profes-
sions through conscious experience, self-discipline, and consensual
planning. To live together in peaceful, comfortable, and accommodat-
ing surroundings.*

Without even realizing it, Maya and Jamal had embedded in their
vision our life-enhancing beliefs. When you write your vision statement with your mate, take time to discuss your highest goals in the
relationship. When you have finished writing your visions, read them
aloud to one another. When you have a vision you can agree on and
you read it together, you're aligning your energy.

In acknowledgment of your deep connection to the spirit, spend time
together daily in prayer and meditation.

To alleviate the ongoing stress of racism, talk to one another about the
racism you both encounter and devise strategies to thwart it. This not
only provides your mind, body, and spirit with relief but takes the
pressure off the relationship.

Many of us have felt the need to shut down emotionally in an attempt
to protect ourselves from further harm; synchronized breathing exercises help us to open our hearts to one another. The following "ah
breath" exercise, taught at workshops conducted by Stephen and
Ondrea Levine, can take you and your mate to a deeper level of connection, beyond any judgments or fears. Begin with one of you
stretching out in a relaxed position, while the other partner sits comfortably beside. The person lying down breathes normally. The person
sitting up matches his partner's. On each exhalation, release an "ah"
sound. Continue for twenty minutes. The next time you engage in
this exercise, switch positions and let the other person stretch out.

Loving Yourself

Make a list of must-do loving actions, such as scheduling an appointment for a Pap smear or breast exam (if necessary), conducting your
own monthly breast exams, wearing seat belts, and giving yourself or
getting regular pedicures and manicures. This list should also include

singing, dancing, painting, or any other creative outlet that allows you to celebrate your unique inner voice. Schedule something from that list weekly. You'll want to keep track of this list for your work with the next chapter, which focuses on controlling behavior. As we learn to stop managing the behaviors and lives of others, we have more time to devote to our self-care.

8

You Don't Have to Be
Your Mate's Mama

Sister Spirit Rosa Parks (b. 1913) is best known for her refusal to give up her seat to a white man on a bus in Alabama, in 1955. Her arrest led to the mass boycott of Montgomery city buses and galvanized the Civil Rights Movement. Few people realize that Mrs. Parks had a loving, mutually sustaining love relationship, which was, in part, the catalyst for her act of heroism. Early in their forty-five-year marriage, her husband, Raymond Parks, a barber, introduced his then shy young wife to black activism. Throughout their union, even when Mrs. Parks's civic responsibilities made it necessary for them to be temporarily separated, they kept their emotional connection intact. A decade after her husband's death in 1977, she founded an institute in their names, dedicated to helping youngsters realize their highest potential. As we work to end controlling behavior, Rosa and Raymond Parks's relationship is a reminder that intimacy flourishes in an atmosphere of mutual respect.

> ***Anti-intimacy belief explored in this chapter:***
> **I have to control everyone and everything around**
> **me to protect myself from being hurt again.**

Sure, some sisters seem to have found faithful mates, but how do they really know? There's a story going around about a woman who hatched a plan. On the night of the annual Halloween party, she begged off with a headache and insisted her man go without her. After he left in his devil outfit, she disguised herself and went to the party. When she arrived, he was up in some woman's face. Worried her man would recognize her voice, she gestured that she wanted to dance. That fool twisted and rubbed himself against her, but she played along and finally led him to a back room, where he whupped something on her.

Back home in bed when he returned, she asked about the party. When he said it was "all right," she snarled, "Just all right?" He said, "I missed you so much, I didn't feel like partying." She yelled, "Didn't you at least dance?" He said, "Actually, no. I went into the back and watched TV. Then I lent my costume to Booker's sixteen-year-old son. He said he had the time of his life."

More than amusing, this story reminds us that fear prompts controlling behavior, which usually backfires, leaving us feeling out of control. The word *controlling* can be confusing. Before we offer an explanation, we'd like you to check out the list below, and, being as candid as possible, mark the behaviors you've engaged in during a past or current relationship. Do you do any of the following:

- Offer unsolicited advice about your honey's clothes, weight, manners, job, speech, and so on?

- Stay abreast of where he goes and what time he arrives and leaves, and ask him for details?

- Feel your lover can't survive without you?

- Buy lots of gifts and take really good "care" of him?

- Feel resentful when he wants to spend his free time with anyone else?

- Check his briefcase, mail, pockets, or wallet for "insider" information?

- Threaten to hurt yourself if you're unhappy with his behavior?

- Tell him or suggest through body language that he's the reason you have a headache or feel ill?

- Suggest he has no right to feel a certain way?

- Pout, stop speaking, or withhold sex if he doesn't do what you want?

- Blow up when he disappoints you?

- Expect him to wait whenever you want as long as you want while you get ready?

- Ask him to lower his voice when he's angry?

- Make excuses for why you didn't do what he expected of you?

- Insist he attend religious services with you or read the Good Book?

- Scold him as if you were the parent and your mate the child?

- Show your impatience when he's a few minutes late?

As you continue reading this chapter, you'll discover that all of these behaviors are controlling. Like someone setting a VCR, a controlling person tries to program the lives of others. One of the most familiar controlling black women is "Maureen." Featured in television commercials, she buttonholes strangers and relatives alike, asking, "You're not going to take that laxative, are you?" If someone hesitates, Maureen drives home her point: "Don't you know nothing's better than Phillips' Milk of Magnesia?" Her beleaguered husband, humiliated by her shaming queries, shakes his head, adding, "She never takes a vacation."

Does Maureen remind you of someone you know? We who are controlling have convinced ourselves that we're trying to manage the lives and behaviors of others for "their own good," because we know best. In truth, it's another unconscious attempt to protect ourselves from being hurt again. Among all the creatures in the animal kingdom, only human beings can anticipate the future. The price we pay for that is fear. As we try to predict the unpredictable—concerning anything that might harm us—we attempt to impose control over others.

Those of us who were traumatized as children, and that accounts for most human beings, became controlling because our subconscious mind developed a belief such as: "If I keep a tight grip on everyone and everything around me, I can avoid being hurt again." When we focus on others, as if by magical sleight of hand, our fear is diverted. Often we're not even aware when we're afraid. Unfortunately, events in our lives can tap into our subconscious fears and trigger the compulsion to control. Men often complain that controlling mates make them feel like boys being scolded by their mothers, which causes many of them to bolt. Being deserted is the opposite of what a controlling person wants, but it's the inevitable outcome.

The relationship between Sharon and Nate, a couple with whom Dr. Wade worked, illustrates the vicious cycle of fear of abandonment, control, and actual abandonment. Sharon, the thirty-nine-year-old wife of a prominent attorney, looks like someone who has got it going on, from the top of her freshly permed hair to the tips of her pedicured toenails. Yet she admitted to Dr. Wade, "Except on weekends, for the last ten years my husband has lived eight hundred miles from me and our two children. The only thing he and I do together is make appearances." As Sharon began working to improve her life, she realized that her husband's determination to live in another city was his attempt to avoid her controlling ways. When he was home, she would make suggestions about the clothes he wore, schedule his tennis games, plan dinner parties, and greet him with a list of chores he had to accomplish.

Sharon had been raised in a prominent St. Louis family. Her father, a politician, was a compulsive gambler, and her mother spent her life guarding this family secret. Sharon learned to pretend that her life was as picture-perfect inside as it appeared to be from the outside. For families struggling with addiction, controlling behavior is an attempt to keep the lid on potentially explosive situations. As the addictive illness progresses, family members work harder to compensate for the addict's underfunctioning. Sharon grew up never knowing when her father would fail to show up for one of his public appearances and fearing that the family would come apart completely.

She eventually convinced Nate to join her for a session with Dr. Wade. Cold and withdrawn, he said bitterly, "I'm very grateful to Sharon. She has made me who I am today—the only problem is I can't remember who I was." Too angry, hurt, and alienated to work toward improving their relationship, Nate later filed for divorce, leaving Sharon to face her worst fear, being alone.

People who feel controlled in a relationship don't always defect. We shared this story to show just how enraging this behavior can be. If you're in a relationship and you're the one being controlled, you know just what we're talking about. One man who left a controlling woman said the relationship felt more like "deadlock" than wedlock.

Other controlled mates stick around but are filled with resentment. You've seen marriages like these and heard comedians make jokes about them. A husband might become so turned off to his wife's constant interference that no matter how often she speaks to him, he doesn't answer. And of course there are controlling men who exert power by choosing their wives' clothes and dictating where and how they live and how they will raise their children. In more openly bitter warfare, the husband might interrupt his grim silence by suddenly telling his wife to "just shut the hell up," before sinking back into his own despair.

Sex is often a major playing field in the control wars. Dr. Gwendolyn Goldsby Grant calls one group of sexually controlling men "studs." These are the men, she explains, who have convinced themselves they're great lovers. She writes: "To him, every act of lovemaking is like some kind of heavyweight championship. He's defending his title, and he wants each bout to be a knockout." The biggest problem with studs, Dr. Grant explains, is that they don't bother to find out what a woman really needs to be sexually pleased, because they're certain they already know.[1] Women, of course, also use sex as way to control. As most of us have learned, however, this is a game with no winners: We're ultimately left unsatisfied.

When the subject of controlling behavior was discussed in our abundance group, several members saw that their own fears had led them to (as one member phrased it) "tighten the noose around men's necks." Dr. Wade reminded the group that their controlling behaviors were created in self-defense, as a way to get the love and recognition they craved. Our painful history provides a key to understanding our controlling ways. Too often, our mothers and grandmothers had to step up to the plate to create order from chaos, when no one else volunteered for the job, and that is still true for many of us today. But if we hope to create satisfying relationships, we must learn to stop being mamas to our mates.

ONE FAMILY'S HISTORY/ONE FAMILY'S FEAR

To help you understand how some of us became controlling, we have demonstrated the effects of our collective history on one family. As you read their story, which is punctuated with grief, note how the accumulation of tragedies leaves each successive generation in a state of chronic fear. Stunned by their losses, these family members came to believe they had to use any means necessary, including violence, to control one another. But just as you are doing, one young woman found the strength and courage to change life as her family had known it for more than a century.

Maxine, a resident of Baltimore, isn't one of Dr. Wade's former clients or an abundance group member or workshop participant. She is a friend of Brenda Richardson. Maxine is familiar with details of her family history dating back as far as her maternal great grand-mother, who was the daughter of a former slave from Georgia. A family of sharecroppers, they lived in fear of marauding nightriders and other racially motivated violence.

At first glance, Maxine's present life seems far removed from that of her ancestors. At twenty-eight, she is a realtor who spends her free time reading self-help books and volunteering at a literacy program. One of the first things anyone would notice about her was Maxine's love for her longtime boyfriend, Dondre, thirty-one, a postal carrier and karate aficionado. Unfortunately, he also likes to fool around with other women. But Maxine had decided to "give him some space."

Maxine felt there was something special about Dondre. He has a shaved head, hazel eyes, chocolate brown skin, and a wiry, muscular body. But it is more than just his looks that impress her. "He knows how to talk to women," she said. "One night, walking on the beach, he pointed at the sky and said each star represented one of my attributes. Then, one by one, he began to name them. I appreciated myself in ways I'd never thought of." Maxine sighed. "We're soul mates," she remembers thinking.

As she waxed poetic, it sounded as if she had just seen him yes-terday, but actually it had been three months. At Maxine's insistence, the couple took four months off so he could get other women out of his system. "My friends say I'm a fool, but I waited a long time for someone like Dondre." Maxine said she's nonjudgmental because she has made so many mistakes herself.

Tall, slender, and heavy-breasted, with a slim waist, raven black hair that reaches to her hips, and a Mediterranean complexion, Maxine, like all of the sisters we've profiled in this book, is a variation of beautiful African sisterhood. She gets a lot of play from men of all races, whom she describes as being "hung up on hair and breasts." But she says, "I'm just not into that. It's sick. People say men would pay to go out with sisters who, quote, look like me. But I've strived to be the total opposite of that image."

That was one reason she noticed Dondre. He was the postman on the route where she and three other women were working to turn a run-down storefront into their realty office. "When he walked in, I had on a head rag and my body was swallowed up in Goodwill rejects. He said he fell in love with my soul. I felt the same way about him, but I did notice those thighs of his."

According to their agreement, Maxine was not due to see Dondre for another month, but in the end, she saw him sooner than she had scheduled. It wasn't just the phone calls she had been getting from his brothers, assuring her he was a changed man, or even her minister's report that Dondre had been coming in for Bible classes. It was business. A woman on his new postal route was selling her house, and Dondre had convinced her to let Maxine sell it. Having spoken with the prospective seller, Maxine was looking forward to meeting her, almost as much as she wanted to see Dondre. "I bought a new dress," she said.

Ten years ago, at eighteen, Maxine couldn't even have bought shoes. At that age she'd already been a mother for three years. "I had a baby because I wanted to know how it felt to have someone love me back." Maxine's earliest memories date back to the apartment she shared with her brother, mother, maternal grandmother, and grandmother's husband.

"My grandmother was the oldest of twelve kids in a family of sharecroppers," Maxine said. "Her parents practically sold her to a local white family. She had to live with them as a domestic. The white wife was like a sister to my grandmother, but her husband raped my grandmother repeatedly. She had nine kids by him. Then she met the man I call my grandfather, the neighborhood handyman. The white wife helped my grandfather get my grandmother away, but that same white man knocked him upside the head, making him deaf in one ear."

Maxine's grandfather may have rescued her grandmother, but he too proved to be physically abusive. "She had to run away from him with her kids, and that's how my mother came to Baltimore as a child," Maxine said. "When my grandmother married again, it was to another wife-beater. Now that I've been in therapy, I understand it was almost inevitable that without intervention she couldn't love a gentle man, only one who had a past like hers." Grandpa Bobby, who had been brutally beaten by his father, tried to impose absolute control over the people in his life. Maxine said, "My mother told me he used to line up the kids and make them watch while he beat their mother. It was like the slavemasters did, so the other slaves would be afraid to cross him."

As an adult, when Maxine's mother moved away, she also married a man who beat her. She left him, but not before she had two children, Maxine and her older brother, Tommy Dee. Having internalized both racism and her family's issues, Maxine's mother was extremely color conscious and rejected her son, who has skin that is a deep brown. She controlled him by shaming him about his looks.

When Maxine's mother fled from her husband and returned with her children to her mother's house, the violence continued. As far back as she can recall, before each fight, little Maxine would try to control the situation. "I'd beg my grandmother to please stop nagging Grandpa Bobby, because I knew he'd explode. She practically dared him to beat her, then he would, and she would quiet down as if she'd gotten what she wanted." Young Tommy Dee would stand silently by watching his grandmother get beaten.

Filled with self-loathing and despair, Maxine's mother was barely able to care for Maxine. At the age of six, Maxine fell and broke her arm and was taken to an emergency room, where an African American physician commented that he and his wife would love to have a daughter like her. "Right then and there, without knowing anything about this man, my mother gave me to him. I've been over this in therapy a thousand times, and it still hurts. But at least I had love and stability at Papa and Ma Gibson's house. They showed me black people could have lives of love and prosperity. For six years I was their child."

Her mother came to get her when she was twelve, insisting that the Gibsons give her back. "Part of me was glad that my mother wanted me; the other part was terrified. I was leaving safety." She was right. When the battles at her grandmother's became life-threatening, Maxine's mother would take her to the home of a woman in Washington, D.C. "I would stay for a while, but when Mama didn't send money, this woman would put my stuff in a bag and tell me to get out. I'd stand in the rain sometimes, waiting hours for my mother." Maxine learned during these times to control her feelings as a way of controlling others. "When Mama arrived, I wouldn't let her know I'd been crying, and I wouldn't complain. I just wanted her to be happy."

For two years, Maxine stayed at the homes of her mother's acquaintances, and even in these places, her terror of being abandoned made her desperate to control others. "The families I stayed with didn't want me, so I became extremely neat and I cleaned up after everybody. This way, I hoped they'd want me to stay. By then, I definitely believed that nobody wanted me."

At the end of the eighth grade, when no one in her family showed up for graduation festivities, Maxine quit school. "I was too depressed to concentrate." That same year, when she became pregnant by a schoolmate and gave birth to a baby girl, her mother let her return to the family home. Then, on the night of her daughter's first birthday party, when her grandparents began fighting, Tommy Dee's rage burst open. "He shot Grandpa Bobby and killed him. My brother was sent to prison for twenty-five years."

Desperate to control her own life, Maxine found work as a live-in baby-sitter. A year later, when her employers moved away, Maxine was terrified that her daughter wouldn't survive. "There was a drug dealer who was always after me. I gave in and became his girl." Drug earnings changed her life. "I went from having nothing to rolling in money. We bought a big house, I drove a big car, and everything extra I had I gave away to kids in my old neighborhood, thousands of dollars, because I knew just how a lot of those kids felt."

Federal authorities caught up with them two years later. Maxine was alone when officers knocked on her door and announced themselves. Racing to the attic, she hid in the rafters as she heard officers yelling for her to come out. When they reached the attic, Maxine, wanting to give herself up, pounced to the floor. Six guns pointed at

her, ready to fire. She was a millisecond from death when a black officer shouted, "Hold your fire!" Maxine recalled, "This agent put his
arms around me, and said, 'Let me hug you, you're just a baby, and we
almost killed you.'"

Arrested and taken to jail, she tried calling her old friends from
her drug life. "They begged me to forget I knew them." Her mother
and grandmother, citing other obligations, said they couldn't visit or
help in any way. "I'd never felt so alone," Maxine said. When her case
was assigned, her cellmates warned she had the toughest, most racist
of all the judges and told her to expect the maximum, fifteen years.
Her public defender concurred. Maxine said, "I was scared for my
daughter, that she'd grow up like me, with no one in her corner."

A few days before sentencing, she was visited by an elderly
woman from her old neighborhood. "She told me to pray, said that no
matter what that judge said, only God could judge me. She said God
knew I'd done wrong but that he also knew I'd helped people. She
told me, 'God's gonna whisper in that ol' judge's ear.' I wasn't religious,
but you know facing fifteen years in prison can sure change your
mind. I began praying and I gave my soul to God."

When she went to court for sentencing, her arms and ankles were
in chains. Looking back, she finds it ironic. "I hadn't come much further in life than the people in my family who had been slaves." As she
stood before the federal magistrate, he pronounced, "I'm sentencing
you to fifteen years. . . . " Maxine stopped listening. She wanted to
hear the one still small voice of God within, telling her she would be
all right, and she answered back in silent thanks for her life, for a soul
that was saved, and for a healthy daughter for whom God would provide. It was during that instantaneous prayer that she heard the
judge's voice still coming at her. He said, "I'm suspending the sentence. You'll report to a parole officer, and if you get in any trouble,
you'll do your time."

The prosecutor objected, but the judge said, "She has never been
in trouble before, and my chamber is filled with letters from children
and their mothers telling me how this young lady helped them out. If
she can do that while she's doing wrong, the court has to consider all
the good she'll do when she's doing right. Maxine, this may be your
last chance. Use it well."

She returned to a life of financial impoverishment. Her home and car had been seized, and she refused further contact with her drug dealer acquaintances. But she no longer felt alone. "Coming out of jail, my hands and legs free, I saw life in Technicolor. I could hold my daughter again. I was awakened to God's grace."

In addition to working menial jobs and saving every extra dollar, Maxine began reading self-help books, studying real estate sales, doing volunteer work, and requesting free counseling from a local mental health clinic. "I never missed an appointment. . . . You know, Iyanla Vanzant was on *Oprah* the other day, and Oprah quoted a line from one of her books: 'If you don't heal the wounds of your past, you will continue to bleed.' I really agree. If I had done nothing to help myself, I'd have continued standing in front of speeding trains; then my daughter would have done the same."

Two years ago, Maxine began working with a private therapist, and they have often discussed her relationship with Dondre. "Therapists don't tell you what to do. It's like they lift a veil so you can see better. She helped me see that Dondre was like a drug to me." In the course of their three-year relationship, Maxine's fear of abandonment had led her to control him with kindness. With business techniques she had learned, she taught him to save his modest salary. She laughed. "You know me. I gave him everything I could. I helped him buy clothes, a car. I cleaned his apartment. That's just the way I am."

Dondre, who had been abandoned by both parents at birth, couldn't seem to get enough of her nurturing—at first. After a year, he began cheating on her. For more than two years, Maxine suffered through his infidelities, then, still unable to let go, she called a temporary halt to their relationship. Bolstered by his assurances of change, she looked forward to seeing him at the business meeting he had arranged. When she arrived, she wasn't surprised to learn the owner was out of town and that it would be just she and Dondre. Pretending this was strictly business, Maxine followed him through the house, which was filled with expensive African artwork.

But she saw something else, too. She had described her therapy as having a veil lifted from her eyes. That image is especially apropos when you consider that a veil is usually worn by someone who's grieving. The healing work that Maxine had been engaged in brought her life into focus. She hadn't seen Dondre in several weeks, and during that time, although she had certainly missed him, she had begun to live her own life and focus on her own needs. In the meantime, he was in the same old groove, the world revolving around him, expecting her to fall back in line. He didn't realize his "sweet baby girl" had changed.

"I demanded that Dondre tell me the real story. Why would someone leave her key with her mail carrier? And how come he knew his way around the house? It was obvious he'd been sleeping with her. He tried to assure me that he didn't love her, which only made it more insulting. That was probably what he told her about me, too.

"Every word he spoke was like a shovel full of dirt on a coffin. I felt like I was dying inside. This house was the kind of place I'd always wanted. And this woman had snapshots on her bureau. She was gorgeous. So was her family. They looked like people who wanted her, not the kind who would give you away to a stranger, then snatch you back when you're happy. I was thinking, 'Oh my God, she's got all this; I can't let her have Dondre too.' I felt like falling in bed with him so he'd stay in my life. Then I heard myself and realized I was desperate to control him, to keep him coming back."

She did what she has learned to do in difficult moments; she asked God to help her put to use all that she had learned in therapy. "I realized that even though the woman in those photos looked happy, she had to have been hurt too, or why else would she also be in love with the same empty man?" Maxine told Dondre that she had decided not to represent the house and that she had also decided not to take him back. She hoped he would beg her to stay; it was something she'd been waiting to hear all her life from someone she loved. But he didn't plead. In fact, he held the door open; as if he wanted to assist her in leaving; she left. This was the first time in her life she had found the strength to choose to let go.

In the weeks following the encounter, Maxine's therapeutic work gave her the strength to realize there are worse things than feeling lonely and horny and that one of them is being with a man who destroys your self-esteem and beats you down emotionally. While Dondre's behavior can't be condoned, it's important to understand he had the same abandonment fears, which is why he was so controlling. Keeping someone waiting and hoping and desperate is like playing the role of a cruel puppet master. But Maxine had been playing the role of "mama," and when we mother our mates, they often respond by asserting their autonomy. For many that means infidelity.

Looking back, Maxine summed up her relationship clearly. She said, "All those gifts I gave him, even refusing to get upset when he slept with other women, were my way of controlling him and forgetting my own needs and feelings. I was willing to do anything to keep him." She has prayed that she would be able to remain strong and keep Dondre out of her life. The universe seemed to be offering help.

One night, while Maxine was standing on a supermarket line, a young man waiting behind her confided that he'd seen her in that store on several occasions but had always felt the time wasn't right to introduce himself. When Maxine asked what had prompted him finally to talk to her, "he said he had a feeling that I was just getting around to being ready for someone like him." Short, slightly heavy, with glasses, Drew isn't the kind of man Maxine ordinarily would have taken the time to get to know. But as they continued to chat, she realized that all the work she'd done on herself wasn't in vain, that she was finally beginning to attract the kind of men she didn't have to control to keep.

"There's nothing flashy about Drew," she said. "He's a good churchgoing brother and a hardworking man. My daughter loves him. What makes him unusual is that he has actually stopped to think about his own emotional stuff. I can't believe it! He runs a class at the county jail teaching men how to be respectful and loving to their mates."

It's too soon to know if their relationship will take off; Maxine's just happy to have pulled herself out from the vicious circle of fearing abandonment, controlling a man, and then driving him away. "I feel really safe telling Drew about my needs, and he tells me about his. We even tell each other when we feel frightened about things." That's really something when you consider that this may be a first in her family's painful history.

OUR EMOTIONAL INHERITANCE

We hope this chapter has helped you to consider your own family history and how fear can be passed down intergenerationally and lead to controlling behavior. The following questions will help you focus your thinking: Have you created relationships in which you and your partner are equals? Do you struggle with issues of control? If you do, consider your family patterns and childhood experiences to discover your unconscious fears. What beliefs did you form as a result of your childhood experiences? Some of the responses we've heard, include: "I can't let anyone get the best of me," "I have to control everyone and everything around me," and "If I can anticipate what might happen next, I can keep myself from being hurt."

Sometimes controlling behavior seems to work out, for a while anyway. Your honey might be crazy about all the meals you cook, the fact that you do the laundry and lots of caretaking. But even if he doesn't have his own abandonment issues, he will eventually feel suffocated. Keep in mind that controlling people are often attracted to one another. In fact they can turn their homes into battlefields: There's nothing a controlling person hates more than being controlled by others.[2]

Now that you're more familiar with controlling behavior, you can learn to spot it in your life. If you are controlling, this is a good time to ask yourself what you're afraid of. If it's your mate who is controlling, it will help you to know he's fearful too. In general, there are four controlling styles: There are the *blamers,* who are angry; the *rationalist-intellectualizers,* who don't allow themselves to feel anything and don't want others to either; the *distractors,* who are emotionally disjointed, making connection impossible; and the *placaters,* who are anxious and resentful, alternately trying to please and resenting all the effort they feel they are making. Following is a list of controlling sentences and a description of the emotions hiding the fear:

The Words	*Type of Message*	*Feeling That Masks the Fear*
"You made me hit you."	Blaming	Anger
"I know how you can lose that weight."	Intellectualizing	Numbness
"I'm not going to put up with this shit!"	Blaming	Anger
"I don't want to discuss that when every light in the house is on. We'll never pay the bills!"	Distracting	Frustration

"I know I'm late but we need the extra money."	Placating	Anxiety
"How can you envy him; be thankful for what you have."	Blaming	Anger
"I don't know." "Maybe." "Nothing."	Distracting	Frustration
"You're right, Honey, now calm down.	Placating	Anxiety
"_____" (refusal to answer)	Distracting	Frustration
"Maybe I shouldn't have bought you the tickets. I'm broke."	Blaming	Angry
"Why get so excited? Just consider the facts."	Intellectualizing	Numbness

If you are not currently in a relationship and you're controlling, you can begin now to change. Become more aware of your true feelings and observe your interactions with children, coworkers, and other people in your life. If you hear yourself saying, "You should . . ." or "I insist that you . . . ," slow yourself down and consider what you might be feeling. Controlling behavior is always a signal that you're feeling fear. When Ondine, an abundance group member, tried this approach, she realized that when working with other medical personnel, she had assumed the mantle of "commander in chief" so her coworkers would feel she was indispensable and always want her around. But when she started asking for their opinions, her coworkers were more supportive and receptive.

If you are currently in a relationship, discuss what you've learned with your partner and ask for feedback regarding your style. Rather than saying, "Do you think I'm controlling?" simply ask, "How do you think this subject applies to me?" Don't be surprised if your partner has a lot to say and is angry about it. Listen without formulating an argument; then summarize the gist of this person's response. Then apologize, if necessary. Don't make any excuses. Later, it will be important to share information about your feelings and needs, or you will end up perpetuating the cycle in which your feelings and needs go unacknowledged. At that time, it is fair to speak about what parts of your mate's behavior trigger your fears. But don't offer an analysis of your partner's wrongdoings. Let him figure out how he wants to change. Just assure him of your intention to change and follow through. Once your mate sees that you've stopped trying to control him, he will be much more likely to want to work with you to do more healing in your relationship.

Healing Fear/Embracing Love

The Breath of Life

One of the first physical responses to fear is holding the breath. You'll realize how true this is when you think of a baby who has been frightened. She might catch her breath and hold it, sometimes turning red before she releases a wail. While our screams cease as we grow older, we do respond to fear in the same manner. "Half breathing" keeps us alive, but we want more than that; we want lives of abundance, and that means giving our spirit/mind/body what it needs: room to breathe. Most of us who learned to hide our fears never learned to self-soothe (although some of us have tried with behaviors such as overeating, -spending, or -drinking). Conscious breathing is something we can learn to help calm ourselves. It takes a little practice because it feels like doing the opposite of what we've grown accustomed to. Practice this deep breathing when you feel fearful about money or work or relationships, and especially when you find yourself acting in a controlling manner.

Begin by standing and placing your palm on your lower stomach. As you inhale, feel your stomach expanding as you push it out like a balloon. As you exhale, feel your abdomen relaxing and being drawn in. Keep practicing this throughout the day, especially when you find yourself acting in a controlling manner.

Questioning Yourself

When you find yourself acting in a controlling way, use this quick four-step process: (1) Start taking full breaths, (2) ask yourself what you're afraid of, (3) acknowledge the fear to yourself, and (4) ask yourself what you need to feel peaceful and comforted.

Here's an example of how this process works: You're in a restaurant holding hands across a table with a man you love, and he's gazing affectionately into your eyes. Suddenly, a beautiful sister enters the room, and his eyes move in her direction, taking in every curved inch of her body. You're thinking, "Get your eyes back down here, I want to wipe that stupid grin off your face."

In the "old days," you might have controlled him by pouting or pulling away emotionally. But since you're learning to live abundantly, you admit to yourself that you feel hurt and insecure. When you ask yourself why, you tell yourself you feel scared that he'll leave you for someone else. When you ask yourself what you need, the answer is probably as simple as some reassurance. You can tell him what you're feeling and say you need a hug, or you might try candor with a little humor mixed in. "Her suit is fabulous, but I hope you also noticed the huge wart on her nose. . . . Yes, I'm feeling insecure, but it's nothing one of your hugs couldn't soothe." That's emotional freedom and intimacy, and it's what you deserve.

Role-Playing

When you're struggling with long-term problems that you find yourself "overmanaging," try this role-playing technique. It can help you get to the bottom of a problem quickly. Find a quiet place where you can be alone and ask yourself what fears from the past the given situation is bringing up for you. Accept the first answer that comes to mind, and then play the roles of the people involved. The following is an example of how it works.

Marie was locked in battle with her husband, Walter, over his fifty-pound weight gain. He was depressed, and he ate constantly. Dr. Wade suggested that Marie stop nagging him about his weight and focus on fear from her past that might be associated with this situation. Marie connected the pain to the death of her older sister, who had died of a stroke at thirty-one when she weighed nearly four hundred pounds. This sister had been like a mother to her after their mother's early death, and when her sibling died, Marie was left to struggle with a double abandonment. Marie secretly was terrified that she would also lose her husband because of his eating habits. She needed to express her feelings concerning her childhood experiences.

Though she initially insisted that pretending to have a conversation with her deceased sister would do her no good, "because there's no way I could be angry with her," she soon discovered the power of this exercise. Sitting comfortably, she played herself as a child, verbalizing to an empty chair (imaginary stand-in for her sister) what she had wanted to say back then; then she switched seats and verbalized what her sister would have said if she'd spoken the truth about her eating.

LITTLE MARIE: Please stop eating. I'm so tired of hearing the kids in the neighborhood make fun of you. I hate the way our brothers make grunting noises like a pig when you eat. I look up to you, but you're embarrassing me. Stop eating right now!

SISTER: I'm going to eat anything I want. Too bad for you. My life has been miserable, and if I have to step in and take Mama's place, I'm going to give myself all the food I need to feel better. Pass the meat and biscuits.

LITTLE MARIE: Stop! I can't stand to see you stuff your face again. You look horrible, and I'm ashamed of you. Put that food down now!

SISTER: I have to eat, I'm so scared. I'm so stupid and ugly, no one is going to want me. This is the only happiness I have. Give me back that pie. I want to crush it in my face, eat like a hog because that's what I am, a filthy hog!

LITTLE MARIE: Stop saying horrible things about yourself. I feel so guilty about having a better life than you. If only we could trade lives and you could have mine, so I could be protecting you. If only I could have controlled our lives, you wouldn't have to be so unhappy. Why can't you just stop? Use some discipline. Stop, damn it. [*Marie began to cry.*]

ADULT MARIE: I miss you so much. There's not a day I don't miss you. I couldn't stop you from eating and I couldn't stop you from killing yourself. You were all I really had when I was a kid, but I'm an adult now and I have to take care of myself, and not try to run my husband's life. I'm going to love myself and give myself what I need.

As you can see, this exercise cuts right to the quick. It has a way of exposing old fears for what they are. In the future, every time Marie became overfocused on her husband's eating, she repeated this exercise. Eventually, as her old fears and anger over this situation were resolved, she was able to stop policing her husband's weight. He hasn't lost any weight, but he has stopped gaining.

This method will work for you, too. Every time you've completed the exercise, consult that "self-loving list" that you compiled when reading the previous chapter and find something that you can do for yourself, even if it's something as simple as rubbing lotion on your hands, reapplying lipstick, or hugging yourself and saying "I love you and I'm going to take care of you."

The next chapter, which explores sexuality, demonstrates that giving up controlling behavior is one of the most significant steps you can take toward a more fulfilling sex life.

9

Your Body and Your Sexuality Are Yours

Sister Spirit Judith Jamison (b. 1943) is a personification of elegant sensuality. Although told by whites that she was too tall and too "African looking" to be a ballet dancer, she knew these characteristics contributed to her allure. Raised by loving parents and trained in dance from the age of six, Jamison endured years of rejections until she was spotted by the gifted choreographer Alvin Ailey. He must have taken one look at Jamison, a lovely, fleshed-out, breathing stroke of midnight, and imagined the captivating dances he would create for her, which is just what he did. Eventually, Jamison's masterful dancing was praised the world over. A New York Times dance critic described her as an African queen. And so are we all —a rhapsody in brown. As we reclaim our sensuality, coming fully alive from the tops of our heads to the tips of our toes, we are inspired by the story of Jamison, who after Ailey's death, in 1989, succeeded him as his company's artistic director.

> **Anti-intimacy belief explored in this chapter:**
> **My body is not my own.**

We want to tell you about a sister who grew up poor and feeling ugly in the South, but who transformed herself into one of the most sensual women we know. While she's certainly an individual in her own right, her story reflects pieces of our own. As a child she was abandoned and sexually abused. She was worn down with shame, and her resulting anger, depression, and insufficiency of self-love led her to abusive relationships and into the habit of compulsive overeating. Her weight peaked at more than two hundred thirty pounds. Still, she never let her hurtful experiences stop her from achieving professionally. But a successful career wasn't enough. Craving abundance in every area of her existence, she decided to change her life.

She engaged in therapeutic work, read self-help books, and talked with supportive friends to heal her shame so she could love herself and work through her fear and anger. She also began reconnecting with the spirit within, paid homage to her slave ancestors, meditated to bring peace into her life, thanked God for her abundance, and gave back much of what she was given. The change was total. She went from everybody's big sister to sensuous goddess.

Though she gave up dieting, she has lost a great deal of weight. These days when we see her, she has often exchanged her elegant business clothes for something soft and loose, much of her makeup removed. In addition to regular exercise, she takes brisk walks as she listens to the crackling of fall leaves beneath her feet and the sounds of her dogs' heavy breathing. Weather permitting, she dangles her bare toes in an icy cool lake as she watches the sun setting behind the trees. Although she has a man she loves and who loves her, she enjoys time alone, especially in a candelit bathroom, luxuriating in a delicious bath, warm water lapping her sable-toned skin as she inhales the scent of fragrant soaps and bath salts.

Psychologist Marilyn Mason would describe this woman as having "come to her senses." By that, Mason means she has become someone who is open to hearing and being heard, to seeing and being seen, to touching and being touched, to smelling and being smelled. Mason believes that when we allow ourselves to be connected to life's energy, "we know that our being is within, relentlessly nudging us to be fully human."[1]

The sister we are describing is Oprah Winfrey. We use her story not simply because she is someone we have all heard about but because she represents so many women who have become fully alive. If you're thinking, "Sure Oprah transformed, she's rich," remember that her change involved eating less, engaging in physical exercise, and meditating; it had nothing to do with money. We don't change because of what's in our pocket, but because we want to get better at being human. All of us can aspire to finding the sensual-sexual goddesses within us.

For many of us that will require healing. Although our sexual experiences may vary, many of us remain bound to our past, unconsciously believing our bodies are not our own. Some of us have been traumatized by sexual abuse and may be turned off completely by sex. Or raised in overly strict households. We might live in secret terror of being "whorish" and become so uptight we feel naked without a pair of panty hose. Or maybe, rebelling from this image, we have allowed others to define us purely in sexual terms. These reactions leave no room for sexual spontaneity, or for the possibility of getting in touch with our essential sensual self.

Sensuality and sexuality are different and yet inextricably linked. Some artists have found that if they lose their interest in sex, they lose their creative ability. Being fully sexual means feeling more alive and whole.

Sexuality has been described as "the human/psychic energy that finds physical and emotional expression in the desire for contact, warmth, tenderness, and love."[2] Scheming against our lovers or worrying (Should I have shaved under my arms? What about the lights?) makes us uptight and reactive, so we can't fully feel, taste, smell, and hear. By working to heal ourselves and create unions that provide a sense of safety, we can offer our whole selves, including our spirituality. The ancient Eastern practice of tantric yoga—the spiritual practice of sexuality—has as its goal the union of two spirits merging on all levels of consciousness. This merging creates sexual ecstasy. In Western society, we're conditioned to self-centered sex; either our orgasm becomes the focus or we show what great technicians we are so we can wow our partners. Beyond the concept of technical prowess is the idea that two beings merge into one, to give the experience of being one with God.

When we recognize that our sexuality extends beyond our genitals, our lovers can touch parts of us we didn't even know existed. Intercourse becomes a sacred act that allows us to bring into lovemaking a sense of deep compassion for ourselves, which can be shared with our partner. Sometimes we don't want our partner to touch us or look at us because we don't feel good enough about ourselves or feel judgmental about some part of our body. But this lack of self-acceptance only makes our mate feel judged too.

All of us have heard racist suggestions that our men are the best lovers and that black women can really get it on. So what's up with that? As we'll discuss in this chapter, those are lies that bind us. Here's the gospel truth from the sisters Wade and Richardson: No matter what the color or gender of our partner, when it comes to lovemaking, one of the greatest gifts of healing is that we can draw on the finest aspects of our culture, including the musical tradition of call and response.

We might start out wailing from the stage, but our audience always joins in: first with whispered tones, followed by throaty laughter and purrs. Calling our names, they implore us to descend, and together we become rhythmically agile. There's the sudden shout of trumpet, foggy moan of horn, somebody finds the "G" spot and keeps on strumming. "Taking a ride with the spirit" is the way Malidoma Somé and his wife, Sobonfu, describe this act of love. The ride ends with a burst of passion, followed by long stretches of silence, and we fade out with a sigh.

How do we get to this place of freedom? We have already begun, by working through the grief we have addressed, and here, we work on another piece of the puzzle. We examine our views on sexuality. When we raised the subject of sex at an abundance group meeting, we found that it brought up more immediate sadness than any we had introduced. Women recalled instances of sexual abuse and terrible misuse. Some had completely given up on their dreams of ever having a sexually fulfilling life. Their sadness mirrored that of many of the women Dr. Wade has worked with through the years. The stories of four women that follow illustrate the challenges we face in transforming our sexuality.

Judy, thirty-six, a court reporter, confided, "I'm just not into the sex thing. I cringe when my husband tries to touch me." A petite woman, she shook her shoulder-length hair, which was styled and highlighted to frame her delicate face. When asked when she had last had intercourse with her husband, Judy said, "Who knows, who cares?"

Her response was particularly ironic given that she and her husband hoped to have at least one child before her "biological clock" ran out. Although it was obvious they would have to have intercourse more frequently, that seemed to be the last thing on Judy's mind. She had tried convincing her fertility specialist to recommend an expensive procedure in which her eggs, fertilized in the lab with her husband's sperm, could be implanted into her. But her doctor, insisting she was capable of having a baby naturally, recommended she work with Dr. Wade.

After a therapy session, the pieces of Judy's puzzle began to fall into place. She used abstention from sex as a weapon to punish her husband, to thwart intimacy, and to protect herself from her mother's fate. Her mother had married at sixteen, and before the age of twenty-four had given birth to seven children. To support his large family, her father maintained two factory jobs and spent weekends moving furniture. He died at forty from a stroke, when Judy was thirteen. She believed her beloved father would still be alive if her parents "hadn't been so eager to jump into bed."

But there was much more to Judy's reluctance. When her mother began dating again, she brought home a man who molested Judy on several occasions. "I told my mother, and she believed me and threw him out," Judy said. "Then she spent the rest of her life alone, struggling financially. But at least she didn't have to put up with no mess. I will never let a man get the upper hand on me."

Before her work with Dr. Wade, Judy had never been in therapy for her sexual abuse and her other childhood losses. She described herself as "frigid," and though her husband, Cedric, tried to remain faithful, two years into their union he strayed, and Judy caught him in bed with his coworker, a young white woman. They separated, but when Judy finally agreed to come home, she was unable to let go of her anger and forgive him. He was condemned to his side of the bed, never to venture across the Grand Canyon–sized invisible divide. Truth be told, if he had tried to test the temperature, Cedric might have frozen to death. "Don't get me wrong," Judy said. "I respect him and all that, but I don't want his damn hands on me."

The disproportionately high poverty rate, coupled with its twin, oppression, has forced some black women, such as twenty-eight-year-old Carmen, into the sex industry. Born in the Dominican Republic, Carmen was raised in the Bronx; she moved to California to escape a physically abusive boyfriend. With her short platinum blonde hair and hip-length skirts, she attracted lots of attention from men on the street. A mother of three, she was a recovering crack addict and met Dr. Wade in a court-ordered halfway house therapy group. During their first meeting, Carmen proudly displayed a dog-eared photo of her parents, her sisters and brothers, and her own kids taken during a family reunion.

Her father, the owner of a neighborhood bodega, had been kind and loving when his daughters followed his household rules. But for him, there wasn't a right way and a wrong way, just *his* way. The smallest infraction of his rules meant severe punishment. When Carmen was sixteen and her father discovered she had a boyfriend, he threw her out of the house. Her boyfriend, a crack addict, put her out on the street to turn tricks, and she eventually adopted his drug habit. Speaking in a heavy New York accent, Carmen said, "I got three sisters. My father guarded our virginity like a mad dog. We weren't allowed to date, wear lipstick, boys didn't exist. My sister raises her kids like that. I thought it was crazy, now I wouldn't mind. It's hard out there, but I can't afford to stop. I got mouths to feed. You figure it, Doc. Clean houses for five bucks an hour or sell Miss Poosie for two hundred dollars a night. . . . Guess I'm the bad woman my father warned us about. Shit, what can I do?"

"Sex with him is sooo good," thirty-four-year-old Violet said. "I know you think he's doggin' me, but deep down he really cares." This otherwise intelligent young woman, a nurse, was trading her self-respect for sex with a hurtful and dishonest man, a white physician at the hospital where she worked. On the job, he was cold and aloof toward Violet and told her he didn't want any commitments, but he often came to her apartment unannounced, late at night, when they had hot, passionate sex. Against her better judgment, she found herself sitting around nights waiting for him.

Violet originally enlisted Dr. Wade for help in ending the relationship, but after a few visits she abruptly ended her appointments, saying she was unable to break away from her lover. Her parents, a proud, hardworking couple who had raised their son and daughter "in the church" with rigid rules, would have been shocked to learn about her lifestyle. She said, "Two things my folks and my minister hammered into my head: not to have sex before marriage and to leave white men alone."

Although the relationship with the white physician was her first experience with a man of a different race, this behavior was really a continuation of a pattern of one-sided relationships. Violet was accustomed to not feeling loved. At first she resisted the advances of her white "night visitor." She said, "I thought I wouldn't be able to stand the idea of a white man touching me, after all the terrible things they've done to black women, and I'd heard they weren't very good in bed. But he kept pressing, and I was so lonely, I let him rock my world." Violet was filled with self-loathing and shame over the pseudorelationship, and she still grieved the two abortions she'd had while in nursing school. "I'd have those kids now," she said, "and I probably wouldn't be so lonely."

Terry and Grace, a lesbian couple, have been together for a decade after meeting at a political fundraiser. Grace, a thirty-four-year-old jewelry designer who is Japanese American, had been open with her sexuality since high school. Terry, forty, an architect who is African American, revealed to her mother that she was a lesbian when her mother was on her deathbed. "It turned out that she'd always known and that she'd always loved me," Terry said. Six feet tall, slim, and shapely, with a wide sixties afro, Terry lived with her lover in a town house surrounded by a high fence. Only close friends were invited inside. This sanctuary was the one place Terry revealed her true self. Hiding her sexuality from the world, Terry would say, "Who I sleep with is no one's business but my own."

She and Grace began working with Dr. Wade because Terry insisted their lives remain shrouded in secrecy, complete with separate phone lines and bedrooms. All along Terry had insisted that her business would be hurt "if we flaunt the intimate details of our lives," but Grace wasn't buying that. She had been livid when, during an office Christmas party, Terry flirted with one of Grace's coworkers, a tall and handsome African American man.

During their first session, Terry assured Grace that she did love her and wanted to make a life with her. But, she cautioned, she couldn't swear to be faithful. After all, Terry pointed out, she had been raised in a very liberal household. Her father had been known as the neighborhood Romeo; her mother bore the hurt silently. As their therapeutic work continued, Terry realized she was sorrowful over her father's infidelities—a secret hurt that fueled her own lack of commitment. At some point she had vowed she would never be made a fool of like her mother. Not committing also meant she could keep anyone (including Grace) from getting close enough to hurt her the way her father had. Children of unfaithful parents feel betrayed by their parents' infidelity.

All four of these women believed they were independent women who did as they pleased: Judy, who was sexually abused; Carmen, the sex industry worker, was victimized by both her father's Victorian standards and her drug-addicted boyfriend; Violet, who was filled with shame over her lopsided affair and past abortions; and Terry, who modeled her father's inability to make a commitment. They didn't realize that when it came to sex, they were anything but free. For too many of us, sex has become a weapon, or a tool, or a symbol for the closeness and love we never received and that we still crave.

We might "mistakenly" become pregnant and keep our unplanned baby, hoping a child will create a permanent bond with a lover. Or we might try to assuage our loneliness and fears by sleeping with partners we don't love or respect—sometimes men who won't even remember our names—as we use sex addictively to fill the emotional hole. But we never walk away from sex scott free. Sex is more personal to us than to men, and there's a reason for that. The results of preliminary research suggests that when we have orgasms, our bodies release oxytocin, the same chemical that's produced during breast-feeding, and that heightens feelings of bonding.

Our desperation to be loved and held and to connect costs us big time. Dr. Wyatt, the professor of psychiatry who is the leading researcher in the area of black women's sexuality, has found that too often we do not exert control over our bodies because we defer to our partners' needs. The need to please shows up in our earliest sexual experiences. Ninety-one percent of black adolescent girls interviewed about their first sexual experiences said they did not have sex for the sake of their own gratification.[3] Although we tend to have fewer partners over the course of our lifetimes than do white women, fewer than half the women in Dr. Wyatt's studies reported using contraception.[4] One of the common reasons is that they don't want to interrupt the moment or ruin the "naturalness."[5]

The consequences of this behavior are dire. We suffer a higher incidence of sexually transmitted diseases, including a risk of AIDS that is ten to fifteen times higher than that of white women. We also have more unplanned pregnancies.[6] A sociological rule of thumb is that the less education and money women have, the more likely they are to have unplanned pregnancies. When there's little else to look forward to, many women of varying races have babies who they hope can give them the love they crave; they also may hope the fathers will stick around to care for them and the child. The high pregnancy rate among impoverished girls is in large part attributable to their wish to "have a baby to find out what it's like to be loved."

If ever there was proof of our unmet emotional needs, it's this: Although many of us view abortions as genocide, and although our religious convictions cause many of us to oppose abortion,[7] we behave in a very different way. On the average, we have had at least two unplanned pregnancies compared with one for white women. "By age 20, nearly 40 percent of all American women and about 60 percent of American black women have been pregnant," Dr. Wyatt writes. "Minority women in the United States (mainly blacks and Latinas) have an abortion rate of 57 per 1,000 women, 2.7 times higher than that of white women."[8] Putting ourselves at risk sexually in exchange for love is not a recent trend. Prior to the 1973 *Roe v. Wade* decision, African American women accounted for 75 percent of deaths from illegal abortions.[9] The conflict between what we believe and what we do leaves many of us burdened with unexpressed guilt concerning our sex lives. Our reproductive organs often express that emotional conflict.

Niravi Payne is a mind-body fertility therapist in Brooklyn, New York, who has tremendous success in helping her clients work through unconscious conflicts concerning pregnancy and sex: many of her clients who have been medically diagnosed as "infertile" eventually conceive, carry to full term, and give birth to healthy infants. As Payne explains in *The Language of Fertility*, which she coauthored with Brenda Richardson, her work is based on research that validates that thoughts and beliefs can affect functioning in cells, tissues, and organs. In recent decades, scientists have learned that much of human perception is based not on information flowing into the brain from the external world but on what the brain, based on previous experience, expects to happen next.[10] That means that if we unconsciously believe that sex is "shameful" or something to be feared, that belief can be reflected in our reproductive organs by throwing off hormonal functioning, which regulates pregnancy, or in our immune system, which governs our ability to maintain a pregnancy, or even in our menstrual flow, which if malfunctioning can lead to fibroid tumors.

Payne believes our high rate of fibroids—three to nine times higher than among white women[11]—is related to childhood conflicts. For example, one of her clients was raised by parents who were so terrified their daughter would "sin" and have sex before marriage that each month, until she graduated and moved away from home, she was forced to show her mother that she was actually menstruating. This humiliating and controlling practice left her feeling so uptight about sex that even after marriage, when her husband touched her sexually, she felt every muscle in her body tense. Payne believes this extreme sexual tension and rigidity was reflected in her client's fibroid condition.

What is there about our sexual history that has led to a damaging belief so powerful that it affects our reproductive functioning and leads us to ignore our own needs, betray our ideals, and risk our health? We can find answers only by going back and looking carefully at the time when our ancestors became convinced that their bodies were not their own.

OUR HISTORY/OUR SEXUAL SELVES

Most of us are aware that our ancestral history includes the callous use and abuse of enslaved women as "bed warmers" and "breeders" and progressed through the incidents of rape that we recounted earlier. What many of us do not know is that before being forcibly transported to this country, most of our people lived in African societies in which the human body was considered sacred, women were treasured and protected, and there were strict sexual boundaries.[12]

Imagine, then, the degree of emotional and physical trauma of African women who were sexually abused by crew members even before they landed on these shores. Arriving in the "New" World, they suffered the indignity of auctions, where strangers poked, prodded, and examined their breasts and genitals. Later, they were punished by having their clothes stripped from their bodies so they could be whipped and clubbed publicly. Though they could be raped at will, they were forbidden by law from disclosing the names of their white abusers. Knowing that violent fighting back could cost them their lives, our ancestors learned to control their physical and emotional reactions. All they could do with their feelings was to numb themselves completely or turn the anger inward, and on rare occasions explode.

For more than two hundred years, our great grandmothers and then their female offspring taught their daughters how they could (1) avoid sex or (2) pretend that the rapes they endured weren't really occurring. The better a girl became at pretending to disregard her abuse—not crying or discussing it with other slaves—the more she was admired for her strength. It was a survival strategy, and the good Lord knows it was needed.

In addition to sexual exploitation, an enslaved woman had to contend with the jealous fury of white wives who, for the sake of their own survival, had to look the other way when their husbands had sex with African women. They went as far as to pretend that their husbands' mixed-blood offspring were proliferating because black women were wanton temptresses who preyed on white men. Many of these wives punished our ancestors for their husbands' infidelities. They locked female captives in barns, beat them, or sold them off to faraway plantations.

Keep in mind, too, that some white men (as well as white women) fell in love with slaves and risked their lives to create homes with them. In the 1830s, for instance, Zephaniah Kingsley married his former slave, and they and their sons moved to the Caribbean to escape mounting racial tensions.[13]

Generally, however, white men explained their desire for our ancestors by blaming them for being hypersexual. It was a lie that stuck. Even at the end of the Civil War, union soldiers who came South raped our women.[14] What's most significant is that the myths created by whites concerning the sexuality of black women extended way beyond the antebellum South and affected the manner in which generations of free black parents would raise their children.

When African Americans were emancipated, they were determined to refute the demeaning lies about our women, and so they clamped down on their daughters' sexuality as if with lock and key.

Black families often made great financial sacrifices to keep their daughters out of domestic work to protect them from the husbands of white employers. This practice is viewed as one of the most significant reasons so many impoverished black families scraped together money to pay for their daughters' college education. Teaching school meant they could work someplace that was safer. This tradition of educating our daughters has, of course, carried on, and there is still a discrepancy in the numbers of educated black women versus men.

Of course it's not unusual for families of various cultures to devote energy to protecting a daughter's chastity, but African American parents could not easily be matched in the level of fear induced by their antisex messages. The bottom line they espoused was that there were only two kinds of women: good, *clean*, churchgoing girls, or whores. Most girls raised in black middle-class or working-poor households were locked rigidly in the "good, clean" category.

As if parental tongue-lashings weren't enough, the black church also engaged in this crusade. We heard the message from preachers and Sunday school teachers. For generations, hundreds of thousands of us—meticulously scrubbed ebony girls, braids so tight our faces were pulled up in permanent smiles, patent leather shoes mirror bright—sat in Sunday schools where we heard warnings about sex. Dr. Wade recalls hearing this from one Sunday school teacher: "I've been married thirty years, and praise Jesus, my husband has never seen my naked body. It's a sin against God to let a man see your body. Don't ever let a man make you a cheap woman." Among other pearls of wisdom, she admonished the girls, "Never, never sit on a boy's lap. That . . . "—the teacher's voice lowered to a whisper as she looked over her shoulder and then back at the girls—"is how girls end up pregnant."

Ever mindful of the need to outrun racist stereotypes, we were taught to avoid red clothing and, above all, red lipstick, which one mother scathingly called "the bite of blood." We kept our hair "neatly dressed" with Royal Crown or Dixie Peach, our legs Vasolined, our African bottoms girdled, and our well-concealed bosoms sprinkled with baby powder.

One of the biggest problems is that despite all this lecturing, few black parents issued factual information about sex, often because they feared that we would put what we knew into action.[15] This was certainly Dr. Wade's experience. She grew up hearing that men only want "one thing" from women, but no one explained what the one thing was. In her family's case, the strict sexual rearing was coupled with the family belief that the three most important acts in life included breathing, praying, and going to college. But in many other black families, especially when the parents were not educated and there were no clear goals set for their daughters, this lack of information was a severe detriment. A sense of hope for the future can make all the difference as to whether or not a girl abstains from sex.

As Dr. Wyatt explains, "When children receive only fear-inducing information or warnings that they cannot understand, it may serve only to increase their fear and shame rather than prohibit them from engaging in forbidden behavior."[16]

Given the terror of sex that was instilled in so many of us, it's not surprising that one of the most frightening images was of the hot black mama. Writing in *Essence* magazine, author Bebe Moore Campbell drew a compelling picture: "Skin-tight red dress, thigh high, back out, cleavage showing. Blonde wig all askew. 'Hey, sugar! Come on and party with me.' High, round fanny. Gum-chewing. Streetwise. 'Hey, baby. You wanna party with me?' We know her too well. She haunts us. We move far away from where she struts, and breathe a sigh of relief. Then we turn on our television sets, and there she is again."[17]

Campbell's allusion to finding this "fallen black woman" on TV is no coincidence. The myth of our sexual insatiability has been fed by the media. The image of the black prostitute is so often used in the media that popular black actresses complain that they are so frequently asked to portray hookers that they have to turn down roles. And few of us have escaped the humiliation of being affronted by some white man either calling from a car, stopping us at clubs or in hotel lobbies, or propositioning us on the assumption that we are prostitutes.

The shame many of us feel concerning sex has been exacerbated by poverty and abuse. These factors have driven some of us—as happens among members of all races—into the sex industry. This should not be surprising since a direct outcome of being shamed is acting shamelessly. Selling sex is a powerfully rageful (and self-destructive) way of defying the narrow confines of black "ladyhood." Even more, many who make this choice are trying to escape lives of devastating poverty and hopelessness. In addition, many sex workers feel shame about having been sexually abused in childhood.

Clearly, only a small percentage of us are driven to prostitution, but others among us suffer with sexual dysfunctions connected to childhood incest or sexual abuse. Reactions can range from shutting down sexually to acting out sexually.

Though our individual experiences differ, our collective history and the resultant childhood experiences that caused us to feel fear and shame have taken their toll on our sexual freedom. And even a normal, healthy sexual response becomes a double-edged sword when wielded by a woman deprived of love and emotional nurturing.

Our Emotional Legacy

As a result of our brutal history, many of us have lost the beautiful and sacred part of our sexual selves. In ancient spiritual practices, the feminine spirit played an important role in rituals. In some cultures, priests and priestesses chose the men or women they desired as partners and joined with them in sacred rituals to create a union of their spirits as a way to experience and draw closer to the divine. Today, the idea of honoring the feminine spirit may seem strange. Those of us raised in various Christian denominations weren't even allowed in the pulpit.

In the late sixties, Brenda Lane Richardson, the first woman to aspire to the ministry in a small black Baptist seminary, occasionally delivered fiery sermons in local parishes. Some of her male colleagues believed it was sinful for a woman to lift her voice in the church. One male seminarian, infuriated by her ambitions and determined to "bring her down," drove her out to a country road, demanded sex, and, when she refused, pushed her out of the car, telling her to walk home. Months later, a small contingent of her harassers made a speech on the steps of the main building of the school, denouncing her with lies concerning her "whorish sexual life." (Among the charges: She was said to have been spotted dancing in a New York disco, and she wore miniskirts.) When administrators failed to come to her defense, she left the school.

Although some churches have adopted more liberal attitudes, women's femininity and sexuality are still feared and suppressed in most religions. This loss affects the way we view ourselves and our sexuality. What are your views today concerning sexuality and spirituality? Do you feel your body and spirit are separate? Have you ever given yourself, as a spiritual being, permission to be sensual and sexual?

Like all feelings, sexual feelings are energy, and when energy is suppressed, it builds and bursts out in destructive ways. In Eastern medical practices, the unobstructed flow of energy forms the basis for good health. Once energy is blocked, the body no longer has the ability to renew itself and maintain optimal vitality. Unexpressed grief or rage, as well as unexpressed sexual feelings, blocks the energy flow. Repressed sexual feelings may even show up in the reproductive difficulties we talked about earlier. If you've had fibroid tumors, fertility problems, or any physical difficulties concerning your reproductive system, consider how they might be connected to your sexual history or attitudes about sex.

Some of the questions you might ask include: What did I learn about sex as a child? What were my mother's and father's views about sex? Through actions or words, did my parents communicate the message that sexuality was something that could be ignored or something to look forward to?

If you believe sex is better when you're high, ask yourself: What experience from my past am I trying to block out?

In looking back on your childhood and the experiences that affected your sexuality, consider what you learned about masturbation: the rhythmic, self-stimulation of your genitals or breasts. So many of us have been taught that we exist to take care of and give pleasure to others that the idea of masturbation may run counter to our view of ourselves as caretakers. Studies indicate that we are far less likely to masturbate than our white counterparts. Like many people, a lot of us were taught that the practice was sinful. But if you consider that women are possessors of the only organ that exists solely for sexual pleasure—the clitoris[18]—you begin to realize that God wouldn't have given us something this wonderful and then posted a "hands off" sign.

When Dr. Jocelyn Elders spoke out in favor of masturbation, she was removed from the office of surgeon general. But masturbation is perfectly normal and healthy, and it is not something we do "instead of." In fact, self-stimulation is simply a different kind of pleasure that can be enjoyed whether or not we're in a relationship. Studies indicate that women who masturbate reach orgasm 95 percent of the time, have increased sexual desire and more positive feelings about sex, and are more orgasmic with their partners.[19] If you're still hesitant about masturbation, try to keep the subject in perspective. It sure is preferable to (1) putting up with men who don't appreciate you or whom you don't respect or (2) being numbed out and insisting that you no longer care about sex. Whether as an addendum to a sexual relationship or as something to keep you content while you're (temporarily) solo, remember that your genitals, as well as all of your sexuality, belong to you. Claim them and care for them lovingly.

If you're married or in a long-term relationship, be aware that after a while the sexual appetite between two long-term partners undergoes a change. Although the partners lose their ravenous hunger for one another, the heat does not have to die down. The key to long-term passion is to keep your lover guessing about what will happen next. After reading Ken Starr's report on President Clinton's sexual indiscretions, one woman, whose children were out for sleepovers, met her husband at the door wearing a tam and holding two cigars—nothing else. She told him she wanted to speak to him in her "oval office."

In addition to playfulness, we must remember to welcome the Spirit into our sexual relationships. Clinical psychologist Dr. Darlene Powell Hopson has said she teaches her clients an invocation that, in part, she learned from fellow author Iyanla Vanzant: "Dear God, I love you and being your child. You made me a sexual being and I want to experience closeness and fulfillment with my partner. My soul yearns for the pleasure and satisfaction of being spiritually and physically intimate with my partner."[20] You may want to close with the words, "Please continue to remain with me and in me, forever."

Asking God to be with us in our most intimate, committed relationships will also help us to express our sexuality without the guilt and shame many of us have internalized, including lesbian, bisexual and transgender sisters who often struggle for self-acceptance in the harsh climate created by homophobic religious teachings.

It is also shame that can make many of us reluctant to list past and current sex partners, even if we know that list is for our eyes only. How would that feel for you? It can be helpful to do so because a list such as this allows you to evaluate how you have changed over the years. Lovers reflect your emotional state. As you move through this list, remember that most women have had the hurtful experience of having men pursue them and then, after giving in and making love, never hearing from the men again. If this has happened to you, write down beside this man's name how you felt at the time. While compiling this list, also consider whether you have used sex to control a partner. If so, make this notation alongside that name. What was the outcome?

If you are currently in a sexual relationship and you find that you often argue soon after having sex or the next day, keep in mind that the sense of intimacy that sex provides can be so frightening that you might be devising ways to keep your partner at arm's length. You might want to discuss this tendency with your partner, stating that next time you hope to build on this intimacy rather than discourage it.

Other areas you will want to begin exploring may include past incidents of sexual abuse or rape. We realize this may be an extremely painful issue for you, but now that you have worked through some of your major issues of shame and abandonment, you will feel empowered to heal in this area. Begin by considering whether you blamed yourself for these horrendous incidents.

If you shared the information with someone else, how did she or he handle it? Also, how might this abuse have affected your choice of sexual partners? If you have been sexually abused, we urge you to talk with a therapist and join a survivors' support group (such as Incest Survivors Anonymous). Like so many of our deep wounds, this is not something you can simply put behind you on your own.

HEALING OUR SEXUALITY/ EMBRACING FREEDOM

Sexual Rage Release Work

If you have been sexually abused, use cushions to represent your perpetrators and speak to each in turn. Hit each pillow with a long-handled wooden spoon, tennis racket, or rolled towel. Be sure to speak each time you land a blow. Yell, curse, or scream at them, but release this pain from your body. Be assured that this person (or people) deserves to have the hell knocked out of him, and oblige him by doing just that, even if this was a family member you loved. Repeat this exercise as often as is necessary, being sure to follow up by comforting yourself with loving words and hugs.

Be aware that there may also be adults from your past who failed to protect you from this predator. If so, be sure to include these individuals in your rage work, hitting the pillow and saying something such as, "I was just a little girl. You should have protected me."

Abortion Grief Ritual

This ritual is adapted from one created by fertility therapist Niravi Payne.[21] You'll want to invite a lover, friend, or relative to support you during this ritual, or it can be performed during an abundance group meeting. You may also want to dedicate this service to your ancestors who lost children when they were kidnapped or sold away; although you haven't endured this kind of loss, you can grieve for your ancestors in a way they never could allow themselves to. To prepare the room for your service, you will need some comforting background music, candles, a vase of fresh flowers, small cushions, and candles to represent the souls of fetuses you have aborted. Finally, include in your dress an African head wrap, kente scarf, or any jewelry that may symbolize to you your African heritage, in homage to the hundreds of thousands of now-departed ancestors who either were taken away from their infants or had their children sold away.

Before the ritual begins, write a letter to the unborn soul (or souls) explaining why you couldn't welcome him or her into your life at that particular time. You may want to explain the circumstances of your pregnancy, especially in light of what you now understand about yourself concerning your healing work. You can read this letter during the ceremony.

Begin by lighting candles for the soul of each fetus you have aborted. Sitting comfortably and breathing deeply, invite the spirits of your ancestors into the room. Tell them you want them there because you know they can understand some of the more painful aspects of your life. Thank them for their wisdom, support, and strength. Then begin reading aloud the letter you wrote for your unborn.

Finish by saying, "Please forgive me. I release your soul with love and I wish you well on your journey." Remember that it's just as important to forgive yourself. You made the only choice you could at the time. No woman with better options chooses abortion. You must let go of the guilt that you feel and allow yourself to grieve and move on.

If you find yourself crying, don't try to "pull yourself together." God gave us our tears to cleanse our souls and release emotions. Let them work their magic.

Considering Weight and Sex

Weight gain is sometimes connected to the excess warnings many of us heard about sex, or it may be an unconscious attempt to put "armor" on our bodies to protect ourselves from further sexual abuse. Did you gain a great deal of weight during childhood or adolescence that you have retained? If you have struggled with being overweight, take out your journal and write a letter to your body explaining why you felt the need to protect yourself from sexual attention, and describe your intention to change and how you can make loving, self-affirming decisions regarding your body and sexuality.

Talking to Your Body

Rejecting your sexuality and your body perpetuates the old notion that there's something intrinsically wrong with you. We wear the stamp of Mother Africa. Many of us have lovely high derrieres. Some of us have long Masai legs or soft rounded curves, and all of us have been painted by the sun in an ever-fashionable palette of earth tones: beiges, tans, and browns. Demonstrate love for your body with warm, fragrant baths or showers, and afterward, rub yourself down with a rich lotion or oil. Start with your toes. Tell them to be fully relaxed and energized, thank them for all that they do for you, then tell them, "I love you." Gradually work your way through every area of your body, relaxing and thanking each part and stating how much you love it.

When you have finished with your face, stroke your hair lovingly. Look in your mirror and affirm: "Dear Body, I love you! Thank you for all that you do for me."

Your body's functioning constitutes one of nature's greatest miracles. Recognize your body as sacred, truly the temple of your soul.

The sense of being sacred—internally and externally—which we have worked toward in this and preceding chapters, will be tremendously helpful to you as you work through the action-oriented steps detailed in part three.

PART THREE

The Keys to Self–Love

10

Forgiving Those
Who Hurt Us

One of the most important aspects of forgiveness is that it provides a sense of relief for ourselves. There's an old saying: "Holding on to resentment is like drinking poison and expecting the other person to die." Our resentment doesn't hurt others, but it does hurt us. A lot of people mistakenly believe that forgiveness means that we accept our perpetrators' damaging behavior. We believe that their acts may be unforgivable but that we can forgive the flawed human beings who committed them. Seen this way, forgiveness can set us free to move on and love unconditionally.

In this book, we have shown that the road to forgiveness and emotional freedom begins with the larger picture, that is, with those originally involved in the slave trade. This includes sellers and buyers and owners as well as those who created the lies that would justify keeping our people in bondage and would seal our fate for the next three centuries. We're also talking about those who looked the other way and ignored the injustices of slavery and the racism that ensued, as well as any latter-day racist teachers, counselors, neighbors, bosses, realtors, salesgirls, delivery men, or bus drivers—in short all those who robbed us of peace and served as barriers to better jobs, safer neighborhoods, and higher education.

Of course this doesn't mean that we're including in this embittered portrait the face of every nonblack person we've known. There are husbands and lovers, friends and colleagues, famous as well as unknown righteous whites from the past and present who could be included in our own family portraits. As Toni Morrison has pointed out, we don't paint white America with a broad brush; we've always known how to distinguish white allies from white enemies, because our lives depended on it.[1] Despite these notable exceptions, the people who have a history of hurting us are white.

Many of us hoped that white America would jump at President Clinton's suggestion that our nation owes the descendants of slaves an apology. Can you imagine crowding around a TV set with your family and loved ones to listen to the president say what we have longed to hear: "It's true. Terrible crimes were committed against your ancestors, and as a result, our lives are better than they would have been had these tragedies not been perpetrated, while your life is worse off as a result. We deeply regret the pain we have caused you and your ancestors and we intend to redress the wrongs."

However, many of us responded angrily to Clinton's suggestion, understandably, because we sensed the apology would not include these sentiments and that anything else would be less than heartfelt. We are distrustful because we are constantly being rewounded. As Nobel laureate Wole Soyinka has written: "It is futile to pretend that the scars are not real or that contemporary actualities . . . do not re-open the wounds."[2] Equally as infuriating is the fact that white Americans often refuse to see the realities of our lives and their part in our pain.

Many rejected the notion of an apology by claiming that since their ancestors weren't slaveholders, they were not culpable. In general, white Americans are unwilling to accept the notion of white privilege, the idea that they are more likely to be in positions of power simply because of the color of their skin. There are some white liberals who may believe this, but many others are so convinced they don't have anything to learn about race ("some of my best friends are black") that they remain mired in prejudice. It is part of the process of denial. After all, apologies could lead to reparations or restitution and to the necessity of debunking the old myths and acknowledging that we are truly equals. The chances are slim that a full apology will occur in our lifetimes, which leaves us wondering how we can forgive the unforgivable.

As we have demonstrated in this book, forgiveness is an out-

growth of the healing process. In Parts I and II, we formed a foundation for forgiving: We worked at peeling away the layers of history,
expressing our feelings, and gaining understanding into the ways we
have coped—for good or ill. As a by-product of this work, we came to
understand some of the factors that influenced those who hurt us.
We can't understand all the factors that contributed to what was done
to us and to our ancestors, but it's awe-inspiring to consider that we
who have been victims of senseless violence—victims of a nation's
greed, rage, and desperation—have the power to grant ourselves the
freedom we need and desire.

One of the most important lessons that comes from this work is
the recognition that we are shaped by the world around us.
Forgiveness presumes a violation of justice, as well as brokenness and
fragmentation that need healing. It does not blindly excuse or casually ignore injustice; forgiveness is God's answer to the pain of injustice. It is the power of healing, the possibility of an open future in
spite of what has gone wrong.

Forgiving also means we finally get to cancel a debt that's more
than four hundred years old. When someone hurts us, we're left with
the sense that something—peace, joy, dignity, happiness—was stolen
from us and that the other person owes it to us to give it back. An attitude such as this puts us in the position of being a miserly banker,
holding an IOU against someone who can never pay us back. But
when we forgive, we release the transgressor from his debt and the
showdown is over.[3]

Of course forgiveness is not as simple as willing ourselves to
absolve others. One place to start is to consider the hidden benefits of
our resentment. As weird as it sounds, we can develop attachments to
painful feelings; living without them might feel scary and leave us
feeling empty.[4]

Dr. Wade asked one of her clients, Maveleen, age thirty-seven,
what it would feel like to assume that every person she encountered,
regardless of race, was her potential ally. At first, Maveleen said that
was impossible to imagine, but when pressed, she stood to demonstrate her thoughts. Balling her hands into fists and wildly swinging
them in a protective posture, she said, "In my mind, this is what I
always have to do to protect myself in the world. I never know when
the next hit will come, so I have to be prepared." Dropping her hands,

letting them hang in a relaxed position by her sides, she added, "And this is what it would be like if I didn't have to always be on guard and protect myself from enemies." When asked how it felt to not be on guard, Maveleen said, "Very vulnerable, scared really, unprotected. I feel better with my fists flying."

Her response was quite typical. We developed defensive postures so we could survive in this world, and our personalities and behaviors were shaped around these defenses.[5] When we consider a task as major as forgiving a nation of people who have hurt us but who are largely unwilling to admit that they have, it becomes apparent that putting our "fists down" requires a radical rethinking. Perhaps our mistake has been waiting for the world to change, when forgiveness requires that *we* change. Here's what we mean by that.

Just for a minute, think back to a time when you felt powerful, in control, and admired. It may have been during childhood when, for example, out of all the students in class, you correctly guessed the number of gumballs in a jar. Or maybe it was a time when you made a speech and held the audience rapt. Or perhaps it was commencement day or even a quiet moment after mastering a technique that you had been laboring to understand. One woman, who had been raised in a predominately white neighborhood and attended schools where all the children, except her, were white, recalled visiting her cousins down South and spending a day at their segregated school, where she was revered for being a girl from the big city. Whatever the occasion, travel back in your mind to that time, and feel the glow. Listen to the applause and cheers even if they were your own hurrahs.

Now hold on to the glowing warmth of that moment as you contemplate the present. You can take this positive feeling with you when you go out into the world. *Assume* that the people you encounter, of every race and ethnicity, are wise enough to admire you for your many gifts. Accept the fact that there will always be at least one person out there who is unwilling to congratulate you, who in fact resents you. Still basking in your glow—which provides peace, joy, and comfort, and even lightens your load—say to yourself, "I am empowered to forgive this person for her shortcomings. I choose to do so."

Breathe in that freedom. Know that you are letting go, canceling the debt. Because now you have the answer as to how you can forgive so many: It is one person at a time. Use this technique as many times as you need it, and you will find your negative thoughts softening and your load lightening. Remember what Dr. Martin Luther King, Jr. told his followers: "Don't ever let anybody bring you down so low that you hate him." Forgiveness allows us to rise above those who hate us.

Your growing sense of empowerment will allow you to narrow your focus as you work to forgive the significant people in your life who have hurt you. For some of us, that may be even more difficult than forgiving a group of anonymous people. But for the sake of your own healing, it is equally as important to forgive the people you love. It has been written that forgiveness "does not settle all questions of blame and justice and fairness; to the contrary, often it evades those questions. But it does allow a relationship to start over."[6]

During one of our abundance group meetings, we introduced the subject of forgiving loved ones who have hurt us. We are sharing some of the members' responses because we believe their work can give you a sense of how this process works.

When Dr. Wade brought up the subject of forgiving parents, Mary Ann, whose mother rejected her for having browner skin tones than her sister, was quick to say, "I know I've already forgiven my family." When members of the group immediately questioned this, Mary Ann admitted she hadn't completely faced her anger about the abuse, but added that she felt willing to let her anger surface. "I understand the connection," she said. "If I can't let the anger up, I can't really forgive because I'm still holding on." Dr. Wade offered an enthusiastic "yes."

Minutes later, everyone seemed surprised by Ondine, who had insisted in the past that she couldn't get angry with her parents because it would be disrespectful. She said, "I'm good and angry with my mother and father!" The members of the group cheered. She added, "And I'm not ready to forgive. Last night I confronted my father about abandoning me, and he told me I was too nice a person to get caught up in worrying about my own feelings, that I had to think of others. I know he doesn't care about me or my feelings. He's always bragging about me being a doctor, but I told him I wasn't going to let him continue telling his friends he raised me. He didn't, and I won't let him take the credit for it."

After the cheers had died down, Dr. Wade congratulated Ondine on setting boundaries, telling her father what she would no longer allow in their relationship. Dr. Wade then suggested that they all take the time to symbolically confront relatives who had hurt them. With each member moving to a different location in the room, they engaged in release work: striking pillows, confronting their perpetrators. The room was filled with their shouts. "I matter!" "My feelings count!" "I deserve love!" "It wasn't my job to take care of you!" The anger, hurt, and pain seemed to flood out as everyone wept and pounded. This was the deepest release work anyone in the group had achieved.

When the women were spent, they worked through the three-step forgiveness process, which follows this section. They continued by visualizing a shower of violet fire washing down around and through them, clearing their energy fields so that their bodies, emotions, minds, and spirits returned to a peaceful state. Finally, members responded to the questions: "How did I gain? What lessons did I learn by going through the hurt and trauma my parents inflicted on me?" This was an opportunity, as Oprah Winfrey has said, to actually feel grateful for our abuse.

Marisa, who was raised in foster care, said: "Because I had to do everything for myself, I learned to be a very hard worker. And I'm very independent."

Eva, whose mother moved her from one predominately white town to another, where she was taunted about her African features, said, "I always remember how it feels to suffer, so I'm careful of others' feelings."

Mary Ann added: "I have a close relationship with God that began when I was a child because I had nowhere else to turn."

One by one, they accepted the gifts born of the hurt and pain and that reached back across generations.

Members of the group incorporated six significant elements in their forgiveness work. These elements include recognizing their injuries, expressing how particular experiences caused one to feel, expressing their hurt and anger, setting boundaries to protect themselves from further pain, considering the possibility of reconciliation,[7] and identifying the gains that occurred as a result of their traumas. As you work to forgive those you love, use these elements as guidelines, making certain to consider the gifts that grow out of your losses.

We have found that the short meditation "Letting Your Light Shine," presented in chapter 7, can help you feel centered and quiet inside, in preparation for forgiveness. Be sure to take time to ask your Higher Power the following questions: What happened that hurt me? What did this event (or series of events) cause me to feel? How did those around me respond to my feelings? What decisions did I make as a result of this experience? (After each question, listen for an answer.)

Then proceed by saying the following (inserting the name of the person who hurt you), while still in a meditative state, with as much feeling as possible:

1. I forgive _____ for anything and everything he has [they have] done to hurt me in any time and any space.

2. From the bottom of my heart, I ask _____ to forgive me for anything I may have done to hurt _____ in any time or any space.

3. From the bottom of my heart, I forgive myself for anything I'm holding against myself that relates to _____ from any time or any space.

Keep in mind that forgiveness is a process. For example, it would be impossible genuinely to forgive your lover on the day you found out he had cheated on you. You would need time to grieve the loss of trust, experience your anger and resentment, and bolster your inner resources. Eventually, with the passage of time, you might begin to work toward forgiveness. Trigger-happy forgiveness, as author Lewis Smedes calls it, is actually controlling, because it is a way of trying to show the wrongdoer how much more magnanimous you are. The other person ends up feeling ashamed, not forgiven.[8] Meanwhile, you still carry the burden of resentment.

When you're engaged in the three-step forgiveness process, don't worry if anger surfaces. Use the emotional-release exercises introduced in Part II. Anger can not only weigh you down but turn inward and close your heart. Even if you feel you don't want to forgive, you can continue working toward it by at least praying for the willingness to open your heart.

Keep in mind that the forgiveness process can also be extremely helpful in dealing with any resentment that you continue to hold about the way your ancestors were treated. Andrea, a client struggling with depression and a long history of abandonments, was able to trace this pattern back to her great grandmother. Every generation of her family fell into a pattern of leaving children behind for one reason or another. During an emotional-release exercise, Andrea used a pillow as a stand-in for a white slaveholder because she felt deeply that her unknown great-great grandmother had been sold off by this person. Speaking as this great-great grandmother, she began to express her grief over the loss of her children. It wasn't until Andrea began working on forgiving this imaginary historical figure that she began weeping. It felt as if the weight of centuries was being washed away.

A special issue arose for Andrea because her husband is European. She had to forgive him because his life was easier simply because he automatically enjoyed white privileges. In addition, if you are in a love relationship, you may have to practice forgiveness on a daily basis because it's easy for people who are close to rewound one another.

Pay special attention to forgiving yourself if you are holding past actions against yourself. No matter what mistakes you feel you've made, it's time to let go and free up the energy you need to create a better life for yourself. When the self-blame comes up, remember to neutralize the message by talking to yourself lovingly.

It will help if you think of forgiveness, not as forgetting, but as a kind of remembering centered in God, an opportunity for your own self-transformation, and an acceptance of and appreciation for the lives we have formed over time. The Creator has taken the people we have become, shaped by our loves, our desires, and our suffering, and graced us with an alternate set of beliefs that also grew directly from our slavery experience. We call these *life-enhancing beliefs,* and in the next chapter you can learn how to tap into them and make yourself simply irresistible.

11

Using Life-Enhancing Beliefs

Our ancestors were able to survive the ordeal of slavery and the Jim Crow years because they carried within them a set of what we call "life-enhancing beliefs," which could not be destroyed. Existing alongside the anti-intimacy messages formed during slavery, these beneficial messages are the jewels of our slave legacy. Tunnel deep into our souls, and they can be found in abundance. When first extracted, some may look dull from disuse, but once polished they have the power to reflect the greatest light. Most of us have always known these beliefs existed; our parents and grandparents often exhibited them in flashes of brilliance. It is now our turn to call forth all of these positive beliefs so that we can create the lives we desire, and attract and maintain love.

THE SEVEN LIFE-ENHANCING BELIEFS

God Loves Me

Our faith in the divine, which sustained our ancestors, lives on in many of us. An estimated 80 percent of us profess to be regular churchgoers; a figure that's significantly higher than the general population.[1] And as we heal and grow we can learn to put our faith into action. Della Reese, star of television's *Touched by an Angel* and an ordained minister, did just that.

After suffering through a physically abusive first marriage and several more failed relationships, she met a man named Franklin Lett, who seemed kind but too "light-skinned" for her taste. Reese eventually realized that she was tired of being alone, and one day, she told God, "I don't choose well and you know I don't choose well. Everything about me wants to be loved, to be held. I want to be kissed. I want to be swayed. You choose for me." She knew that God would help her if she was willing to change, and she did. She opened her heart and learned to look beyond what she could see; no more rigid demands about dark skin, tall frame, muscular build. She waited and continued praying that her heart would remain open. The next time she ran into Franklin Lett, she saw him for who he really was: a loving, steady, and faithful brotherman. They married in 1983, and today Reese views her husband as an angel who came into her life. Her message to other sisters is that if they're willing to do their part, the Divinity "will do the same thing for you."[2]

By opening our hearts and remembering that God is not a dating service with which we can register desired physical and material characteristics, we too can attract the love we need and desire. Begin by writing a letter to God explaining the qualities that you need (not want) in a relationship, such as a sense of humor, kindness, and spirituality. Don't worry about your penmanship, spelling, or grammar. Just write from your heart. Close your letter by thanking the Creator. Just above your signature, write, "Thy will be done." Place this letter inside your Good Book: a Bible, the Koran, or any work that you find inspiring. When you need it, visualize the union you anticipate. And always, as you return it to its sacred space, repeat aloud, "Thy will be done." When you have healed sufficiently to open your heart to a lover, you and your mate can read this letter aloud together and enjoy knowing that you manifested your heart's desire.

Please take this exercise to heart. It's more than simply a letter. It is your soul's cry, a hope-filled, winged, airbound prayer sent to one who is omnipotent. The Creator wants us to ask and has made us a promise, one that we may have forgotten but surely have heard—perhaps while sitting on a back porch along a country road or in a city kitchen, the air filled with the scent of Sunday's chicken. The word has been passed on from mother to father, down to daughter and son. And if we but listen, we can hear it. For the great God Almighty keeps promises and has pledged to help us if only we help ourselves.

I Can Make Something from Nothing

If you look back on your childhood and the people you admired, there's a good chance that you knew someone who seemed capable of making "something from nothing." A history of scarcity forced our people to hone their creativity. Black women are the inventors of everyday items, such as the ironing board and hairbrush. And keep in mind women like Henrietta Bradberry, a homemaker who invented the submarine torpedo discharger; and more recently, Dr. Patricia Bath, the opthamologist who invented a revolutionary laser technology device for removing eye cataracts. Now that we have removed barriers that once kept us from accepting the generosity of the universe, we can also use our creativity to make ourselves more attractive, and that includes everything from creating financial freedom to devising ways to have more time so we can plant a beautiful flower garden.

Some people don't believe that everyone has a creative streak. Vonnie, thirty-one, the single mother of a fifteen-year-old boy and a practical nurse who spent much of her time doing "grunt" work at the hospital, couldn't imagine that she would ever be anything but impoverished. Her son worked hard after school, saving every extra penny, hoping one day to attend college. Motivated by her son's ambitions, Vonnie began to envision a better life for herself.

Her life had certainly been no picnic. She had dropped out of high school at fifteen, when she became pregnant, at which time her mother had repeatedly told her that she was ruining her life. When Vonnie was twenty, her husband was murdered in a fight, and she began to believe her mother's assessment.

But her attitude shifted. She asked God to help her develop the best of what was in her and gave thanks for her abundance: good health, a steady job, a roof over her head, and a son who wanted to make something of himself. She realized she had so much that she could help others, and so early one Thanksgiving, she put together a food basket for a sick and elderly shut-in from her church. Vonnie cooked and baked, and she added a jar of homemade ginger-peach preserves and watermelon rind pickles. As an afterthought, she walked to the woods to find acorns, pine cones, and colorful leaves for decorating the basket. The forest may have looked dead to someone else, but Vonnie felt like a wonderstruck girl as she took in the autumnal colors and woodland textures. She prepared a stunning basket for her friend. Looking back, she realizes that was the day she officially started her business: filling, decorating, and delivering customized gift baskets.

It wasn't long before her business was thriving. Three years later, she sent her son to college and was able to start putting funds away for her future. Now engaged to be married, Vonnie met her future fiance when she advertised for a bookkeeper to help manage her growing business. Like Vonnie, we can't know for sure where our creativity will lead us, but we can be assured it's always someplace exciting and worthwhile.

If you already make a living using your creativity, you will find that removing existing barriers and freeing up the creative force, which is the Great Creator within us, will put an end to artistic blocks you may have encountered. Whether you use your renewed creative drive to be a better artist, mother, lover, businesswoman, office worker, or laborer, it will bring positive change to your life.

There are four important steps you can follow to develop the artist within you:

1: *Reject limitations.* On a strip of toilet paper, write down all the reasons you think you *cannot* be creative. This list might include objections such as "I've never been creative," "I don't have time," or "I should be happy with what I already have." When you have finished with your list, ball up the toilet paper or rip it to pieces and flush it down the toilet, where it belongs. Repeat this process every day, until you have tamed any inner voices that might be blocking you. Replace them with the affirmation: "God in me is my creative power."

2: *Study nature's handiwork.* You can hone your appreciation for the Creator's talents by walking in a garden or forest, stopping by the local pet shop and checking out the varieties of tropical fish, or doing something as simple as pausing momentarily at the flower stand in your local supermarket. While doing so, say to yourself, "I welcome God's creative force in my life."

3: *Recognize the creative spirit within you.* Give the artist within you a name, a face, a healthy body, and a home filled with abundance and love. You may find it easier, as others have, to imagine this spirit as an innocent, unwounded child who has a pure and trusting spirit. Envision her in Africa or in any favorite place you associate with good times and happiness. Give her permission to feel and express her anger: Creativity involves passion, not "niceness." This life-filled spirit will seem more real if you write about her in the journal you've set aside for your emotional work or draw a picture of her. Or when you're on your way to or from work, envision her in your mind's eye.

4: *Run away with your imagination.* Set aside time each week when you can commune with the artist within: Write, sketch, create lyrics or poetry, think up creative solutions to office problems, sew, cook for fun. The better you know your creative spirit, the more you can invite your true self into your work life and love relationships. This is a wonderful way to celebrate yourself and a powerful way to build your self-love.

I Can Make a Way When There Seems to Be No Way

"I have a dream that one day my four little children will live in a nation where they will not be judged by the color of their skin but by the content of their character."[3] Dr. King's unforgettable words motivated hundreds of thousands of us to follow him despite the water hoses, dogs, and police batons that were turned on us. Because he held up a torch allowing us to look into the darkness, we saw that our hearts craved freedom, dignity, and justice.

What motivates you to keep working for change? When Dr. Wade asks women what incentives they used to make a way when there seemed to be no way, they offered answers similar to Dr. King's. Many said their children were great motivators. Maggie, thirty-seven, said, "I don't want my girls growing up believing everyone except black folks can have success and marry." Many of us had parents who viewed us as their prime motivation. Their desire for us to have better lives kept them going through times that were far darker than those we live in. Other women say their own personal needs are prompting them to change. Edith, fifty-nine, put it bluntly: "Before I die, I want to know what it's like to have something of my own, and I'm talking about love."

We all need inspiration, and we can provide it for ourselves by reading books about famous African Americans who triumphed against the odds. For quick fixes, post photos over your work space of famous black leaders. Their stories can be particularly helpful as you work through specific blocks. For example, if you're struggling with scarcity issues concerning money, put a small photo of Mary McLeod Bethune in your wallet. Her image can remind you that abundance is in the eye of the beholder. In October of 1904, Bethune had only $1.50, but she used that to start a school for "Negro" girls, which eventually evolved into what is now the highly respected Bethune-Cookman College.

If you feel too tired to exercise, place a photo of track star Wilma Rudolph (1940–1994) on your nightstand. Although polio and scarlet fever left her unable to walk without braces or orthopedic shoes until she was twelve, she became the first American woman to win an Olympic gold medal.[4]

A good source for quick motivation is the African American Knowledge Cards. The size of playing cards, they are packaged in decks and contain photos with condensed biographies. Knowledge cards are available in novelty shops or by writing to Pomegrante Publications, P.O. Box 6099, Rohnert Park, CA 94927.

To motivate yourself for any life-changing project, you can follow this quick action plan:

1: Write down a specific goal, such as "I am a successful business owner." (It's important to write your goal in its completed form, because the subconscious is quite literal.)

2: Take one specific action step each day toward that goal.

3: Call a supportive friend or relative and tell her about your goal; then ask her to check in with you each week to help you measure your progress and help you talk through any fear that might derail you.

4: Chant over and over, "I am a success, I am a success. I will persist until I succeed. I will persist until I succeed." Use the power of repetition to build a new belief.

You'll get there!

My Heart Will Guide Me if I Listen

If our ancestors hadn't been intuitive, we would not be here today. Their inner guidance system was necessary for their survival. A lot of us were taught there was something sinful about psychics who use their inner vision to predict the future. No matter how you weigh in on the subject, know that what we're talking about is something different. Our intuition actually speaks to us all of the time. For instance, it was a hunch that convinced Brenda Richardson to accompany her friend to Grand Central Station on the afternoon that she met her future husband. It's the voice that told you to check on a loved one when your presence made all the difference in the world.

The problem is never that our intuition is "out of order"; it's that we don't know how to encourage and listen to it. In case you think this area is flaky, you should know that some business schools offer courses on intuitive management. We can and should use our intuitive gifts to improve our lives; this is what they were intended to do. Unfortunately, most of us now have unfocused inner vision and rely solely on our emotions and intellect.

You'll find that once you combine feelings and intelligence with intuition, you'll be empowered to change the course of your life in general and your love life in particular. Your "third eye" can help you make the right first impressions, choose topics of conversation that can draw others to you, and help you pick up on someone else's strengths and flaws so that you can decide whether or not you want to invest your time in a particular relationship. Think of all the occasions when you've said: "How could I not have known when all the signs were there?" Or you might have thought: "If only I'd been aware of the mistakes I was making, I could have kept him in my life." Your inner vision will help you know in advance instead of when it's too late. Our intuition gives us constant feedback. The problem for most of us is that we don't listen to it.

Learning to tap into your intuition takes practice, but it's not difficult, especially now that you're engaged in healing work. In fact, since the second chapter in this book, you've been talking to your intuition, referring to it as your Higher Power. Here's the method Dr. Wade teaches her clients for accessing intuition:

1: Visualize light flowing from the top of your head down and out through your body, down and out through your feet, forming roots that connect you to the earth. See this light forming a nine-foot shield all around you. Relax, breathing deeply.

2: Focus on a question or dilemma for which you would like an answer. Ask inwardly, addressing your intuition directly: "Higher Power, please tell me or show me the answer I need."

3: Simply let go. Don't try to "think" up an answer. Keep your mind quiet by focusing on the light between your eyebrows.

4: Take the first image (a thing or color, for instance) or perception that comes to you. You will know whether the answer is a thought or an intuitive answer by considering whether your message came to you in a "flash" or in a linear narrative. Intuition always feels like this: "Aha! I've got it." It's instantaneous, and you will feel as if a light has just turned on. If your image or color seems too cryptic, ask your Higher Power for clarity and more detail.

5: Write down your answer and put it to use.

Intuition is like a muscle. The more you use it, the stronger it becomes. To learn more about using your intuition to create love, read *Practical Intuition in Love*, by Laura Day (New York: HarperCollins, 1998).

I Bring Humor and Joy to My Life

We are the descendants of people who used humor in the Motherland to defeat enemies as well as to entertain friends. In various African cultures, people used "aggressive humor" to defuse hostility and check antisocial behavior, according to historian William Piersen.[5] "A victim of African public ridicule was obliged to give and bear the mocking allusions in somewhat the same manner that in Western society a man is expected to be able to take a joke at his expense whereas he would be justified in avenging an insult."[6]

When our ancestors arrived in the "New" World, they used their humor as a coping mechanism. Langston Hughes called it our "unconscious therapy."[7] Through the years, no matter how bad times were, it seems there have always been many among us who could place our hands on our hips, sway back, and laugh from the soul. If it's true, as Mark Twain observed, that sorrow is a greater source of humor than happiness, it should not be surprising that there are so many famous comedians among our people.

Many of us employ humor unaware that we're doing so. Research suggests that one of the best ways to help someone solve a problem is to tell them a joke. Laughing helps us make connections we might miss otherwise.[8]

In troubled relationships, there is an absence of fun and laughter. Nothing seems funny, unless it's one person making fun of and putting down another. When we have a good sense of humor, and use it, it cools us down when we're angry and soothes us when we're disappointed. And humor unites. As Laura Day explains, joy makes us more attractive to prospective mates and draws them to us. She writes: "The biochemical principles are identical. When we laugh our body produces the same kind of chemicals as when we have a massage, dance, or do other pleasure-producing activities. You look different. You smell different. You're producing different chemicals. . . . Smiles and laughter are powerful aphrodisiacs. . . . Even a simple smile creates profound changes in your biochemistry."[9]

Whether or not you're in a relationship now, remember to lighten your load by seeing funny movies, listening to recordings of famous comedians, and saving jokes, funny stories, and cartoons to share with one another.

In addition, plan relaxed loving moments. If you or your honey have had a hard day, take turns pampering one another. Offer him a massage, and once he's under the covers, pour him a cup of honeyed tea and read to him. Being babied occasionally is something we all need.

I Can Inspire Others to Achieve

We've all seen it. We're watching the Academy Awards. The star steps up to accept the award, and the camera zooms in on this person's spouse. What we don't see, as we listen to the star thank a beloved mate, is all that has transpired between them on the road to success. A mate who can inspire is a force of nature. Such a mate makes us feel as if we can achieve anything we want to. Just listen to D. L. Hughley, star of the TV hit *The Hughleys,* talk about his wife of thirteen years, LaDonna: "She has really made me. She's made me better than I ever could have been by myself."[10] That's the kind of relationship everyone deserves to have.

Ours is a history of inspiring others, and inspiration has been provided by preachers, teachers, and legislators, among others. When it comes to love, once we have worked through the fears that cause controlling behavior, we can learn to give our mates positive, loving support as we encourage, listen, and share our wisdom. Be sure not to confuse support with control. Controlling sounds like this: "Why don't you accept that job offer? The benefits are so much better. You're so smart and creative, they're sure to promote you." Essentially, despite the compliments, this is an order. Telling your honey what to do will generate resentment rather than inspiration.

If you want to offer advice to a lover, first ask if it's okay to make a suggestion. If the response is *yes,* start with provisional language, such as "I wonder . . . " or "It seems . . . " or "Do you think it's possible . . . ?" This is how a suggestion might sound: "Sweetheart, may I make a suggestion related to your career?" If the answer is *yes,* proceed. "I heard that company is really a great place to work. I'm wondering if you're interested in checking it out. I was intrigued when I heard about their benefits." Leave it there—no follow-up questions, no nagging. If your lover is to feel authentic and validated about his career choices, they must be his own.

We're sure you already know that when it comes to trying to inspire anyone, you don't spell out your intentions. If you met someone and said, "I'm going to help you become the person you want to be," his only response would be his back, which is what you'd see as he turned to walk away. According to Drs. Connell Cowan and Melvin Kinder, the authors of *Women Men Love, Women Men Leave,* although men greatly benefit from mutually inspiring relationships, they're so wary of being controlled by women that they might misunderstand. But once they begin to see that they've survived our suggestion with their manhood intact, and they have benefited from our words, "they feel an exhilarating sense of relief because there is some-one with whom they can share burdens, dreams, anxieties, and hopes. They feel larger, fuller, and stronger."[11]

The flip side to all this, of course, is that we, too, get devoted partners who will support us when we most need it. Picture yourself sitting in the audience when he blows you a kiss and says, "This is dedicated to you, my love." (Just make sure, when the camera lights hit, that you ain't wearing no funky dress.)

My Friends Are My Sisters

Our notion of kinship ties, born in the African tribal system, gave rise to the now famous proverb, "It takes a village to raise a child." There is a traditional African song, "Sansa Kroma," which assures children that they will be taken in and provided for by a relative or family in their vil-lage should the need ever arise. Our kinship ties were nourished during slavery, when suddenly-sold mothers had to trust others to step in to raise their children and knew they would do the same. That sense of kin-ship continued in our childhood homes, where we often lived with grandmothers, aunts, or cousins (or people we treated as such). Accustomed to forging "sisterly close" relationships, we can use our notion of extended family to create support groups, help one another to heal, and introduce one another to prospective mates.

While it is crucial for you to continue to pray, affirm, and visualize on your own, it's also of great importance that you begin to organize a support group to add more octane to your efforts. Your group should be composed of other women—whether single, married, or divorced—who believe that together women can transform them-selves and create and sustain healthy relationships.

When looking for prospective members, ask for inner guidance, and trust your intuition. Placing an announcement in a church bul-letin is a good way to start contacting others. Also, contact other women whom you respect, asking them to join and recommend their friends as well. Another method of finding members is to post flyers at locations of weekly twelve-step meetings, such as Al-Anon. You can also post flyers at a local college or university.

What's most important is that you have members who can lovingly and nonjudgmentally support you in your transformation; don't expend too much energy on building up a large group. One or two other members are enough to get started. As time passes, you can continue to recruit members, and as word spreads of your meetings, others will seek you out.

A body of research indicates that praying in a group yields powerful results. United, we can create energy and momentum to fulfill our intentions. Of course, these groups do much more than pray together. There's a scene in the film *Beloved* that reminded us of why our San Francisco abundance group is such a powerful force. In the film, some of the women in the community come to the yard of Sethe, whose life has been destroyed by a ghost from her past. Sethe's neighbors seem to be mindful of the biblical passage (Exodus 14) in which God encourages the Egyptians to stop waiting for divine intervention and to take action. These women have done that, sending food to Sethe and her family, and now they march down the road together, singing God's praises, and they keep on singing, until they run Sethe's ghost away. This act clears the way for Sethe's future, and she has room for love. That's what we're doing in our group: coming together to heal our past, so we can make room for love.

As members of our San Francisco abundance group came together, they found they were able to take steps in their lives that they would not have taken without the group gently prodding and encouraging them. Group members can share experiences, wisdom, passion, and pain. And with so many external pressures, the members will feel stronger working together. As motivational speaker Napolen Hill has explained, the individuals' combined intention multiplies the power exponentially.

As you heal together, members of your group will become like-minded family members. You will exchange details about triumphs in your lives and share late-night and early-morning support.

ABUNDANCE GROUP OPERATING INSTRUCTIONS

Strive to be democratic. Individuals should take turns monthly serving as speaker and secretary. The secretary types up membership lists, contacts people with news about upcoming meetings, and locates bookstores where you can order books you might like to discuss.

Find meeting places (homes, offices, or church settings) where you have enough privacy to share your deepest feelings. Ask members to call in advance when they are unable to attend. Begin each meeting with a prayer, your hands joined as you stand in a circle. Sit in a circle and have members introduce themselves by first name.

Members should be reminded at each meeting that confidentiality is an absolute must. They should refrain from discussing one another with friends or spouses. If members feel they can't trust in the privacy and discretion of the group, they will not feel safe sharing their deep feelings. Repeat the twelve-steps confidentiality motto: "Who you see here, what you hear here, when you leave here, let it stay here."

Take turns reading an excerpt from this book. A designated speaker should share her thoughts and experiences for ten to fifteen minutes at each meeting. Following the speaker's offering, encourage others to discuss issues brought up during the talk or reading.

During these meetings, members should refrain from offering one another advice and, especially, criticism. Each member gets to speak (with an agreed-on time limit) without interruption. Nurture and support one another concerning individual triumphs and opportunities for growth. Encourage women to continue attending meetings, especially when they are feeling discouraged, as well as after beginning relationships.

Depending on the needs of the group, you may elect to have a potluck or rotating dinner at each meeting. (Our San Francisco group had food delivered from local restaurants.)

Group Activities

It's crucial that members either work together as a team of volunteers in various community groups or volunteer as individuals. At each meeting, members should take turns briefly discussing what they have done to help others.

Volunteer work is critical in this transformational work because it enables us to feel a sense of humility. It's no coincidence that most of our religious figures were born and raised in humble circumstances. Humility is a state of being that opens us to God's grace. It gives us a proper sense of ourselves in relation to a larger purpose. Humility opens the door to truths we might otherwise not see.

There are many ways in which we can make a difference in the lives of one person—young or old—or several people. Many people become turned off to volunteer work because they choose jobs that are sheer drudgery to them. That's why it's important to brainstorm with other abundance group members about where and how to find exciting volunteer opportunities that are flexible enough to fit into even the busiest schedules. Working together as a group—sponsoring one family, one classroom, or one Sunday school class—is a fun way to get a lot accomplished.

Your group may also want to consider joining or setting up a chapter of Single Volunteers, an organization that brings singles together. While doing good works, volunteers get a chance to meet other singles who care about helping others. There are Single Volunteer chapters in Washington D.C.; Bucks County, Pennsylvania; southern Florida; Cleveland; the Dallas–Fort Worth area; and western Massachusetts. Founder Anne Lusk began with several women volunteers, then joined a local dating service so she could get a list of bachelors and invited them to join. For information on starting your own group, contact Anne Lusk via the Internet at AnneLusk@aol.com.[12]

If you're someone who enjoys working with clothing, consider hooking up with Dress for Success, an organization that accepts and distributes clothing for low-income women looking for work. For more information, contact the organization at their website: www.dressforsuccess.org

An emotional shift occurs when we stop focusing on how much we need someone and, instead, focus on sharing the love that is within us. The effect is similar to the attraction to a light in a dark forest: People are drawn to us when we are filled with God's luminosity.

After your group has been meeting for a few months and the members have worked through many common issues, you may want to plan a party. Invite men that you know and admire, including single brothers or cousins, office friends, and so on. You can also send out letters to friends asking them to recommend any "emotionally healthy" men they might know, whom you can invite. Over the years, many of us have learned how to network for business purposes; we can use that skill to improve our social lives.

You'll want to start compiling your guest list at least two months in advance. When our San Francisco abundance group planned a party, the friends we'd written to took weeks to respond. Along with our letter, which began with the words "I'm looking for a few good men," we included postage-paid postcards. Many women sent them back with the names and addresses of men to whom they'd talked in advance, and they included encouraging comments such as "What a great idea!" "This one's a cutie; hope someone snaps him up." One woman sent the names of her two sons. One man wanted to travel eight hundred miles for the affair. As much fun as these parties can be, limit social events so your group's emphasis is on healing.

You can close the regular meetings by singing familiar spirituals and offering prayers of thanks. One possible prayer might be this: *Immortal Mother—Father God of truth, beauty, and love, send your light into our hearts, heal our wounds, help us to share our many gifts, give us the courage to live so that we love more each day and inspire others to love. So be it, dear God. Thank you.*

It is essential that you remain mindful of the life-enhancing beliefs that nourished our ancestors like manna in the desert. You may recall that one of our greatest leaders, Harriet Tubman, who led so many to freedom, was called "Lady Moses." Like the Hebrew slaves who were led through the desert by Moses, many of us still feel unsure of the future. As our ancestors learned, freedom involves uncertainty. All they knew for sure was that freedom would give them the chance to use their many natural gifts.

We have illustrated the fact that the tremendous hostility and abuse directed at our ancestors made it impossible for them to reach their full potential. But because of the legacy we inherited from them—their wounds as well as their gifts—we can strengthen ourselves emotionally and create the lives they dreamed of. We've learned that we don't have to go it alone. We will always need God and the support of our community.

Fortified by this knowledge, we take our communal legacy out into the world with an affirmation powerful enough to connect us to our faith, our creativity, our determination, our intuition, our humor, our ability to inspire others, and our kinship ties. Before we present to you the affirmation, however, we'd like to give you background information, so that when you say the words you truly can connect with them, as if you've plugged into an electrical outlet.

First, think back to the biblical story of Moses asking the burning bush, "Who are you?" God responded: "I am that I am." Used in sacred religious texts the world over, the words "I am" have to do with identity; God was essentially saying to Moses, "I am the source; I cannot be reduced to anything else."

As we go out into the world, we know we are descendants of people who kept the inner divinity alive and that it lives within us. We can invoke that spirit when we say, "I am." That's why we begin this life-enhancing affirmation with "I am."

Because rhythm and vibration deeply penetrate the subconscious and help us to remember, we also chose words from a famous song, although not just any song. The one we've chosen was used in the film *Pleasantville;* it reminds us of the positive impact that we as a people and as individuals have on this world. The movie tells the story of white citizens in a 1950s town who have color magically added to their monochrome lives. They become filled with passion, which allows them to love deeply, risk their lives for freedom, and use anger as an instrument of awareness. (Although viewers never see a black person in the film, director Gary Ross apparently found it impossible to make a point about passion in contemporary culture without alluding to us. From music to medicine, whatever we put our heart into, we infuse the field with our energy, intelligence, focus, and verve.)

The song we have chosen is played in *Pleasantville* in a transformative scene as life turns from shades of gray to Technicolor. As the scene unfolds, a smitten young man sits beside his girl while he drives a convertible, top down, on a beautiful spring day. The trees have leafed, sun-pinked blossoms whirl down, and the landscape lies about them like a temptress. The setting is brought to life by the voice of Etta James as she sings "At Last." This sister's voice is a study in adaptability. She can sing in all keys, and here her voice is pensive, haunted, and it tells us everything we need to know about her life. We "hear" that she has been abandoned, learned to sing in a gospel choir, and knows all about hurting and rage, and that she has given her heart to men who misused her. But we also hear that she has known love and joy and laughter, and because of her assurance that she would prevail and triumph, she could sing "At Last."

The history of this song also tells us something about America's love-hate relationship with us and how we can transcend that ambivalence. James recorded "At Last" in 1960, a time when white record promoters insisted that black music was "too passionate" for white audiences and, because of racism, black artists were not considered acceptable. African American hits were often redone by white artists, who recorded them in more "conservative," less spontaneous, heavily orchestrated styles. Often these songs became huge moneymakers for white artists and their recording studios. But things were about to change. Baby boomers—raised by parents influenced by Freud, and taught to believe in the importance of the inner life—were coming of age and demanded the "real thing." They had a taste for music that was filled with drama and emotion, a style so provocative it could eventually be the underlying impetus for a social revolution that would lead young blacks and whites to join together and battle the old order. "At Last" was James's first big hit. Thirty-eight years later, audiences from around the world still ask her to sing it.[13] Its success was one of the first musical trickles in what would become a social storm.

Apart from the song itself, consider how we normally use the words *at last*. You might worry that something or someone important is missing from your life, and when you see that person you heave a sigh of relief and say "at last." Well, truth be told, *we* are those longed-for people, and *you* are that longed-for person. The world has always had a secret love affair with our people, and we can't simply wait to hear about it from others. If we acknowledge this and love ourselves, "at last" is the phrase others will utter as we enter the boardroom or club, go for a job interview, or greet our lovers.

The affirmation that summarizes all of our positive ancestral gifts begins with "I am" to acknowledge our inner Spirit. And because we are no longer stuck in the past but fully here in the present, we say, "here." Then we include the essential "loving myself," and we finish with "at last."

We affirm ourselves by saying, "I am here, loving myself, at last."

Epilogue

Hi, Mama:

It's early, even by your standards. But I'm up before everyone else, writing in my journal, because Mark and I have invited the San Francisco abundance group members over for dinner. The kids have pitched in by convincing our neighbors to let them pick lots of their lemons, so we're going to serve real lemonade, and I'm baking some lemon-scented yeast bread and making a pot of bouillabaisse. Dr. B. will bring a few of her beautifully arranged salads.

In one way at least, you'll be here with us. I'll be using your mother's cut glass serving dishes and your favorite dinner plates, the gold-rimmed ones. That's one reason I'm up so early. I have to wash them by hand. I'm sure the plates will put me in mind of how you used to pull them out every time there was a new beau in your life, and you wanted to impress him with a good meal. . . . Come to think of it, your cooking may be one of the reasons you didn't remarry. You should have served Kentucky Fried and tried to dazzle them with your brilliance. Mama, I can hear you laughing.

Our family just returned from New York. While there, we visited Grand Central Station so Mark and I could show the kids where we first met. They didn't seem all that impressed. But Mark and I did have Carolyn take a photo while we stood under the elevated clock. I have so enjoyed looking at that snapshot.

Twenty years have passed since that day when we met, and of course we look more world-weary, but I couldn't be happier about our changes. Just think, if we had taken a photo on the day we first met, rather than standing side by side, we would have had to stand far apart to make room *for the ghosts of our ancestors who stood between us for so long. What a crowded house we lived in.*

But in this snapshot, it was just me and my guy, our arms about one another, holding on for dear sweet life. So just between the two of us, this party today is a celebration of my emotional freedom too. There's an old slave saying that I scrawled on the back of the photo: "We ain't what we ought to be, and we ain't what we want to be, and we ain't what we're going to be, but thank God, we ain't what we was." Maybe decades from now, our great grandchildren will read it, point at us, and say, "That was the generation when everything changed for the better."

I'd best get up from here. The sun is rising. Have you ever noticed something special about early mornings? They're so full of possibilities you can practically taste them on your tongue. Thank God for taste buds.

Your daughter always, BLR

Resources

Assistance for Individual or Group Abundance Work

Affirmations: "I am Light & Energy" and other uplifting vocals included in our healing exercises; by Dr. Brenda Wade, music by Myumi.

Meditations: "Queen of Light" and other vocals; by Dr. Brenda Wade and Brenda Lane Richardson.

Spirituals: "Can't Nobody Turn Me Around" and other uplifting and healing ancestral songs. Vocals by Dr. Brenda Wade and Lawrence Beamen; arranged by Jacqueline Harriston.

To order any of these tapes, send $17 (this includes $2.00 for postage and handling) to Doc Wade, 2443 Fillmore St., Box 250, San Francisco, CA 94115. Please make checks payable to Heartline Productions, Inc. To order by phone, call 1–888-DOCWADE.

The voices of former slaves: Little-known recorded interviews that date back to the 1930s are available in the book and audiotape set *Remembering Slavery*, edited by Ira Berlin et al., $49.95 at local bookstores.

Dr. Brenda Wade and Brenda Lane Richardson are available to lead workshops for groups of twenty or more. For more information, call 1–888-DOCWADE.

Recommended Films for Viewing the Emotional Legacy of Slavery

Beloved

Down in the Delta

4 Little Girls

Mental Health Organizations

Association of Black Psychologists
P.O. Box 55999
Washington, D.C. 20040
202-722–0808

Black Psychiatrists of America
2730 Adeline St.
Oakland, CA 94607
510-465–1800

National Association of Black Social Workers
8436 W. McNichols Ave.
Detroit, MI 48221
313-862–6700

Sisterly Support

The Circle of Sisters is a network of support groups that offers membership for individuals and organizations. For more information, you can write to Circle of Sisters at 405 W. 147th St., New York, NY 10031, or phone 212-459-4806. You can e-mail this organization at www@CircleofSisters.com.

Dr. Wade and Brenda Richardson would love to hear your stories of transformation, as well as ideas that may grow out of your individual or group abundance work. Please write to them in care of HarperCollins, Editorial Department, 10 East 53rd Street, New York, NY, 10022-5299.

Notes

Introduction

1. Bonnie Angelo, "The Pain of Being Black," *Time,* May 22, 1989, 120.

2. Annie Murphy Paul, "The Cost of Coping," *Psychology Today*, November/December 1998, 12.

3. Stephen and Ondrea Levine, *To Love and Be Loved*, audiotape (Niles, Ill.: Nightingale-Conant Corporation, 1997), side 1.

4. We are aware that some readers have been blessed to have known or to have a record of earlier ancestors. This program can be helpful to you whether or not you have that information.

5. bell hooks, *Sisters of the Yam: Black Women and Self-Recovery* (Boston: South End Press, 1993), 131.

6. Gail Elizabeth Wyatt, *Stolen Women: Reclaiming Our Sexuality, Taking Back Our Lives* (New York: Wiley, 1997), 25.

7. Nancy Boyd-Franklin, *Black Families in Therapy* (New York: Guilford Press, 1989), 10.

8. "White Man Who Altered Himself to Look Black Reveals Chilling Accounts of Racism, Oppression," *Jet*, December 26–January 2, 1995, 26–27.

9. *Boston Globe* Wire Service, "Whites Still Privileged, Race Panel Tells Clinton," *San Francisco Chronicle*, September 18, 1998, A17.

10. Boyd-Franklin, *Black Families in Therapy,* 10.

11. bell hooks, *Sisters of the Yam,* 62.

12. William Grier and Price Cobbs, *Black Rage* (New York: Bantam Books, 1968), 22.

13. Grier and Cobbs, *Black Rage,* 172.

14. Joe R. Feagin and Melvin P. Sikes, *Living with Racism* (Boston: Beacon Press, 1994), 16.

15. Toni Morrison, *Beloved* (New York: Random House, 1987), inside jacket cover.

16. T. Lindsay Baker and Julie P. Baker, eds., *Till Freedom Cried Out* (College Station: Texas A&M University Press, 1997), xi.

17. Eudora Ramsay Richardson, director of the Virginia Writers' Project and a white woman who was considered a liberal radical, wrote to a colleague in 1937 concerning one manuscript: "It is not reasonable to believe that slaves were fed only cornbread and fat-

back and sometimes only corn bread and that rations would be exhausted before the end of the week and then the slaves for several days would have nothing to eat."

This information was included in *Weevils in the Wheat*, edited by Charles L. Perdue Jr., Thomas E. Barden, and Robert K. Phillips (Charlottesville: University Press of Virginia, 1976), xxii.

Chapter 1

1. George M. Fredrickson, "Of Human Bondage," *New York Times Book Review*, October 4, 1998, 9.

2. Lerone Bennett, Jr., *Before the Mayflower: A History of Black America* (Chicago: Johnson Publishing, 1987), 44.

3. William D. Piersen, *Black Legacy: America's Hidden Heritage* (Amherst: University of Massachusetts Press, 1993), 3.

4. Bennett, Jr., *Before the Mayflower*, 45.

5. Beverly J. Armento et al., *Across the Centuries* (Boston: Houghton Mifflin, 1991), 152.

6. Armento et al., *Across the Centuries*, 153.

7. Piersen, *Black Legacy*, 75.

8. Fredrickson, "Of Human Bondage," 9.

9. Delores S. Williams, *Sisters in the Wilderness: The Challenge of Womanist God-Talk* (Maryknoll, N.Y.: Orbis Books, 1995), 70.

10. Jewell Handy Gresham and Margaret B. Wilkerson, "The Burden of History," *The Nation*, July 24/31, 1989, 115.

11. "Africans in America: America's Journey Through Slavery," Public Broadcasting System, October 22, 1998, Part IV.

12. Lerone Bennett, Jr., *Before the Mayflower*, 153.

13. Ann McGovern, *The Defenders,* (New York: Scholastic), 1970, 48.

14. Mary Helen Washington, *Invented Lives* (New York: Doubleday, 1987), 73.

15. Darlene Clark Hine and Kathleen Thompson, *A Shining Thread of Hope* (New York: Broadway Books, 1998), 63.

16. Mary Ellen Butler, editor, *Black Women Stirring the Waters*, from an essay, "When Diversity Comes Naturally," by Maybelle Broussard, (Oakland, CA: Marcus Books Printing, 1997), 1997, 11.

Chapter 2

1. Joyce Nelson Patenaude, *Too Tired to Keep Running, Too Scared to Stop* (Boston: Element Books, 1998), 9.

2. Erica Goode, "A Computer Diagnosis of Prejudice," *New York Times*, October 13, 1998, D8.

3. Patenaude, *Too Tired to Keep Running*, 29.

4. Wayne W. Dyer, "The Secrets to Manifesting Your Destiny," audiotape (Niles Ill.: Nightingale-Conant Corporation [7300 North Lehigh Ave], 1996), side A.

5. David Ewen, *Ewen's Musical Masterworks: The Encyclopedia of Musical Masterpieces* (New York: Arco, 1954), 577.

6. Velma Maia Thomas, *Lest We Forget* (New York: Crown, 1997), 2.

7. Thomas, *Lest We Forget*, 3.

8. Thomas, *Lest We Forget*, 2.

9. Thomas, *Lest We Forget*, 5.

10. Monica McGoldrick and Randy Gerson, *Genograms in Family Assessment* (New York: Norton, 1985), 29.

11. J. Keith Miller, *Compelled to Control* (Deerfield Beach, Fla.: Health Communications, 1992), 11.

12. Some of the information related to colors and chakras was taken from *Mother Wit: A Feminist Guide to Psychic Development*, by Diane Mariechild, (Trumansburg, N.Y.: The Crossing Press, 1981), 41.

Chapter 3

1. Richard Fields, "John M. Gottman, Ph.D.: Saving Marriages from the Apocalypse," *Professional Counselor*, February 1997, 8.

2. Delores S. Williams, *Sisters of the Wilderness: The Challenge of Womanist God-Talk* (Maryknoll, N.Y.: Orbis Books, 1994), 36.

3. Darlene Clark Hine and Kathleen Thompson, *A Shining Thread of Hope* (New York: Broadway Books, 1998), 169.

4. United States Department of Commerce, Bureau of the Census, *The Black Population: Historical View From 1790 to 1978* (Washington, D.C.: Bureau of the Census, 1979), 58.

5. Leon F. Litwack, *Trouble in Mind* (New York: Knopf, 1998), 149.

6. Gail Elizabeth Wyatt, *Stolen Women* (New York: Wiley, 1997), 24.

7. Hine and Thompson, *A Shining Thread of Hope*, 243.

8. Lerone Bennett, Jr., *The Shaping of Black America* (Chicago: Johnson Publishing, 1987), 272.

9. Hine and Thompson, *A Shining Thread of Hope*, 244.

10. Wyatt, *Stolen Women*, 97.

11. Dr. Rosie Milligan, *Why Black Men Choose White Women* (Los Angeles, CA: Professional Business Consultants), 1998, 27.

12. Milligan, *Why Black Men Choose White Women*, 30

13. Williams, *Sisters in the Wilderness: The Challenge of Womanist God-Talk*, 57.

14. Mary Helen Washington, *Invented Lives: Narratives of Black Women 1860–1960* (New York: Doubleday, 1987), 73.

15. Linda Villarosa (ed), *Body & Soul: The Black Women's Guide to Physical Health and Emotional Well-Being* (New York: HarperPerennial, 1994), 430–31.

16. Jason DeParle, "Welfare Overhaul Initiatives Focus on Fathers," *New York Times,* September 3, 1998, A1.

17. David L. Miller, "It's Simpler than You Think," *The Lutheran,* August 1998, 11.

18. Niravi B. Payne and Brenda Lane Richardson, *The Language of Fertility,* (New York: Harmony), 1997, 98–99.

19. Margo Maine, *Father Hunger* (Carlsbad, Calif.: Gurze Books, 1991), 8.

20. Sam Donaldson, *Prime Time Live,* ABC-TV, June 17, 1998.

21. Geneen Roth, *When Food Is Love* (New York: Penguin Books, 1991), 3.

22. Mary Roach, "The Dieter's Paradox," *Health,* November/December 1997, 99.

23. Roach, "The Dieter's Paradox," 99.

24. Roth, *When Food Is Love,* 3.

25. Charles Perdue, Jr., Thomas Barden and Robert Phillips, *Weevils in the Wheat* (Charlottesville: University Press of Virginia, 1992), 190–91.

26. Jane E. Brody, "Children Who Skip Breakfast Pay a High Price," *New York Times,* October 6, 1998, B10.

Chapter 4

1. Julia Boyd, *In the Company of My Sisters* (New York: Penguin Books, 1997), 26.

2. Mary Ellen Butler, editor, *Black Women Stirring the Waters* (Oakland, CA: Marcus Books), 1997.

3. bell hooks, *Sisters of the Yam: Black Women and Self-Recovery* (Boston: South End Press, 1993), 137.

4. Fahizah Alim, "Hair Debate: First Hippie, Then Bushy, Now Nappy," *Oakland Tribune,* December 13, 1998, B1.

5. Alim, "Hair Debate," B4.

6. Jill Nelson, "Stumbling upon a Race Secret," *New York Times,* November 28, 1998, A31.

7. Katti Gray, "Against the Grain," *Essence,* February, 1999, 66.

8. Alim, "Hair Debate," B1 and 4.

9. hooks, *Sisters of the Yam,* 134.

10. Kathy Russell, Midge Wilson, and Ronald Hall, *The Color Complex* (New York: Bantam Doubleday, 1992), 95.

11. Francine Klagsbrun, *Mixed Feelings* (New York: Bantam Books, 1992), 175–6.

12. Klagsbrun, *Mixed Feelings,* 174.

13. Fox Butterfield, "Southern Curse: Why America's Murder Rate Is So High," *New York Times,* July 26, 1998, 1.

14. William H. Grier and Price M. Cobbs, *Black Rage* (New York: Basic Books, 1968), 20.

15. Bonnie Angelo, "The Pain of Being Black," *Time,* May 22, 1989, 121.

16. Darlene Clark Hine and Kathleen Thompson, *A Shining Thread of Hope* (New York: Broadway Books, 1998), 84.

17. Velma Maia Thomas, *Lest We Forget* (New York: Crown, 1997), 17.

18. Russell, Wilson, and Hall, *The Color Complex*, 15.

19. Dr. Roxie Milligan, *Why Black Men Choose White Women*, (Los Angeles: Professional Business Consultants), 1998, 33-35.

20. Thomas Hart, *Hidden Spring* (New York: Paulist Press, 1994), 25.

21. Hart, *Hidden Spring,* 24.

22. Joseph M. Murphy, *Working the Spirit* (Boston: Beacon Press, 1994), 2.

23. Hine and Thompson, *A Shining Thread of Hope*, 169.

24. Richard D. Kahlenberg, "Bench Marks," *New York Times Book Review*, June 14, 1998, 32.

25. Lerone Bennett, Jr., *Before the Mayflower* (Chicago: Johnson Publishing, 1987), 287.

26. "Bush Angered by Secret Service Agent's Scuffle with Condoleezza Rice," *Jet*, June 25, 1990, 6.

27. "The Rule of Law Protects the President, too, A Counsel Tells the Senate," *New York Times,* January 21, 1999, A-16.

28. Pam Belluck, "Doctors in Spotlight are Role Models for Black Youths," *New York Times*, November 22, 1997, A-7.

29. "The Rule of Law Protects the President, too, A Counsel Tells the Senate," A-16.

30. Belluck, "Doctors in Spotlight Are Role Models for Black Youths," A-7.

31. Will Jaynes, "Staying Stubbornly True to a Writers Vision," *New York Times*, October 18, 1999, AR13.

32. Alim, "Hair Debate," B4.

Chapter 5

1. Darlene Clark Hine and Kathleen Thompson, *A Shining Thread of Hope: The History of Black Women in America* (New York: Broadway Books, 1998), 63.

2. *Africans in America: America's Journey Through Slavery*, PBS, October 21, 1998, Part III.

3. Julius Lester, *To Be a Slave* (New York: Dial Books), 1968, 52–53.

4. Lester, *To Be a Slave*, 56.

5. Lester, *To Be a Slave*, 56.

6. Lerone Bennett, Jr., *Before the Mayflower* (Chicago: Johnson Publishing, 1987), 219.

7. Hine and Thompson, *A Shining Thread of Hope*, 150.

8. Richard S. Cooper, Charles N. Rotimi and Ryk Ward, "The Puzzle of Hypertension in African-Americans," *Scientific American*, February, 1999, 59.

9. Jonathan Alter, "The Long Shadow of Slavery," *Newsweek,* December 5, 1997, 83.

10. Jewell Handy Gresham, "The Politics of Family in America," *The Nation*, July 24/31 1989, 119.

11. Brenda Wade, "Fear of Abandonment," *Essence*, April 1995, 80.

12. Ossie Davis, "Challenge for the Year 2000," *The Nation,* July 24/31 1989, 145.

13. This exercise is based on a model from the book *Gestalt Self-Therapy,* by Muriel Schiffman (Berkeley, Calif.: Self Therapy Press, 1971), 195–6.

14. This list was compiled by Charles Whitfield in *Healing the Child Within* (Deerfield Beach, Fla.: Health Communications, 1987).

15. Malidoma Patrice Somé, *Of Water and the Spirit* (New York: Penguin Books), 9.

16. Diane Weathers, "Wisdom of the Somés," *Essence,* December1998, 124.

Chapter 6

1. Nancy Boyd-Franklin, *Black Families in Therapy* (New York: Guilford Press, 1989), 76–77.

2. Bonnie Angelo, "The Pain of Being Black," *Time*, May 22, 1989, 120.

3. Lerone Bennett, Jr., *Before the Mayflower* (Chicago: Johnson Publishing, 1987), 114–5.

4. Bennett, Jr., *Before the Mayflower,* 117.

5. Bennett, Jr., *Before the Mayflower,* 116.

6. *The World Book Encyclopedia*, Vol. 17 (Chicago: Field Enterprises Educational Corporation, 1963), 423.

7. Gerta Lerner, ed., *Black Women in White America* (New York: Random House, 1972), 27.

8. Angela Dodson, "Secrets of the Quilts," *Essence*, February, 1999, 148.

9. Lerner, *Black Women in White America*, 54.

10. Darlene Clark Hine and Kathleen Thompson, *A Shining Thread of Hope* (New York: Broadway Books, 1998), 115–6.

11. Lerner, *Black Women in White America*, 53.

12. Lerner, *Black Women in White America*, 53.

13. Dorothy Sterling, *We Are Your Sisters* (New York: Norton, 1984), 62.

14. Edward Ball, *Slaves in the Family* (New York: Farrar, Straus & Giroux, 1998), 56.

15. Lerner, *Black Women in White America*, 35.

16. Leon F. Litwack, *Trouble in Mind* (New York: Knopf, 1998), 39.

17. Rick Bragg, "Ex-Klansman Implicates Chief in Killing," *New York Times*, August 20, 1998, A12.

18. Lewis B. Smedes, *Forgive & Forget* (New York: Simon & Schuster, 1984), 143.

19. John Hockenberry, "The Color of Money," *NBC Dateline*, September 1, 1998.

20. Anthony Maione, "We Must Walk the Walk, Not 'Just' Talk the Talk," *Oakland Tribune*, April 2, 1994, A13.

21. Warren E. Leary, "Discrimination May Affect Risk of High Blood Pressure in Blacks," *New York Times*, October 24, 1996, A20.

22. Leary, *New York Times*.

23. Daniel Goleman, *Emotional Intelligence* (New York: Bantam Books, 1995), 60.

24. Gail Elizabeth Wyatt, *Stolen Women* (New York: Wiley, 1997), 185.

25. Michael Janofsky, "About-Face in Washington in Furor on Misunderstood Word," *New York Times*, February 4, 1999, A14.

26. Leo Madow, *Anger* (New York: Scribner, 1972), 73.

27. Richard S. Cooper, Charles N. Rotimi, and Ryk Ward, "The Puzzle of Hypertension in African-Americans," *Scientific American*, February, 1999, 56-57.

28. Richard S. Cooper, Charles N. Rotimi, and Ryk Ward, 59, 60, 63.

29. Sarah Lyall, "European Court Orders Britain to Restrict Beatings By Parents," *New York Times*, September 24, 1998, A7.

30. Wyatt, *Stolen Women,* 183.

31. Michelle Joy Levine, *I Wish I Were Thin, I Wish I Were Fat* (Huntington Station, N.Y.: Vanderbilt Press, 1998), 64.

32. Kevin Sack, "To Vestige of Black Farmers, Bias Settlement is Too Late," *New York Times*, January 6, 1999, A12.

33. The idea of keeping a journal of unexpressed emotions comes from the work of fertility therapist Niravi Payne. She detailed her views in *The Language of Fertility*, coauthored with Brenda Lane Richardson, (New York: Harmony, 1997), 41-42.

Chapter 7

1. Dorothy Height, "Self-Help—A Black Tradition," The Nation, July 24, 1989, 137.

2. Gwendolyn Goldsby Grant, *The Best Kind of Loving* (New York: HarperCollins, 1995), 45.

3. Terrence Real, *I Don't Want to Talk about It* (New York: Scribner, 1997), 99.

4. Real, *I Don't Want to Talk about It,* 103.

5. Nancy Boyd-Franklin, *Black Families in Therapy* (New York: Guilford Press, 1989), 22.

6. Linda Villarosa, editor, *Body & Soul: The Black Women's Guide to Physical Health and Emotional Well-Being* (New York: HarperPerennial, 1994), 368.

7. Angela Mitchell with Kennise Herring, *What the Blues Is All About* (New York: Berkley Publishing, 1998), 4.

8. Mitchell and Herring, *What the Blues Is All About,* 4.

9. Real, *I Don't Want to Talk about It,* 68.

10. Mitchell and Herring, *What the Blues Is All About,* 7.

11. Daniel Goleman, *Emotional Intelligence* (New York: Bantam Books, 1995), 175.

12. Mitchell and Herring, *What the Blues Is All About,* 130–1.

13. Lena Williams, "Beyond the Game: A Player's Unsettling End Leaves Others Wondering Why," *New York Times*, January 23, 1999, B15, 18.

14. Elizabeth Start, "Quicker Fixer Uppers," *American Health,* October, 1991, 45.

15. Start, "Quicker Fixer Uppers," 45.

16. Lerone Bennett, Jr., *Before the Mayflower* (Chicago: Johnson Publishing, 1987), 217.

17. David Oshinsky, *Worse than Slavery* (New York: Simon & Schuster, 1996), 21.

18. Oshinsky, *Worse than Slavery*, 23.

19. Leon Litwack, *Trouble in Mind* (New York: Knopf, 1998), 286–7.

20. Loretta V. Britten, ed., *Voices of Triumph: Creative Fire* (Alexandria, Va.: Time-Life, 1994).

21. Brian Robertson, *Little Blues Book* (Chapel Hill, N.C.: Algonquin Books, 1996), 22.

22. Donna L. Franklin, *Ensuring Inequality* (New York: Oxford University Press, 1997), 72–73.

23. Ossie Davis and Ruby Dee, *With Ossie and Ruby: In This Life Together* (New York: Morrow, 1998), 164.

24. *I'll Make Me a World*, February, 2, 1999, Part II, PBS.

25. Franklin, *Ensuring Inequality*, 74.

26. Franklin, *Ensuring Inequality*, 74.

27. United States Department of Commerce, Bureau of the Census, *The Black Population: Historical View From 1790 to 1978* (Washington, D.C., Bureau of the Census, 1979), 98–99.

28. Robert Pear, "Black and Hispanic Poverty Falls, Reducing Overall Rate for Nation," *New York Times*, September 25, 1998, A1.

29. Ethan Bronner, "Study Strongly Supports Affirmative Action in Admission to Elite Colleges," *New York Times*, September 9, 1998, A24.

30. Michiko Kakutani, "From Underground Music to Fashion Statement," *New York Times*, December 4, 1998, B41.

Chapter 8

1. Gwendolyn Goldsby Grant, *The Best Kind of Loving* (New York: HarperCollins, 1995), 151.

2. Muriel Schiffman, *Gestalt Self Therapy* (Berkeley, Calif.: Self Therapy Press, 1971), 89.

Chapter 9

1. Marilyn Mason, *Making Our Lives Our Own* (New York: Harper San Francisco, 1991), 156.

2. Mason, *Making Our Lives Our Own*, 126.

3. Gail Elizabeth Wyatt, *Stolen Women* (New York: Wiley, 1997), 134.

4. Wyatt, *Stolen Women*, 175.

5. Wyatt, *Stolen Women*, 175.

6. Wyatt, *Stolen Women*, 151.

7. Rachelle Johnson, "Unplanned Pregnancies: Stories of Choice," *Black Elegance,* May 1998, 43.

8. Wyatt, *Stolen Women,* 151.

9. Johnson, "Unplanned Pregnancies," 43.

10. Sandra Blakeslee, "Placebos Prove So Powerful Even Experts Are Surprised," *New York Times,* October 13, 1998.

11. Christiane Northrup, *Women's Bodies, Women's Wisdom* (New York: Bantam Books, 1994), 169.

12. Wyatt, *Stolen Women,* 9.

13. Michael Parfit, "Human Migration," *National Geographic,* October 1998, 20.

14. Wyatt, *Stolen Women,* 23.

15. Wyatt, *Stolen Women,* 72.

16. Wyatt, *Stolen Women,* 77.

17. Wyatt, *Stolen Women,* 32–33.

18. Northrup, *Women's Bodies,* 225.

19. Linda Villarosa, editor, *Body and Soul: The Black Women's Guide of Physical Health and Emotional Well-Being* (New York: HarperPerennial, 1994), 462.

20. Marcia L. Dyson, "Can You Love God and *Sex*?" *Essence,* February, 1999, 175.

21. Niravi Payne and Brenda Lane Richardson, *The Language of Fertility* (New York: Harmony Books, 1997), 147-149.

Chapter 10

1. Bonnie Angelo, "The Pain of Being Black," *Time,* May 22, 1989, 120.

2. A review of "The Burden of Memory," *Publishers Weekly,* November 9, 1998, 66.

3. David Stoop and James Masteller, *Forgiving Our Parents, Forgiving Ourselves* (Ann Arbor, Mich.: Servant Publications, 1991), 163.

4. Tian Dayton, *Heartwounds* (Deerfield Beach, Fla.: Healthy Communications, 1997), 109.

5. Dayton, *Heartwounds,* 169.

6. Stoop and Masteller, *Forgiving Our Parents, Forgiving Ourselves,* 159.

7. This is a synthesis of ideas from Stoop and Masteller, *Forgiving Our Parents, Forgiving Ourselves,* 169–78.

8. Lewis Smedes, *Forgive & Forget* (New York: Simon & Schuster, 1984), 149.

Chapter 11

1. Richard Scheinin, "Black Faith in Ferment," *Publishers Weekly,* February 13, 1995, 42-43.

2. Sylvia Flanagan, ed., "Celebrities," *Jet,* November 24, 1997, 38–39.

3. Ira Peck, *Martin Luther King, Jr.* (New York: Scholastic, 1968), 68.

4. African American Knowledge Cards, Pomegrante Publications, Box 6099, Rohnert Park, CA 94927

5. William Piersen, *Black Legacy* (Amherst: University of Massachusetts Press, 1993), 55.

6. Piersen, *Black Legacy*, 55.

7. Michel Marriott, "Rock on a Roll," *Essence*, November 1998, 116.

8. Daniel Goleman, *Emotional Intelligence* (New York: Bantam Books, 1995), 85.

9. Laura Day, *Practical Intuition in Love* (New York: HarperCollins), 1998, 14.

10. "Comedian D.L. Hughley Is a Hit in New TV Sitcom, 'The Hughleys'," *Jet*, December 7, 1998.

11. Connell Cowan and Melvin Kinder, *Women Men Love, Women Men Leave* (New York: Penguin Books, 1987), 206–7.

12. Alex Witchel, "Singles Look for Romance at the Soup Kitchen," *New York Times*, December 7, 1998, B8.

13. Etta James and David Ritz, *Rage to Survive* (New York: Villard Books, 1995), 101.

Index